OCT 2 3 2012

3/19

Discarded By Elk Grove
Village Public Library

fun with the family Texas

hundreds of ideas for day trips with the kids

Seventh Edition

Sharry Buckner

ELK GROVE VILLAGE PUBLIC LIBRARY
1001 WELLINGTON AVE
ELK GROVE VILLAGE, IL 60007
(847) 439-0447

Guilford, Connecticut

The prices, rates, and hours listed in this guidebook were confirmed at press time. We recommend, however, that you call establishments to obtain current information before traveling.

To buy books in quantity for corporate use or incentives, call **(800) 962-0973** or e-mail **premiums@GlobePequot.com.**

Copyright © 1997, 1999, 2001, 2003, 2005, 2007, 2010 Morris Book Publishing, LLC

ALL RIGHTS RESERVED. No part of this book may be reproduced or transmitted in any form by any means, electronic or mechanical, including photocopying and recording, or by any information storage and retrieval system, except as may be expressly permitted in writing from the publisher. Requests for permission should be addressed to Globe Pequot Press, Attn: Rights and Permissions Department, P.O. Box 480, Guilford, CT 06437.

Text design by Nancy Freeborn and Linda R. Loiewski
Maps by Rusty Nelson © Morris Book Publishing, LLC
Spot photography throughout © Photodisc and © RubberBall Productions

ISSN 1542-2313
ISBN 978-0-7627-5340-6

Printed in the United States of America

10 9 8 7 6 5 4 3 2

To my husband, Al, my companion on the trails.

—SB

TEXAS

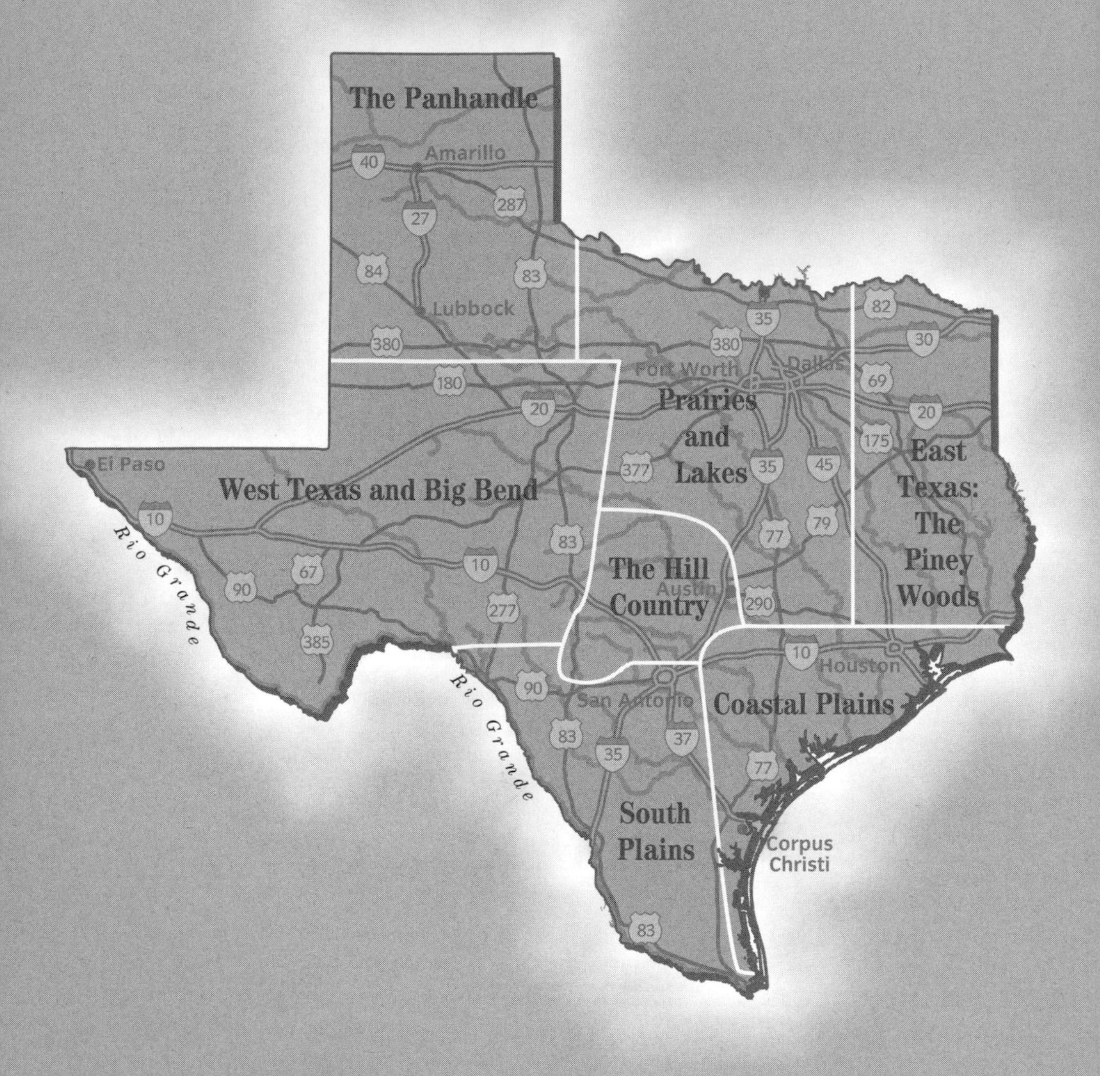

The Panhandle
Amarillo
40
287
27
84
83
Lubbock
380
35
380
82
30
Fort Worth
Dallas
180
20
69
Prairies
and
Lakes
20
175
El Paso
377
35
45
East
Texas:
The
Piney
Woods
West Texas and Big Bend
10
Rio Grande
83
77
79
90
67
10
The Hill
Country
Austin
290
277
385
10
Houston
Rio Grande
90
San Antonio
Coastal Plains
83
35
37
77
South
Plains
Corpus
Christi
83

Contents

Preface vi

Introduction vii

Prairies and Lakes 1

The Panhandle 54

West Texas and Big Bend 72

South Plains 109

The Hill Country 136

Coastal Plains 167

East Texas: The Piney Woods 203

Index 235

About the Author 244

Preface

I love Texas. I love its diverse land, its colorful history, its great food, and most of all its small towns and friendly folks. The back roads of the Lone Star State have taken me through the hills, valleys, deserts, forests, and to the coast, showing me special places and introducing me to people who are true Texas treasures. Texas has its own culture and Texans are pretty much a separate breed. It takes a lifetime to get to know Texas and visitors usually only get a glimpse. This book is intended to help you make good use of whatever time you have to spend in the Lone Star State. Don't believe everything you see in the movies or everything you hear about Texas braggin' . . . just enjoy what you discover!

—Sharry Buckner

Introduction

Texas contains 267,277 square miles, with 624 miles of coastline and 191,000 miles of rivers and streams. But it isn't just size that makes Texas special, it's the incredible diversity of the Lone Star State. Here, America collides with Mexico to create what seems to be a whole new culture. But many more cultures than those two have influenced—and continue to influence—Texas. Germans, Czechs, Polish, Native Americans, English, Irish, Scottish, Scandinavians, Africans, Filipinos, Lebanese, Chinese, Japanese, Canary Islanders, and many others have made their presence felt so strongly in the state that an immense Institute of Texan Cultures had to be established in San Antonio just to pay tribute to them all.

Texas's diversity extends to climate and geology as well. Here the borders reach from balmy, sandy beaches to raw desert, majestic mountains, rolling hills, deep forests, grassy plains, and tropical areas filled with swaying palm trees. Four distinct geographic

Texas State Symbols

- The name Texas comes from tayshas, a Hasinai Indian word meaning "friend."
- The state nickname is the Lone Star State, from the solitary star on the state flag.
- The state song is "Texas, Our Texas."
- The state flower is the bluebonnet.
- The state tree is the pecan.
- The state bird is the mockingbird.
- The state dish is chili.
- The state reptile is the Texas horned lizard.
- The state small mammal is the armadillo.
- The state large mammal is the longhorn.
- The state flying mammal is the Mexican free-tail bat.
- The state stone is petrified palm wood.

Information Centers

During your trip, don't miss stopping at one of the Texas Travel Information Centers run by the state Department of Transportation. These are at entry points scattered around the state on major thoroughfares, and each one is packed with travel literature to make your trip easier and more enjoyable. They are open daily from 8 a.m. to 5 p.m., until 6 p.m. Memorial Day weekend through Labor Day, and closed New Year's Day, Easter Sunday, Thanksgiving, Christmas Eve, and Christmas. Call (800) 452-9292 for automated road condition information 24 hours a day.

- **If you're traveling east from New Mexico or south from Oklahoma,** stop at the Amarillo center at 9700 E. I–40.
- **Traveling from southwestern New Mexico,** stop at the El Paso center on I–10 in the town of Anthony.
- **In Austin,** stop at the Capitol Complex Visitors Center in the restored Old General Land Office Building at 11th Street and Congress Avenue. The building features several exhibits on the history of Texas and the land office, which manages state properties. One display celebrates the land office's most famous employee, William Sydney Porter, who wrote short stories under the name O. Henry.
- **Traveling south from Oklahoma,** stop in Denison on U.S. Highway 75, in Gainesville on U.S. Highway 77 at I–35, or in Wichita Falls on I–44 at U.S. Highways 277 and 281.
- **Traveling south or west from Arkansas,** stop at the Texarkana center on I–30.
- **Traveling west from Louisiana,** stop at the Orange center on I–10 or the Waskom center on I–20.
- **Traveling north from Mexico,** visit the Laredo Visitors Center on I–35 just north of the city, the Harlingen center at the intersection of US 77 and 83, or the Langtry center on Loop 25 at U.S. Highway 90. The Langtry location is especially interesting because it's on the grounds of the historic Jersey Lilly Saloon built by Judge Roy Bean, the "Law West of the Pecos" back in the late 1800s.

regions converge here: the Rocky Mountains, the Great Western High Plains, the Great Western Lower Plains, and the Gulf Coastal Plains.

These regions are home to some huge, modern metropolitan areas, and three of them (Houston, San Antonio, and Dallas) are among the ten largest cities in the United States. Yet Texas has more land dedicated to agriculture, has more farms and ranches, produces more cotton, and grazes more cattle than any other state.

In fact, Texas is so big you really can't see it all in one trip, unless your vacation lasts for months. The best way to see it is in bits and pieces. This book presents a selection of places children will enjoy—but "children" encompasses many ages, so read the descriptions to decide if your family will enjoy the attractions listed. Try some local eateries, "Mom and Pop" places, chicken-fried steak, Texas barbecue (or BarBQ), German sausages, chili, and Tex-Mex food.

If your family likes to drive around scenic areas, the state has helped you out by creating several "highway trails." These are well-marked routes that travel through the most interesting areas of each region of the state. They include the Hill Country Trail in Central Texas, the Tropical Trail in South Texas, the Independence Trail along the Coastal Plain, the Forest Trail in East Texas, the Mountain Trail and the Pecos Trail in West Texas, the Plains Trail in the Panhandle, the Lakes Trail in northeast Texas, the Forts Trail in north-central Texas, and the Brazos Trail in central Texas. For brochures about these trails, as well as a **free** 288-page *Texas State Travel Guide* and **free** state map,call (800) 888-8TEX or visit www.traveltex.com.

Maps provided at the beginning of each chapter of this book are for reference only and should be used in conjunction with a road map. Distances provided are approximate.

If you're driving in Texas, you are required to have liability insurance. Evidence of insurance must be furnished when requested by a police officer. Texas law (www.txdps.state.tx.us/director_staff/public_information/seatbelt.htm) also requires all passengers to wear seat belts, children under five to be secured in a federally approved child safety seat system, and no one under the age of 18 may ride in the open-bed of a pickup truck.

South of the Border

Since Texas shares 1,254 miles of border with Mexico, your family might want to make a side trip south of the border. Before you go, check with the U.S. Department of State at http://travel.state.gov/travel/tips/regional/regional_1174.html for the most current regulations and travel tips. If you are a U.S. citizen, federal law requires a valid passport to travel to Mexico. The passport must be valid for at least six months past entry date. Laws have been changing often, so for the latest rules and regulations, check the U.S. Customs and Border Protection Web site at www.cbp.gov before you go.

Happy Trails

If you're taking a family vacation, it's fun to let the kids help plan it. Let them e-mail or call for tourist brochures and maps from the places you'll be visiting. When the literature arrives, have a "vacation-planning day" and spread it out on the dining room table. If possible, let each child pick one or two places they would like to visit. When traveling, let the kids collect mementos (ticket stubs, brochures, postcards, etc.) and make a scrapbook either during the trip or when you get home. Wherever you go, enjoy!

Lodging, Restaurant, and Attraction Rates

Rates for places to stay and eat, as well as attraction admission prices, are represented with dollar signs and offer a sense of the price ranges at press time. Lodging rates are based on double occupancy and tend to increase seasonally depending on location; many establishments offer family rates and discounts. Restaurant prices pertain to most dinner entrees, and attraction rates are per person.

Lodging

$	up to $60
$$	$61 to $100
$$$	more than $100

Restaurants

$	up to $10
$$	$11 to $20
$$$	more than $20

Attractions

$	up to $5
$$	$6 to $10
$$$	$11 to $20
$$$$	more than $20

Attractions Key

The following is a key to the icons found throughout the text.

- SWIMMING
- BOATING/BOAT TOUR
- HISTORIC SITE
- HIKING/WALKING
- FISHING
- BIKING
- AMUSEMENT PARK
- HORSEBACK RIDING
- SKIING/WINTER SPORTS
- PARK
- ANIMAL VIEWING
- FOOD
- LODGING
- CAMPING
- MUSEUM
- PERFORMING ARTS
- SPORTS/ATHLETICS
- PICNICKING
- PLAYGROUND
- SHOPPING
- PLANTS/GARDENS/NATURE TRAILS
- FARM

Prairies and Lakes

This is a region drenched in history, with a number of fine museums to preserve its past. The Texas Declaration of Independence was signed here, the fledgling republic's first capital was here, the oldest university in the state is here, Dr Pepper was invented here, the West begins here, and the Texas Rangers—both the law enforcement agency and the baseball team—have excellent showcases here.

Except for the bucolic rolling hills along the back roads, this area doesn't have much in the way of dramatic landscapes. But when the wildflowers are blooming in the spring, the area is a festival of color and a great backdrop for photographs of children. The Brazos River Valley offers plenty of outdoor recreation, from canoeing down the river to water sports on the lakes.

Most of the land here is given over to farming, with a giant metropolitan area hulking in its midst. The Metroplex, from Fort Worth to Dallas, is one of the largest urban areas in the nation and offers families an abundance of things to do, from amusement parks to world-class zoos, from art galleries to wax museums, from planetariums to sporting events.

The easiest way to get around the Prairies and Lakes region is on I–35 and I–45, U.S. Highways 281 and 290, and Highway 6. Don't worry if you take a back road—virtually all Texas roads are very well maintained. This area is crowded with cities and towns, perhaps more than any other region, so a travel stop is always just over the next hill. In the Metroplex, the majority of family attractions are adjacent to or very near I–30.

Bastrop, Rosanky, and Smithville

Bastrop is one of the more historically important towns in Texas. The area originally was a meeting ground for Tonkawa and other southwestern Indians, provided a vital river crossing on El Camino Real—the King's Road from Mexico City to Nacogdoches—and was the prime settlement for Stephen F. Austin, the father of Texas.

PRAIRIES AND LAKES

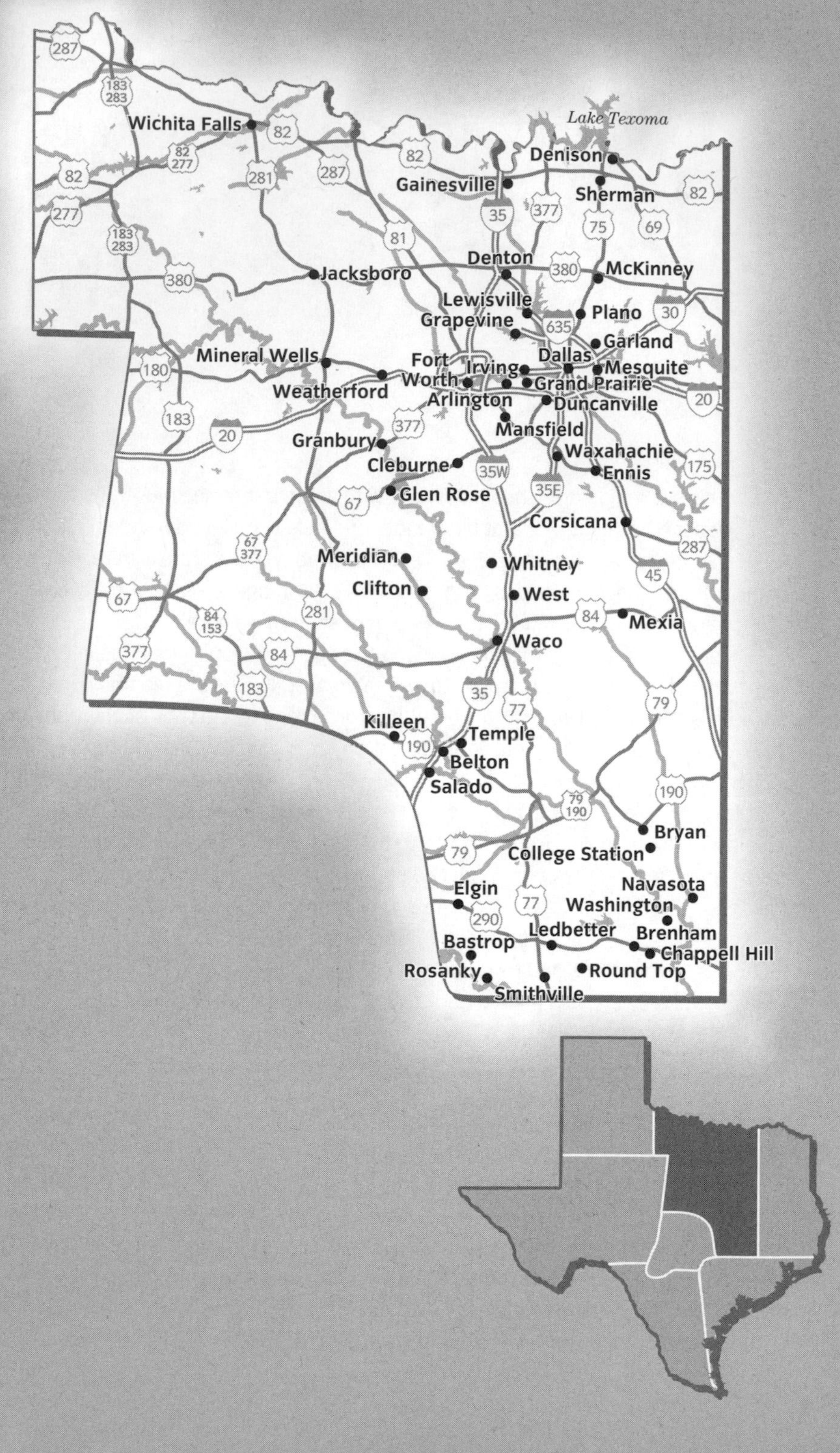

TopAnnualEvents in Prairies and Lakes

- **Southwestern Exposition and Livestock Show and Rodeo,** Fort Worth, January (817-877-2400)
- **Eeyore's Birthday,** Round Top, April (979-278-3530)
- **Bluebonnet Festival,** Ennis, April (972-878-4748)
- **Scarborough Faire,** Waxahachie, April through May (972-938-3247)
- **Red River Rodeo,** Wichita Falls, June (940-704-0514)
- **Comanche County Pow-Wow,** Comanche, September (325-356-3233)
- **State Fair of Texas,** Dallas, October (214-565-9931)
- **Red Steagall Cowboy Gathering,** Fort Worth, October (888-269-8696)
- **Winedale Oktoberfest,** Round Top, October (979-278-3530)
- **Christmas in Chappell Hill,** Chappell Hill, December (979-337-9910)

The city is named for Philip Hendrick Nering-Bogel, a land developer with no royal blood who called himself the Baron of Bastrop. He was instrumental in persuading the Mexican governor of Coahuila y Tejas to allow Austin to bring American colonists into the area in 1827. That was the beginning of events that would lead Anglo settlers and many Mexican citizens to revolt against Mexico and establish Texas as an independent republic just a few years later.

Nestled among towering loblolly pines along the Colorado River, Bastrop is surrounded by parks, ranch land, and meadows alive with wildflowers in the spring. More than 125 structures in town are listed on the National Register of Historic Places. Bastrop's courthouse was built in 1889, the same year as its Opera House.

The nearby city of Smithville has a similar history and was once a riverboat stop on the Colorado River and an important railroad hub. It's known today as a popular place to shop for antiques.

Bastrop Opera House (ages 6 and up)

711 Spring Street, Bastrop (512-321-6283; www.bastropoperahouse.com).

Located in a historic building, the Opera House is home to the Colorado River Repertory and the Spring Street Players. It offers year-round family entertainment at reasonable prices with delightful presentations of children's theater and musicals on Friday and Saturday evenings. Prices vary with the performances.

Bastrop Museum (ages 6 and up)

702 Main Street, Bastrop (512-303-0057; www.bastroptexas.net/around_bastrop/bastrop_museum.htm). Open Monday through Friday 1 to 5 p.m., Saturday 10 a.m. to 2 p.m. $.

Bastrop-Smithville **Annual Events**

- **Yesterfest,** Bastrop, April
- **Smithville Jamboree,** Smithville, April
- **Patriotic Festival,** Bastrop, July
- **Bastrop MusicFest (Concert for CASA),** Bastrop, October
- **Old-Fashioned Christmas Parade,** Bastrop, December
- **Festival of Lights,** Smithville, December

For more information contact the Bastrop Chamber of Commerce and Visitor Center at 927 Main Street, Bastrop 78602 (512-303-0558; www.bastrop chamber.com).

The museum is located in an 1850 house and displays historic documents and photographs, along with frontier tools, artifacts, and Native American relics sure to interest children.

Bastrop State Park (ages 2 and up)

1 mile east of Bastrop on Highway 21, via Loop 150 from Highway 71 (512-321-2101; www .tpwd.state.tx.us/spdest/findadest/parks/bastrop).

The 3,503-acre park is in the midst of the Lost Pines area of Texas, a loblolly pine woodland isolated from the main body of East Texas piney woods. It's the most westerly stand of loblollys in the state. The rugged hills and quiet woodlands are an ideal retreat.

Overlooking a small lake are thirteen rustic cabins with cooking facilities—the perfect place for a family to relax for a day or two. The park also has a swimming pool, two children's wading pools, a nine-hole golf course, picnic tables, and modern restrooms with hot showers. the golf course winds through tall pines and crosses steep ravines.

If you have older children, you might be interested in biking along the hilly park road system that connects Bastrop and Buescher State Parks.

Central Texas Museum of Automotive History (ages 6 and up)

South of Bastrop at 2502 Highway 304, Smithville (512-237-2635; www.ctmah.org). Open April 1 through September 30, Wednesday through Saturday 10 a.m. to 5 p.m., Sunday 1:30 to 5 p.m.; October 1 through March 31, Friday through Saturday 10 a.m. to 5 p.m., Sunday 1:30 to 5 p.m. $, children 5 and under free.

Anyone who likes old cars is going to love this museum full of beautiful and interesting vehicles, all restored and polished to mirror finishes. Usually you'll see 100 to 115 cars on display at any time. The rotating collection traces the development of the automobile and its effect on the social and economic climate of the world. You'll see early European estate cars, town cars, limousines, and sports cars, as well as cutaway engine displays, tools, and diagnostic equipment.

Other displays include gasoline and oil pumps, automotive signs, license plates from around the world, accessories, and a large collection of models and toys.

Smithville Railroad Historical Park and Museum
(ages 4 and up)

102 West First Street, Smithville (512-237-2313). Open during business hours Monday through Friday. Free

Who doesn't like trains, especially kids? This museum in the Katy Depot features Union Pacific and Missouri-Kansas-Texas cabooses, photos, railroad memorabilia, and a vintage motor car. Railroad Park has tree-shaded picnic tables and a children's playground. The park's gazebo is topped by a cupola salvaged from the 1896 city hall building.

Buescher State Park (ages 2 and up)

On Park Road 1, 2 miles north of Smithville off Highway 71 (512–237-2241; www.tpwd.state .tx.us/spdest/findadest/parks/buescher).

Unlike nearby Bastrop State Park, this park on the edge of the Lost Pines has more oaks than pines. It also has picnic areas with tables and grills, a 7.8-mile hiking trail, and overnight camping facilities. Four screened shelters with water and electricity are available at $20 a night, but make reservations well in advance, especially in spring and summer.

While roaming around Buescher (pronounced Bisher), you might see armadillos, bobcats, white-tailed deer, opossums, rabbits, raccoons, and squirrels. The thirty-acre lake is stocked with fish and you can swim in the lake, but the park has no lifeguards so keep a close eye on the kids.

Scenic **Drive**

One of the prettiest drives in the entire Prairies and Lakes region is the 13-mile route through the Lost Pines. Directions are simple: Take Park Road 1 from either Bastrop State Park or Buescher State Park and drive to the other park. Park Road 1A loops around Bastrop State Park. The route splits into Park Roads 1C and 1E, but they both end up in the same place, so travel in one direction on one and return on the other. In some areas, the trees are so thick and the road so narrow, it appears as if you are in a wooded tunnel. Make sure your windows are down as you mosey over the hills, letting in that fresh smell of the pines, a fragrance intensified just after a rain shower. Best times are spring and fall.

Free **Fishing!**

Texas Parks & Wildlife has waived fishing license requirements for anyone fishing inside the property boundary of a Texas State Park. The Free Fishing program is intended to encourage folks to get outside and enjoy fishing—whether you're an adult or child, fishing in a river or creek, from a pier or bank, or even from a boat if the body of water is inside a state park boundary. The program is available at more than fifty state parks across Texas and several even have special events like "learn to fish" classes or kids' fishing contests.

Where to Eat

The Roadhouse. 2804 Hwy. 21 East, Bastrop (512-321-1803; www.kendrasroadhouse.com). Voted best hamburgers in Bastrop County five years in a row—also steaks, chicken, salads and a kids' menu. $

Pocket's Grill. 205 Fawcett St., Smithville; (512-237-5572; www.pocketsgrille.com). Great sandwiches, burgers, pizza, Tex-Mex, Dawgs, dinner entrees, and a kids' menu. $

Where to Stay

Bastrop Inn. 102 Childers Street, Bastrop (512-321-3949; www.bastropinn.com). Swimming pool, HBO, kids under 10 stay **free.** $$

Days Inn. 4102 Highway 71 East, Bastrop (512-321-1157; www.daysinn.com). Pool, **free** breakfast, high-speed Internet. $$

For More Information

Bastrop Chamber of Commerce and Visitor Center. 927 Main Street, Bastrop 78602; (512) 303-0558; www.bastropchamber.com.

Smithville Area Chamber of Commerce. First Street & Main Street, Smithville 78957; (512) 237-2313; www.smithvilletx.org.

Elgin, Ledbetter, and Round Top

Take Route 95 north to US 290, then east.

If you're in the little town of Elgin (pronounced with a hard g, as in begin) in late June, take the family to the city's **Western Days and Rodeo** festival in Memorial Park and the Lost Pines Rodeo Arena. You'll be treated to arts-and-crafts and food booths, dancing on tennis courts, a fun run, a kids' parade, and a championship arm-wrestling contest. Top-notch rodeo entertainment in the evening. Call (512) 285-4515 for information.

By the way, US 290 and Highway 21—roads that connect Austin (home of the Lyndon B. Johnson Presidential Library at the University of Texas) and College Station (home of the George Bush Presidential Library at Texas A&M University)—are now designated the Presidential Corridor, a picturesque drive.

Stuermer Store (ages 6 and up)

On US 290, Ledbetter (979-249-3066; www.ledbettertexas.com/Business/Stuermer-Store.html).

Old-fashioned fun and food can be found at the Stuermer Store, which has been in operation for more than one hundred years. Its old bar has been converted to a soda fountain and ice-cream parlor.

Henkel Square (ages 6 and up)

Downtown Round Top (979-249-3308; www.texaspioneerarts.org). Open Thursday through Sunday noon to 5 p.m. $.

Experience a peek back into pioneer life at this nationally recognized museum village. Artifacts are on display in each building, and often reenactors demonstrate pioneer crafts. Among the forty historic structures you can visit are a double-log house, a schoolhouse, a church, a log store, and several family homes. The apothecary shop serves as the visitor center.

Winedale Historical Center (ages 6 and up)

4 miles east of Round Top via Farm Road 1457, then Farm Road 2714 (979-278-3530; www.cah.utexas.edu/museums/winedale.php). Open Monday through Friday 9 a.m. to 5 p.m. Event admission varies.

The Winedale Historical Center in Round Top is operated by the University of Texas' Center for American History. The center itself is a restored nineteenth-century farm and homestead with log cabins, a fireplace kitchen, a smokehouse, and barns. The center holds a couple of first-rate, family-oriented festivals and special events during the year, as well as several classes and workshops.

Eeyore's Birthday is celebrated in late April with food, children's games, children's costume contests, and a Shakespearean comedy. **Shakespeare at Winedale** offers a revolving repertoire of the Bard's classics in July and August.

Where to Eat

Meyer's Elgin Smokehouse. 188 US 290, Elgin (512-281-3331; www.cuetopiatexas.com). Elgin sausage is legendary. Sample it here along with heaping helpings of ribs, brisket, beans, potato salad, creamed corn, pickles and onions, and bread. Stars here are garlic pork sausage and a fat-free (yes, that's fat-free) barbecue sauce. $

Royer's Round Top Café. On the square in Round Top (979-249-3611 or 877-866-PIES; www.royersroundtopcafe.com). This fun place serves stuff that grazes, oinks, and chirps plus mouth-watering, award-winning pies. $$–$$$

Southside Market. 1212 US 290, Elgin (512-285-3407; www.southsidemarket.com). One of the most authentic, and legendary, Texas barbecue cafes. Dating to the 1880s, the eatery is known far and wide for its German-style sausage. This is old-fashioned fare, with big slabs of meat served up on red butcher paper, side orders in cups, and drinks from a tub of ice. $

Where to Stay

Sunset Lodge. 1113 Hwy. 290, Elgin; (512-285-4689; www.sunsetlodgeelgintx.com). Cable TV, refrigerator, hair dryer. $$

Anderson's Round Top Inn. 102 Bauer Rummel Road off Highway 237, Round Top (979-249-5294; www.andersonsroundtopinn.com). Beautifully restored pioneer buildings, amenities vary according to individual cottage, sleep amid history. $$$

For More Information

Greater Elgin Chamber of Commerce. 114 Central Ave., Elgin 78621; (512) 285-4515; www.elgintxchamber.com.

Round Top Area Chamber of Commerce. 102 E. Mill Street, Round Top 78954; 979-249-4042; www.roundtop.org.

Brenham

Brenham is more than 150 years old and teeming with historic buildings. The downtown area has plenty of antiques shops, and the town has more than thirty bed-and-breakfast inns. The area is filled with bluebonnets and other wildflowers in the spring. Call the local chamber of commerce at (888) 273-6426 and ask for a list of historic sites, info on the bed-and-breakfasts, and a **free** **Bluebonnet Trails** map so you can find the best spots to take those precious photos of your children.

Blue Bell Creamery (ages 4 and up)

1101 S. Blue Bell Road, Brenham (800-327-8135; www.bluebell.com). Open Monday through Friday 8 a.m. to 5 p.m. (tours offered 10 a.m. to 2:30 p.m.), closed major holidays. Tours: $.

The Blue Bell Creamery is the second most sacred place in Texas, just behind the Alamo, and a great family fun place. This is where Blue Bell Ice Cream is made. Somehow, over the years, this state favorite became legendary, and to disparage it in front of an old-time Texan is to risk your health.

The "little creamery in Brenham" was founded in 1907, named for the bluebell flowers that cover the nearby hills in the spring. Time magazine pronounced Blue Bell "the best ice cream in the world." Judge for yourself with a tour and a taste. Tours are given Monday through Friday throughout the year.

Brenham Heritage Museum (ages 6 and up)

105 South Market Street, Brenham (979-830-8445; www.brenhamheritagemuseum.org). Open Wednesday 1 to 4 p.m., Thursday through Saturday 10 a.m. to 4 p.m. $.

The Brenham Heritage Museum is housed in a renovated 1915 federal building. The exhibits preserve area history and feature traveling exhibits throughout the year. Among the attractions is an 1879 steam-powered fire engine.

Texas Trivia

Texas is second only to Alaska in volume of inland water, with 4,959 square miles of lakes and streams.

Monastery of St. Claire (ages 2 and up)

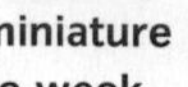

9300 Highway 105, 9 miles northeast of Brenham (979-836-9652; www.monasteryminiature horses.com). Open Tuesday through Saturday 1:30 to 4 p.m. except Holy Week (the week prior to Easter), Thanksgiving Day, and the week preceding Christmas. Open Friday and Saturday only in January, February, and September. $.

The kids will love the Monastery of St. Claire, and they don't have to be religious—they just have to love little horses. The monastery is home to a group of nuns who support themselves by raising miniature horses—some as small as medium-size dogs—and selling handmade ceramics and other crafts in their Art Barn Gift Shop.

Lake Somerville

On Highway 36, 14 miles north of Brenham, Lake Somerville has four Army Corps of Engineers parks (979-596-1622; www.swf-wc.usace.army.mil/somerville), two state parks (Birch Creek: 979-535-7763 or Nails Creek: 979-289-2392; www.tpwd.state.tx.us/spdest/findadest/parks/lake_somerville), and a city park (979-596-1122).

Cool off at this 11,460-acre lake with seven parks and about 500 acres of shoreline developed for boating, camping, fishing, picnicking, and swimming. Lake Somerville State Park is divided into two units, Birch Creek on the north shore and Nails Creek on the south shore. The two units are connected by the 21.6-mile Somerville Trailway System, where you can hike, bike, or ride horses.

Where to Eat

Purcell's Country Style Buffet. 2800 Highway 36 at US 290, Brenham (979-836-9508; www.purcellsbuffet.com). Wide variety of choices. $

Mariachi's Mexican Restaurant. 2522 South Day Street, Brenham (979-830-9015). A local favorite for good Mexican food. $–$$

Tex's Barbecue. 4807 Texas Highway 105, Brenham (979-836-5962). Open pit barbecue; dine inside or in picnic area. $–$$

Where to Stay

Best Western of Brenham. 1503 US 290 E., Brenham (800-WESTERN or 979-251-7791; www.bestwesterntexas.com/hotels/best-western-inn-of-brenham). Pool, hot tub, cable TV, high-speed Internet. $$–$$$

Holiday Inn Express. 555 US 290 W., Brenham (979-836-4590). Pool, gazebo, spa, **free** continental breakfast, **free** WiFi. $$$

For More Information

Brenham Chamber of Commerce. 314 South Austin Street, Brenham 77833; (979) 836-3695 or (888) BRENHAM; www.brenham texas.com.

Chappell Hill and Washington

This area rivals the Hill Country when it comes to beautiful wildflowers in the spring. Take the scenic drive along Farm Road 1155 north to **Washington-on-the-Brazos State Historical Park.** The road winds through beautiful pastoral landscapes filled with bluebonnets, red Indian paintbrush, and pink primroses along a historic route used by early pioneers and settlers.

Chappell Hill has several early Texas and antebellum structures, homes, antiques stores, and crafts shops. One standout is the Chappell Hill Bank. In the same building since 1907, it is the oldest continuously operating bank in the state and features rare historical photographs and documents on its walls, including an original 1899 map of the United States.

Don't miss the **Teddy Bear Parade** during the Christmas in Chappell Hill celebration in early December. Young owners escort the bears and win prizes. City merchants kick off the Yuletide with a number of events, including the arrival of Santa Claus on a fire truck and other entertainment and caroling.

Washington is considered the birthplace of Texas. The city was the site of the signing of the Texas Declaration of Independence and the drafting of the new republic's constitution. From 1842 to 1846 this small town served as the capital of the Republic of Texas.

Chappell Hill Historical Museum (ages 6 and up)

9220 Poplar Street, Chappell Hill (979-836-6033; www.chappellhillmuseum.org). Open Wednesday through Saturday 10 a.m. to 4 p.m., Sunday 1 to 4 p.m. Donations accepted for tours.

Housed in a 1927 school building, the museum exhibits depict plantation life, the Civil War era, life under Reconstruction, local educational institutions, and Polish immigration.

Washington-on-the-Brazos State Historical Park (ages 2 and up)

Off Farm Road 1155, just south of Washington (936-878-2214; www.tpwd.state.tx.us/spdest/findadest/parks/washington_on_the_brazos). Open daily 8 a.m. to sundown. Visitor Center open daily 9 a.m. to 5 p.m. Free.

This 229-acre park on the banks of the Brazos River contains a portion of the original town site, a reconstruction of Independence Hall, an auditorium, a pecan-grove picnic area,

Texas Trivia

Along Texas roads you will find more than a million signs and markers, including more than 2,500 historical roadside markers and more than 1,000 rest areas, picnic areas, and scenic overlooks.

Texas Trivia

The Texas Parks and Wildlife Department manages 123 park areas in the state, including forty historical sites.

an outdoor amphitheater, and Barrington Living History Farm (www.tpwd.state.tx.us/spdest/findadest/parks/barrington_farm), the home of Anson Jones, the last president of the Republic of Texas. The park was recently renovated and the new visitor center has computerized interactive exhibits. History comes alive during the annual **Texas Independence Day** celebration, when volunteers re-create the original Texas Army and display pioneer garb and crafts (usually held on the Sunday nearest March 2).

Star of the Republic Museum (ages 6 and up)

In Washington-on-the-Brazos State Park, Washington (936-878-2461; www.starmuseum.org). Open daily 10 a.m. to 5 p.m. except Thanksgiving Day and December 23-January 1. $, children 6 and under Free

The history of early Texas is preserved at the Star of the Republic Museum, built in the shape of a star. One of the best historical museums in the state, it presents Texas history through exhibits and multimedia presentations depicting pioneer life, agriculture, politics, transportation, and military affairs.

Texas **State Parks**

The Texas parks system is one of the best in the country with 125 state parks and thousands of campsites available statewide. Most parks are generally accessible to the disabled. In addition, there are dozens of State Natural Areas and State Historic Sites from forts to a historic inn to a battleship. Entrance fees vary from $1 to $6 at each park. Camping fees vary considerably. A yearly $60 Texas State Parks Pass allows unlimited entry for everyone in your vehicle, as well as discounts on some camping, park store merchandise, and other special promotions. A **free** lifetime Texas State Parklands Passport allows entry to parklands at half price for senior Texas residents sixty-five and older and to veterans with a 60 percent or greater disability.

Get comprehensive information on state parks in Texas by writing to TPWD, 4200 Smith School Road, Austin 78744; calling (800) 792-1112; or visiting the Web site at www.tpwd.state.tx.us. Camping reservations must be made by calling (512) 389-8900 or visiting www.reserveamerica.com, regardless of the park. A complete Texas State Parks map may be purchased by mail from park headquarters or at most state parks.

For More Information

Washington County Convention and Visitors Bureau. 314 South Austin Street, Brenham 77833; (888) BRENHAM or (979) 836-3695; www.brenhamtexas.com.

Chappell Hill Chamber of Commerce. 5145 Main Street, Chappell Hill 77426; 979-337-9910; www.chappellhilltx.com.

Bryan and College Station

The Brazos Valley Museum of Natural History (ages 6 and up)

3232 Briarcrest Drive, Bryan (979-776-2195; www.brazosvalleymuseum.org). Open Monday through Saturday 10 a.m. to 5 p.m. and the first Sunday 1 to 5 p.m. $.

The museum has displays on archaeology, prehistory, and other subjects and hosts many children's activities and traveling exhibits.

Children's Museum of the Brazos Valley (ages 4 and up)

111 E. Twenty-seventh Street, Bryan (979-779-5437; www.mymuseum.com). Open Monday through Saturday 10 a.m. to 5 p.m. $, children under 1 free.

This hands-on, interactive museum provides a fun educational environment for kids. Daily programs promote reading, recycling, and healthy lifestyles.

Texas A&M University (ages 10 and up)

At Texas Avenue and University Drive, College Station (979-845-5851; www.tamu.edu). Appelt Aggieland Information Center open Monday through Friday 8 a.m. to 5 p.m., Saturday 10 a.m. to 4 p.m. and Sunday 1–4 p.m. Free.

College Station is home to Texas A&M University, which dominates the city as few other colleges dominate towns in Texas. Among the attractions on campus are the Academic Building and Rotunda with its mosaic tile seal and replica of the liberty bell, the Aggie's gigantic Kyle Field, the A&M Sports Museum, the Student Center with galleries and bookstore, and the Sam Houston Sanders Corps of Cadets Center, which honors the past, present, and future of the university, celebrating its Corps of Cadets with miniature cannons, swords, guns, flags, and a Hall of Honor. The center also includes the Metzger-Sanders Gun Collection, featuring antique firearms and other weapons and a collection of Colt pistols.

The university conducts customized family tours of the campus led by students who tailor their presentation based on the ages of your children.

George Bush Presidential Library and Museum (ages 6 and up)

1000 George Bush Drive West, College Station (979-691-4000; http://bushlib.tamu.edu). Open Monday through Saturday 9:30 a.m. to 5 p.m., Sunday noon to 5 p.m. $–$$, children 5 and under free.

The research library and museum is on the Texas A&M campus. It houses thirty-eight million pages of official and personal papers of President George H. W. Bush, as well as one million photographs, 2,500 hours of videotape, and 50,000 museum exhibit items. Included in the exhibits are a 1925 home movie of baby George taking his first steps, as well as memorabilia from his days as a congressman, ambassador to China, head of the Central Intelligence Agency, vice president, and president. Some of the larger displays include a World War II torpedo bomber airplane, a 1947 Studebaker, a slab of the Berlin Wall, and replicas of Bush's offices.

The museum also has a classroom where kids can learn about the presidency and recent American history.

Arctic Wolf Ice Center (ages 6 and up) 

400 Holleman Drive East, College Station (979-693-3900: http://arcticwolfice.com). Call for hours open to the public. $$

This ice rink is home to figure skating, hockey, and broomball as well as some great events including a "kids night out."

Where to Eat

Blue Baker Pizza. 201 Dominik Drive, College Station (979-696-5055; www.bluebaker.com). Award-winning pizza, great deli sandwiches, soups, salads, and pastries. $–$$

Chicken Oil Company. 3600 S. College Ave., Bryan (979-846-3306; www.dixiechicken.com/chickenoil). Great burgers (including the local favorite Death Burger) and sides served in a most unusual atmosphere. Chicken, salads, sandwiches, and a kids menu are available, too. $

Rudy's BBQ. 504 Harvey Road, College Station (979-696-7383; www.rudys.com). Unpretentious, family-friendly, tasty barbecue. $$

Where to Stay

La Quinta Inn. 607 Texas Avenue, College Station (979-696-7777). Outdoor pool, cable TV, high-speed Internet, **free** continental breakfast. $$

Comfort Suites Aggieland. 2313 Texas Ave. South, College Station (979-680-9000; www.comfortsuitescs.com). All-suites hotel near Texas A&M University with fridge, microwave, **free** hot breakfast, outdoor pool, cable TV, and **free** high speed Internet access. $$$

For More Information

Bryan/College Station Chamber of Commerce. 715 University Drive East, College Station 77840; (800) 777-8292 or (979) 260-9898; http://visitaggieland.com.

Temple and Belton

Take U.S. Highway 190 west from Bryan.

Temple grew up around the railroads and still maintains an important railroad shop. The town is now an agriculture center with a growing emphasis on industrial products. Nearby Belton is a smaller town that has retained a rustic charm. Founded in 1850, it was a central stage stop and favorite of cowboys herding cattle up the Chisholm Trail. Many of the city's buildings date to the 1860s and are well preserved, especially in the graceful old downtown area. The city is also home to one of the oldest colleges in the state, Mary Hardin Baylor University, founded in 1845 when Texas was still an independent republic.

Mother Neff State Park (ages 4 and up)

On Highway 236, Moody, 20 miles northwest of Temple (254-853-2389, www.tpwd.state.tx.us/spdest/findadest/parks/mother_neff).

Mother Neff State Park—the first Texas state park—was named for former governor Pat Neff's mom, who donated the land. Developed by the Civilian Conservation Corps during the Depression, the park features tall trees, hills, ravines, and cliffs. There are hiking trails, picnic facilities, campsites, fishing spots along the Leon River, a playground, and plenty of opportunities to see wildlife like armadillos, deer, raccoons, roadrunners, and squirrels.

Annual **Area Events**

- **Belton Youth Fair and PRCA Rodeo,** Belton, February
- **Largest Children's Art Exhibit in Central Texas,** Temple, April and May
- **Central Texas Air Show,** Temple, May
- **Fourth of July Parade, Festival, and Rodeo,** Belton, July
- **Fourth of July Family Fun Fest,** Temple, July
- **Salado Legends,** Salado, July
- **Central Texas State Fair,** Belton, September
- **Temple Annual Model Train Show,** Temple, September
- **Texas Early Days,** Temple, October
- **Scottish Clan Gathering and Highland Games,** Salado, November
- **Tablerock Festival,** Salado, December

Railroad and Heritage Museum (ages 4 and up)

315 West Avenue B, Temple (254-298-5172; www.rrhm.org). Open Tuesday through Saturday 10 a.m. to 4 p.m. $.

Housed in a restored depot, the museum has exhibits devoted to pioneer farm, ranch, and home life; tools; clothing; and the early days of railroading in Texas, including an old Santa Fe steam engine.

Trains are honored in a big way at the Texas Train Festival in September, when the museum puts on special displays and demonstrations and Temple hosts a huge model-train show.

Miller Springs Nature Center (ages 4 and up)

Northside of dam on Farm Road 2271, Temple (254-298-5720). Open dawn to dusk.

When Lake Belton overflowed its spillway in 1992, the water carved out a huge canyon and created wetlands that are being preserved as a natural area that offers hiking, bird-watching, and wildlife photography. Miracle Mile, a fully accessible boardwalk, allows people with disabilities to view the wetlands and restored prairie below.

Temple Lake Park (ages 4 and up)

On Farm Road 2305, 9 miles northwest of Temple.

Cool the kids off on 172 acres along Lake Belton, which features a boat ramp, picnic and camping facilities, fishing, and swimming.

Lake Belton (ages 4 and up)

Headquarters at the dam at the junction of Farm Road 2271 and Farm Road 439, Belton (254-939-2461; www.swf-wc.usace.army.mil/belton).

Lake Belton is the prime source of outdoor recreation in the area. It's noted for numerous arms and coves along its 110-mile shoreline and is surrounded by thirteen public parks offering camping, picnicking, boat ramps, marinas, fishing, and, swimming. For detailed information, visit the Army Corps of Engineers headquarters at the dam.

Summer Fun Water Park (ages 4 and up)

1410 Waco Road, Belton (254-939-0366; www.summerfunwaterpark.com). Open weekends beginning in early May, then daily 11 a.m. to 6 p.m. Memorial Day through Labor Day. $$–$$$.

Summer Fun is a small but classic water park featuring inner-tube rides, water slides, beach volleyball, and horseshoe pits. Locally owned since 2004, it's undergone many improvements and is a favorite place for birthday parties and special events for kids.

Bell County Museum (ages 6 and up)

201 North Main Street, Belton (254-933-5243; www.bellcountytx.com/Museum). Open Tuesday through Saturday noon to 5 p.m. Free.

Housed in a restored 1904 library, the museum focuses on the history of the county, with some interesting exhibits from a restored log cabin to a moustache cup collection. Charley the Longhorn has a couple of special adventures for kids.

Where to Eat

Hank's Town. 4305 South Thirty-first Street, Temple (254-778-1700). Hank's combines an amusement park with an all-you-can-eat pizza and taco buffet. More than 30 fun activities and video games for kids. $

Golden Corral Family Steakhouse. 2113 Southwest H. K. Dodgen Avenue, Temple (254-773-4064). Steaks and all-you-can-eat buffet with special kids' desserts. $–$$

Fuddrucker's. 3111 South Thirty-first Street, #3211 in Temple Mall (254-742-1700; www.fuddruckers.com). This is a chain, but they have fabulous burgers and a kids menu. $

Where to Stay

Best Western Inn. 602 North General Bruce Drive, Temple (254-742-1122; www.bestwestern.com). **Free** cable TV, high-speed Internet, newspaper, and breakfast. Pool and exercise room. Kids 12 and under stay **free.** $$

La Quinta. 1604 West Barton, Temple (254-771-2980 or 800-531-5900; www.laquinta.com). Outdoor pool, **free** breakfast, high-speed Internet. $$

La Quinta Inn & Suites. 229 W. Loop 121, Belton (254-939-2772; www.laquinta.com). Indoor pool, **free** breakfast, newspaper, high-speed Internet, cable TV. $$

For More Information

Temple Convention and Visitors Bureau. 2 North Main Street, Temple 76501; (254-298-5561; www.ci.temple.tx.us/index.aspx?NID=409).

Belton Area Chamber of Commerce. 412 E. Central Avenue, Belton 76513; (254-939-3551; www.beltonchamber.com).

Salado and Killeen

Killeen is just west of Temple on US 190; Salado is south on I–35.

Salado (Suh-lay-doh) was a bustling city when the Chisholm Trail ran through it before the turn of the twentieth century, but when the railroad passed it by things got quieter. The little town is best known today for its quaint shopping area full of galleries and crafts shops and boutiques. If you're here around the first weekend in August, don't miss the annual **Salado Art Fair** in Pace Park, one of the best juried arts and crafts shows in the state. A follies show and an all-you-can-eat fajita dinner are featured in the evening.

The tree-shaded picnic area at **Pace Park** on Thomas Arnold Road beside Salado Creek was once a Native American camp, long before recorded history, and you can still see ruts from wagon wheels in the bedrock of the creek just north of the park.

Fort Hood (ages 6 and up) 

Main gate is on US 190, west of Killeen. Museums open Monday through Friday 10 a.m. to 2 p.m., closed weekends and major holidays. Free.

Killeen is home to Fort Hood, the largest army post in the world, covering 339 square miles off US 190 just west of the city. The post has two museums open to the public at no charge.

The **First Cavalry Division Museum** exhibits more than 150 years of cavalry uniforms, equipment, and weapons, from swords to helicopters, artillery, tanks, and trucks. Located at Building 2218 on Headquarters Avenue; (254) 287-3626.

The **Second Armored Division Museum** features unit history from 1940 to the present and includes some of General George Patton's personal items, along with tanks, combat photos, and dioramas. Located at Building 418 on Battalion Avenue; (254) 287-8811. Visitors should stop for directions at the main gate.

Where to Eat

Stagecoach Inn. Salado exit off I–35, 401 S. Stagecoach Road, Salado (254-947-5111). Known far and wide for its prime rib, hush puppies, and Strawberry Kiss dessert. Servers recite the menu verbally as in the olden days. $–$$

Where to Stay

Stagecoach Inn. Salado exit off I–35, 401 S. Stagecoach Road, Salado (254-947-5111 or 800-732-8994). Texans travel hundreds of miles to stay at the place where George Armstrong Custer, Robert E. Lee, and Jesse James once slept. Historic Inn (circa 1860), restored in the 1940s, now very modern with pool and fitness center. $$$

For More Information

Salado Chamber of Commerce. P.O. Box 81, Salado 76571; (254) 947-5040; www.salado.com.

Clifton, Waco, and West

Take Route 317 north of Killeen to Highway 6 into Clifton, then return on Highway 6 to Waco, for a scenic 35-mile drive through the picturesque North Bosque River Valley.

Waco was named after the peaceful Hueco Indians who lived on the banks of the Brazos River here. The river valley's black soil turned the area into a cotton capital. Later, when the Chisholm Trail was blazed, the city became a cattle center. Today Waco is known as the home of **Baylor University,** the oldest college in Texas and the largest Baptist University in the world.

Go Texan at Waco's **Heart o' Texas Fair and Rodeo** the first week in October. The fair showcases professional rodeo riders, livestock and horse shows, and fine arts exhibits. Located at the Heart o' Texas Coliseum and Fairgrounds; www.hotfair.com.

Waco's **Old Suspension Bridge** was the nation's largest when it was built in 1870 as a toll bridge along the Chisholm Trail. It was the model for the Brooklyn Bridge. Today the

Texas Trivia

When 39 miles of U.S. Highways 81 and 287 south of Ringgold were paved in 1936, sand taken from a pit in the area was mixed with paving material. The sand was found to contain gold in very small amounts. So when you drive down the road here, you're on a highway paved with gold.

bridge, off University Parks Drive, is still used by pedestrians to link **Indian Spring Park** and **Martin Luther King Jr. Park** across the Brazos River. You can enjoy **free** evening concerts in the summer at Indian Spring Park.

Just north of Waco is the tiny town of West, known for its historic Czech cuisine and an annual festival honoring its Czech heritage. Featuring parades, kolache contests, children's games, folk dancing, ethnic food, and an arts and crafts show, **Westfest** (www.westfest.com) takes place on Labor Day weekend.

Bosque Memorial Museum (ages 6 and up)

301 South Avenue Q, Clifton (254-675-3845; www.bosquemuseum.org). Open Tuesday through Saturday 10 a.m. to 5 p.m. Donations accepted.

Clifton is the Norwegian Capital of Texas, and the museum displays the largest collection of Norwegian artifacts in the South. The museum also houses mineral and fossil collections, guns, coins, sailing ship models, pioneer kitchen equipment, farm tools, and Native American artifacts.

Cameron Park Zoo (ages 2 and up)

1701 North Fourth Street, Waco (254-750-8400; www.cameronparkzoo.com). Open Monday through Saturday 9 a.m. to 5 p.m., Sunday 11 a.m. to 5 p.m., closed holidays. Children 3 and under free. $–$$.

The Cameron Park Zoo is the fifty-one-acre home near the Brazos River for antelopes, bison, giraffes, monkeys, rhinos, tigers, wolves, zebras, and other animals. The grounds are covered in native trees—cottonwoods, mesquites, pecans, and oaks—and feature a waterfall. The surrounding park on University Parks Drive at Herring has 328 acres of woods, nature walks, equestrian trails, scenic picnic areas, and a children's playground. Horseback riding is available for an additional fee.

Dr Pepper Museum (ages 6 and up)

300 South Fifth Street, Waco (254-757-1025; www.drpeppermuseum.com). Open Monday through Saturday 10 a.m. to 4:15 p.m., Sunday noon to 4:15 p.m. $–$$.

The soft drink Dr Pepper was invented in Waco by Charles Curtis Alderton, and the recipe has remained unchanged since he first mixed up the concoction at the Old Corner Drug Store in 1885. The Dr Pepper Museum, in the original 1906 bottling plant, honors Alderton and the history of the unique drink. Featured are a restored soda fountain, many interactive displays for children, and a tour through the manufacturing facilities. Admission for the soda fountain or gift shop only is **free.**

Mayborn Museum Complex (ages 4 and up)

1300 South University Parks Drive, Waco (254-710-1110 or 800-BAYLOR-U; www.baylor.edu/mayborn). Open Monday through Wednesday and Friday through Saturday 10 a.m. to 5 p.m., Thursday 10 a.m. to 8 p.m., Sunday 1 to 5 p.m., closed major holidays. $–$$.

The new Mayborn Museum Complex opened in 2004 on the Baylor University campus. It combines the Victorian-era Strecker Museum's natural history collection, a huge hands-on science discovery center for children, and a historic village along the banks of the Brazos River.

Texas Ranger Hall of Fame and Museum (ages 4 and up)

Exit 335B off I–35 in Fort Fisher Park, Waco (254-750-8631; www.texasranger.org). Open daily 9 a.m. to 5 p.m. $–$$, children 5 and under free.

One of the most recognized law-enforcement agencies in the world is the Texas Rangers. The Rangers established Fort Fisher here in 1837, making the region safe for settlers. The Texas Ranger Hall of Fame and Museum is housed in a replica of that original fort at University Parks Drive on the shore of Lake Brazos. The fort serves as headquarters for Company F of the Rangers and also as a museum of the agency's colorful history. Included are an extensive firearms collection, examples of western art, Native American artifacts, dioramas, and a slide show. Many of the docents are retired Rangers, so you can get the history from an expert. Fort Fisher is also a thirty-five-acre park with camping and picnic facilities.

Waco **Annual Events**

- **Central Texas African-American Cultural Expo,** April
- **Brazos River Festival,** April
- **Cinco de Mayo,** May
- **Freedom Frolic,** July
- **Drag Boat Races,** September
- **Heart O' Texas Fair and Rodeo,** October
- **Christmas on the Brazos,** December

For more information call (254) 750-8696 or (800) 922-6386, or visit the Waco Web site at www.wacocvb.com.

Texas Sports Hall of Fame (ages 6 and up)

Next to Fort Fisher, 1108 South University Parks Drive, Waco (254-756-1633; www.tshof .org). Open Monday through Saturday 9 a.m. to 5 p.m., Sunday noon to 5 p.m. $–$$, active military and children under 6 free.

If your kids don't know who Nolan Ryan, Earl Campbell, Lee Trevino, Byron Nelson, George Foreman, or Babe Didrickson Zaharias are, take them to the Texas Sports Hall of Fame, where they'll learn about these Texas heroes and more than 300 others. The museum features several different halls of fame and a video on important sporting events in the history of the state.

Waco Water Park (ages 5 and up)

900 Lakeshore Drive, Waco (254-750-7900; www.waco-texas.com/CITY_DEPTS/parks/aquatics .htm). Open Memorial Day through Labor Day. $–$$ admission determined by height, kids 3 and under free.

A fun park for kids to splash and slide.

Lions' Park Kiddieland (ages 4 to 12)

1716 North Forty-second Street, Waco (254-772-3541). Open Monday through Friday 10 a.m. to 3 p.m., Saturday 10 a.m. to 10 p.m., Sunday 1 to 9 p.m. in the summer. Prices vary with activity.

The kids should like this small amusement park, which has a playground, miniature golf, tennis courts, rides for small children, a swimming pool, and a miniature train that whistles its way around the park.

Where to Eat

Cracker Barrel. 4275 North I–35, Waco (254-799-4729; www.crackerbarrel.com). Southern cooking, huge gift shop in lobby. $–$$

Elite Circle Grille. 2132 South Valley Mills Drive, Waco (254-754-4941; http://elitecircle grille.com). "Where the elite meet to eat" in Waco; specializes in chicken fried steak. $–$$

Rudy's Bar-B-Q. 2510 Circle Road, Waco (254-750-9995; http://.rudys.com). Good Bar-B-Q and "country store" with reasonable prices. $

Where to Stay

Best Western Old Main Lodge. I–35 at Fourth Street, Waco (800-299-9226 or 254-753-0316; www.bestwestern.com). Outdoor pool, free breakfast, cable TV. $$

Victorian Inn. 720 Martin Luther King, Jr. Boulevard (I–35 at exit 335C), Waco (254-752-3388; http://victorianinnswaco.com). Free continental breakfast, cable TV, high-speed Internet. $$

For More Information

Waco Convention and Visitors Bureau. P.O. Box 2570, Waco 76702-2570; (800) 321-9226 or (254) 750-5810; www.wacocvb.com.

Waco Tourist Information Center. Exit 335B on I–35; (800) 922-6386 or (254) 750-8696.

Texas Trivia

The smallest county in Texas is Rockwall County, just east of Dallas, with 128 square miles.

Mexia and Corsicana

Mexia (pronounced *Meh-hay-ah*) is a former oil boomtown at the intersection of Highway 14 and U.S. Highway 84 with three state parks and a lake nearby for family outdoor fun.

Lake Mexia (ages 4 and up)

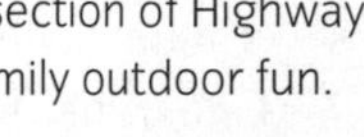

On US 84, 8 miles west of Mexia (254-562-5922).

Lake Mexia is a 1,200-acre impoundment of the Navasota River. You'll find facilities here for boating, camping, fishing, picnicking, swimming, and waterskiing.

Confederate Reunion Grounds State Historical Park (ages 4 and up)

6 miles south of Mexia off Highway 14 on Farm Road 2705 (254-716-3730; www.thc.state.tx.us/hsites/hs_conf_reunion.aspx?Site=Confed).

Confederate Reunion Grounds State Historical Park, now operated by the Texas Historical Commission, has several historic buildings, two scenic footbridges, a low dam, a cannon, and a scenic hiking trail. Reenactments and historical programs are scheduled throughout the year.

Fort Parker State Park (ages 4 and up)

Off Texas Highway 14 on Park Road 28, just south of Mexia (254-562-5751; www.tpwd.state.tx.us/spdest/findadest/parks/fort_parker).

The park consists of 750-acre Lake Fort Parker and the gently rolling oak woodlands surrounding the lake. Here you can boat, camp, fish, hike, swim, or go bird-watching.

Old Fort Parker Historical Park (ages 6 and up)

On Park Road 35, Groesbeck, off Highway 14, south of Mexia (254-729-5253; www.tpwd.state.tx.us/spdest/findadest/parks/old_fort_parker/).

Don't confuse Fort Parker State Park with Old Fort Parker Historical Park, which is a little farther south, near the town of Groesbeck. Kids will love roaming around this reconstructed stockaded fort, a rarity in the West. The fort honors several area pioneers, especially the Parker family and famed captive Cynthia Ann Parker.

Cynthia Ann **Parker**

Cynthia Parker was kidnapped from her family home at Fort Parker in 1836 by Comanches when she was nine years old. In the next twenty-five years, she forgot white ways, married Chief Peta Nocona, had three children, and repeatedly refused to return to white society. Cynthia was recaptured inadvertently by Texas Rangers when she was thirty-four during a raid on a Comanche hunting camp in which Peta Nocona was killed. She was so homesick for her Comanche family that she never settled into white society, made several unsuccessful attempts to flee, and died soon after of a broken heart.

One of her sons, Quanah Parker, became the last war chief of the Quahadi Comanche, a major figure in his tribe's resistance to white settlement and in the Comanches' adjustment to reservation life. Quanah eventually became a wealthy rancher, deputy sheriff, and close friend of Theodore Roosevelt.

Lefty Frizzell Country Music Museum and Pioneer Village
(ages 6 and up)

912 West Park Avenue, Corsicana (903-654-4846). Open Monday through Saturday 9 a.m. to 5 p.m., $, children under age 4 free.

Country-music fans will want to take the family to the Lefty Frizzell Country Music Museum, located in Pioneer Village. The museum houses Frizzell's personal items, including photos, gold records, costumes, and mementos from other country singers. Outside is a life-size statue of this local boy who made it big in country music. Handprints of Merle Haggard and other singers are embedded in the sidewalk in front of the statue. Pioneer Village preserves many restored houses and buildings from the 1800s.

Collin Street Bakery (ages 6 and up)

I-45 at Hwy. 287, Corsicana (903-872-2157; www.collinstreet.com). Open Monday through Saturday 7 a.m. to 8 p.m. and Sunday 11 a.m. to 7 p.m. Free.

Home of the world-famous DeLuxe® Fruitcake since 1896, this new facility has expanded to produce other tasty bakery items and serves sandwiches on homemade bread. The original bakery at 401 W. Seventh Street is also open to visitors.

For More Information

Corsicana Chamber of Commerce. 120 North 12th Street, Corsicana 77510; (903) 874-4731; www.corsicana.org.

Ennis and Waxahachie

Ennis is an unassuming little town today, proud of its Czech heritage, historic building preservation downtown, and its annual bluebonnet crop. In the spring, the local garden club sponsors three **Bluebonnet Trails** in the area, covering a distance of 40 miles through farmlands and rolling hills. On the third weekend in April, the city hosts a **Bluebonnet Festival** featuring an arts and crafts show, horticultural information, Czech pastries, and wildflower seeds.

Waxahachie (Walks-ah-hatchy), a small city south of Dallas, is known as the gingerbread capital of Texas because of its high number of beautifully ornate Victorian-era homes and buildings. It's worthwhile just to wander around the city streets, marveling at the amount of work it took to create these structures. The local chamber of commerce has a map of historic buildings and locations where several movies (*Bonnie and Clyde, Tender Mercies, A Trip to Bountiful*) have been filmed. Of special note is the **Ellis County Courthouse,** built in 1895. With its spires and columns of red sandstone and granite, it is perhaps the most beautiful courthouse in the state. Italian artisans were imported to carve the stone, and the building is covered with ornamental objects and faces, many said to be the face of Mabel Frame, a local woman one of the Italians fell in love with. Ask one of the shop owners around the courthouse square to tell you Mabel's story.

Railroad and Cultural Heritage Museum (ages 6 and up)

105 NE Main Street, Ennis (972-875-1901). Open Monday through Saturday 10 a.m. to 4 p.m. and Sunday 1 to 4 p.m. $, children under 12 free.

Ennis was once the hub for the Houston and Texas Central Railroad, so it's only natural that it's also home to the Railroad and Cultural Heritage Museum. Artifacts include the 1897 edition of the Book of Rules for train operators, photos of trains that stopped in town, and a miniature replica of the train station.

Texas Motorplex (ages 8 and up)

On US 287 between Ennis and Waxahachie (972-878-2641or 800-MOTORPLEX; www.texasmotorplex.com).

If your family likes transportation a little more modern and quicker than trains, go to the Texas Motorplex, a drag-racing mecca east of Ennis. More than 90 races are held annually, along with a number of other auto-related shows and swap meets.

Scarborough Faire (ages 4 and up)

On Farm Road 66, 2 miles west of Waxahachie (972-938-3247 or 888-533-7848; www.scarboroughrenfest.com). $$$–$$$$, children 4 and under free.

There's nonstop fun for everyone in the family at Waxahachie's Scarborough Faire, a Renaissance festival that runs on weekends from early April though the end of May. You'll enjoy hundreds of arts-and-crafts and food booths, seven medieval entertainment stages, and wandering jugglers, wizards, jesters, royalty, and peasants, all in period costumes.

Where to Stay

Best Western Gingerbread Inn. 200 North I–35 East, Waxahachie (972-937-4202; www.bestwestern.com). Outdoor swimming pool, cable TV, high-speed Internet, **free** continental breakfast. $$

Comfort Suites. 400 I-45 South, Ennis (972-872-9898; www.comfortsuites.com). **Free** continental breakfast, high-speed Internet, no smoking. $$

For More Information

Ennis Convention and Visitors Bureau. 2 East Ennis Avenue, Ennis 75119; (972) 878-4748 or 888-366-4748; www.visitennis.org.

Waxahachie Chamber of Commerce. 102 YMCA Drive, Waxahachie 75165; (972) 937-2390; www.waxahachiechamber.com.

Fort Worth

Affectionately called "Cow Town," Fort Worth became one of the largest shipping points for cattle after the Civil War. This was the hub of all those cattle drives. Today it's one of Texas's largest cities and one of the anchor cities—along with Dallas to the east—of the vast Metroplex. The city may be smaller than Dallas and have a more rustic background, but thanks to wealthy patrons over the decades, Fort Worth has museums, art galleries, and fine-arts venues second to none in the state.

Now more than one hundred years old, the **Southwestern Exposition and Livestock Show and Rodeo** (817-877-2400; www.fwstockshowrodeo.com) is a big family event in late January and early February. There's a downtown parade, livestock judging, a carnival, headliner entertainers, and a professional rodeo. Located at the Stock Show Grounds at the Will Rogers Memorial Center, 1 Amon Carter Square. $$$.

Fort Worth Zoo (ages 2 and up)

1989 Colonial Parkway, Fort Worth (817-759-7555; www.fortworthzoo.com). Open daily at 10 a.m. except on Thanksgiving and Christmas, closing times vary, with extended weekend hours during the summer. $$–$$$, half price on Wednesday, children 2 and under free.

The Fort Worth Zoo is a first-class attraction. Your family will go wild over this place, where you can get face-to-face with gorillas, orangutans, and chimpanzees at the World of Primates or watch eagles flying above and around you in Raptor Canyon. Step back into old-time Texas at a one-room schoolhouse, ranch house, and other buildings around which the deer and the antelope do play and the buffalo do roam. Stroll tree-shaded paths that wind around the grounds so you can see more than 5,000 exotic and native animals in natural-habitat exhibits.

The kids will enjoy the **Yellow Rose Express Train Ride** at the zoo. Two ornate miniature trains carry passengers between the Safari Depot and the Texas Wild exhibit. $.

Texas **Bluebonnets**

The official state flower, bluebonnets are a member of the lupine family and have been known as wolf flower, buffalo clover, and el conejo (the rabbit). The name "bluebonnets" came from the flower's resemblance to the sunbonnets pioneer women wore.

The best-known legend surrounding bluebonnets says that a long time ago the Comanches were suffering from starvation and disease. Elders decided the tribe should burn their most valuable possessions as an offering to nature. A young girl overheard the council recommendation, and while everyone was asleep she took her cornhusk doll with its headdress made from blue jay feathers to a hillside, burned it, and scattered the ashes over the hill. The next morning, where the ashes had fallen, the hill was covered in beautiful blue flowers, the same shade as the blue jay feathers. These flowers, the legend says, are the bluebonnets that continue to bloom in Texas every spring.

Botanical Gardens (ages 4 and up)

3220 Botanic Blvd., Fort Worth (817-871-7686; www.fwbg.org). Open 8 a.m. to 10 p.m. Monday through Friday, 8 a.m. to 5: p.m. Saturday, 1 to 5 p.m. Sunday, with extended hours during Daylight Savings Time. The Japanese Garden is a six-acre garden with a pagoda, moon deck, teahouse, and meditation garden. Open 10 a.m. to 5 p.m. and 9 a.m. to 7 p.m. during Daylight Savings Time. $, children under 4 free.

The Botanical Gardens in Trinity Park is a showcase of 150,000 plants in both formal and natural settings. Small waterfalls, ponds, and pathways abound for a relaxing visit. The Conservatory houses hundreds of exotic tropical plants.

Mayfest in Trinity Park (817-332-1055; www.mayfest.org) is a big gathering early in May, with hundreds of arts-and-crafts and food booths, sports activities, competitions for all ages, continuous entertainment, a special children's area, and a concert by the city symphony.

Fort Worth Nature Center and Refuge (ages 4 and up)

9601 Fossil Ridge Road, Fort Worth (817-392-7410; www.fwnaturecenter.org). Open winters daily 8 a.m. to 5 p.m. and summers Monday through Friday, 8 a.m. to 7 p.m., Saturday and Sunday 7 a.m. to 7 p.m. $, children under 3 free.

Not far from the gardens is the Fort Worth Nature Center and Refuge, just west of the Lake Worth Bridge. The 3,500-acre refuge offers an interpretive center, picnic areas, and hiking and self-guided nature trails. Some trails are wheelchair-accessible. The kids will love seeing the bison herd or the white-tailed deer. There's even a prairie-dog town.

Fort Worth **Annual Events**

- **Southwestern Exposition and Livestock Show and Rodeo,** late January/ early February
- **Main Street Arts Festival,** April
- **Cinco de Mayo,** May
- **Mayfest,** early May
- **Chisholm Trail Round Up,** June
- **Pioneer Days,** Labor Day weekend
- **Oktoberfest,** October
- **Parade of Lights,** weekend after Thanksgiving

Museum of Science and Natural History (ages 4 and up)

1501 Montgomery Street, Fort Worth (817-255-9300 or 888-255-9300; www.fortworth museum.org). Open Monday through Thursday 9 a.m. to 5:30 p.m., Friday and Saturday 9 a.m. to 8 p.m., Sunday 11:30 a.m. to 5:30 p.m. $$, hours and prices vary for the Omni Theater and Noble Planetarium, including combination tickets.

Have more family fun at the Museum of Science and Natural History in air-conditioned comfort. The huge museum complex allows kids to dig for dinosaur bones or learn about the wonders of science or history in a number of hands-on, interactive exhibits. Observe the night sky and experience other stellar phenomena at the Noble Planetarium ($). Then experience the ultimate in sight and sound at the Omni Theater ($$), an 80-foot dome that envelops viewers.

Amon G. Carter Museum (ages 6 and up)

3501 Camp Bowie Boulevard, Fort Worth (817-738-1933; www.cartermuseum.org). Open Tuesday through Saturday 10 a.m. to 5 p.m., (Thursday until 8 p.m.), Sunday noon to 5 p.m. Free.

Fine art at the Carter Museum includes one of the largest collections of Western art in America, featuring works by Charles Russell and Frederic Remington. The museum also showcases exceptional traveling exhibits, hosts educational and homeschooling programs, and has an extensive research library.

Cattle Raisers Museum (ages 4 and up)

1501 Montgomery Street, Fort Worth (817-332-8551; www.cattleraisersmuseum.org).

The brand new 10,000-square-foot state-of-the-art museum will open in late 2009 as part of the new Fort Worth Museum of Science and History in Fort Worth's cultural district.

Find out what Fort Worth was all about at this very kid-friendly place. The colorful history of Texas ranching is portrayed with photos, cowboy artifacts, and interactive displays and video games.

Cowtown Rodeo (ages 4 and up)

121 East Exchange Avenue, Fort Worth (817-625-1025 or 888-COWTOWN). $$.

Everyone enjoys a rodeo, and Fort Worth puts one on every Friday and Saturday night at 8 p.m. in the **Stockyards Historic District** at the **Cowtown Coliseum,** site of the first indoor rodeo in 1908. In addition to regular rodeo events, **Pawnee Bill's Wild West Show** features trick roping, riding, and cowboy songs and stories in the summer. Occasionally they feature "Free Kids on Fridays" specials, so check it out.

The **Stockyards Historic Area** captures the Old West with a number of shops and restaurants along Exchange Avenue. A new handheld GPS multimedia computer "tour guide" is available in several languages for rent at the Stockyards Visitor Center. Stockyards Station (817-625-9715) is a large western festival market housed in the renovated hog and sheep pens of the original stockyards. It's the perfect place to buy souvenirs. To see authentic cowboys waxing poetic, make an effort to attend the annual **Red Steagall Cowboy Gathering** in October at the Stockyards. The three-day event is filled with western songs, lore, and poetry.

Performing **Arts** (ages 10 and up)

For a bit of culture, catch a show by one of the city's excellent fine arts companies.

- **The Texas Ballet** (817-212-4280; www.texasballettheater.org
- **The Fort Worth Opera,** the oldest in Texas (817 731-0726; www.fwopera .org)
- **The Fort Worth Symphony** (817-665-6000; www.fwsymphony.org)
- **Bruce Wood Dance Company** (817-927-6500; www.brucedance.org)

These and other organizations perform at several performing arts venues including the **Nancy Lee and Perry R. Bass Performance Hall in Sundance Square,** the downtown **Convention Center,** and **The W.E. Scott Theatre** in the Cultural District.

Fine theater productions may be seen at **Casa Manana** (817-332-2272; www.casamanana.org), **Hip Pocket Theatre** (817-246-9775; www.hippocket .org, or **Stage West** (817-784-9378; http://stagewest.org).

Grapevine Vintage Railroad (ages 2 and up)

130 East Exchange Avenue, Fort Worth (817-625-7245; www.gvrr.com). $$–$$$.

The vintage steam train (see: Grapevine) makes round-trip excursions from Grapevine to Fort Worth's Stockyards Historic District on weekends, except in January when it's closed for maintenance. You may purchase a one-way ticket at the Stockyards Station Depot or take a short afternoon excursion ride in Fort Worth.

The Fort Worth Herd (ages 2 and up)

East Exchange Avenue in the Historic Stockyards District (817-336-HERD; www.fortworth herd.com). Daily at 11:30 a.m. and 4 p.m. Free.

Watch the world's only daily cattle drive! Bring your camera! Watch genuine cowboys drive a herd of authentic Texas Longhorn cattle down Exchange Avenue twice a day to and from their grazing grounds. Educational and family programs are offered throughout the year.

National Cowgirl Museum and Hall of Fame (ages 6 and up)

1720 Gendy Street, Fort Worth (817-336-4475 or 800-476-FAME; www.cowgirl.net). Open Monday through Saturday 9:30 a.m. to 5:30 p.m.; Sunday 11:45 a.m. to 5: p.m. $–$$, children 2 and under free.

It wasn't just cowboys who won the West. Women played just as important a role. The Cowgirl Hall of Fame honors those women who helped make the West great—the pioneers, the performers, the rodeo stars, and the ranch owners. The Cowgirl Hall of Fame moved into a new, impressive facility in the museum district of Fort Worth, and it's full of stuff that will take hours to see.

American Airlines C. R. Smith Museum (ages 6 and up)

4601 Highway 360, at FAA Road near the Dallas/Fort Worth Airport, Fort Worth (817-967-1560; www.crsmithmuseum.org). Open Tuesday through Saturday 10 a.m. to 6 p.m. $, children under 2 free.

You'll discover all kinds of things about passenger airplanes at the American Airlines C. R. Smith Museum. Named for the "Father of American Airlines," the museum has a number of interactive displays, films, videos, and hands-on exhibits.

BC Vintage Flying Museum (ages 6 and up)

At Meacham International Airport, Fort Worth (817-624-1935; www.vintageflyingmuseum .org). Open Saturday 10 a.m. to 5 p.m., Sunday noon to 5 p.m. $$, children under 6 free.

Want to see more airplanes? Go to the BC Vintage Flying Museum at the south end of Meacham International Airport, where you'll see lots of World War II memorabilia and a B-17 Flying Fortress.

Texas Motor Speedway (ages 8 and up)

On Highway 114, at I–35 West, Fort Worth (817-215-8500; www.texasmotorspeedway.com). Call for events and prices.

A state-of-the-art track north of Fort Worth showcases NASCAR and Indy Car races on the big track, Legends Cars on the quarter-mile oval, and auto shows and concerts. Racing takes place spring through summer.

Bureau of Engraving and Printing (ages 10 and up)

9000 Blue Mound Road, Fort Worth (817-231-4000 or 866-865-1194; www.moneyfactory.gov). Open Monday through Friday 8:30 a.m. to 3:30 p.m. (last tour at 2 p.m.) with extended hours in June and July. Free.

See billions of dollars being printed! Take a fascinating 45-minute guided tour or watch the video, see the exhibits, and visit the gift shop. Security screening to enter facility.

Where to Eat

Kincaid's. 4901 Camp Bowie Boulevard, Fort Worth (817-732-2881; www.kincaids hamburgers.com). This former neighborhood grocery store makes big, juicy hamburgers that are consistently voted the #1 burger in the Metroplex. $–$$

Riscky's Barbecue. 300 Main Street, Sundance Square (817-877-3306); 140 East Exchange Avenue, Historic Stockyards District (817-626-7777); and 6701 Camp Bowie, Cultural District (817-989-1800). Jim Riscky is famous in these parts for his "Riscky Dust," a meat rub of eighteen secret spices first concocted by his grandmother. $

Romano's Macaroni Grill. 1505 South University Drive, Fort Worth (817-336-6676; www.macaronigrill.com). Plentiful Italian food, and the kids get to color on the tablecloth with crayons. $–$$

Where to Stay

Park Central Hotel. 1010 Houston Street, Fort Worth (817-336-2011 or 800-848-PARK; www.parkcentralhotel.com). Convenient location directly across the street from the convention center in downtown; swimming pool, fitness center. $$$

Stockyards Hotel. 109 East Exchange Street, Fort Worth (817-625-6427 or 800-423-8471; www.stockyardshotel.com). Luxurious Old West décor, convenient to everything in the Stockyards District. $$$

Holiday Inn Express. 2730 Cherry Lane, Fort Worth (877-863-4780; www.hiexpress.com). Good budget hotel just west of downtown, free breakfast. $$

For More Information

Fort Worth Convention and Visitors Bureau. Sundance Square (downtown), 415 Throckmorton Street, 76102, (800) 433-5747 or (817) 336-8791; Stockyards National Historic District, 130 East Exchange Avenue, 76106, (817) 624-4741; Cultural District, 3401 West Lancaster Avenue, 76107, (817) 882-8588); www.fortworth.com.

Arlington and Mansfield

Just east of Fort Worth is Arlington, home to three of the best family attractions in all of Texas: Texas Rangers baseball, Six Flags Over Texas, and Hurricane Harbor.

Texas Rangers (ages 4 and up)

1000 Ballpark Way, off I–30 at Highway 157, Arlington (817-273-5222; www.texasrangers.com). $$–$$$.

The American League Texas Rangers play at Ameriquest Field, a ballpark that combines a very traditional look with modern comforts and conveniences, including a full-service restaurant with great views of the diamond. The architectural details are exquisite. Behind the bleacher area are several gift shops, an art gallery, and the **Legends of the Game Museum** (817-273-5600). Your children will love the Learning Center in the museum, with several interactive exhibits. A **Walk of Fame** encircles the upper promenade. And you get to watch baseball, too. Most games start at 7:35 p.m. The bleacher seats are a bargain, given the grand view of the game and park and the proximity to the museum and shops. The area around Ameriquest Field have been developed into a parks area with picnic facilities, a Hall of Fame, and a state-of-the-art youth ballpark similar to the big one next door.

Six Flags Over Texas (ages 4 and up)

At I–30 and Highway 360, Arlington (817-530-6000; www.sixflags.com/parks/overtexas). Hours vary considerably with the seasons and days of the week. $$$$.

Six Flags Over Texas is the most popular tourist attraction in the state. The park is full of gravity-defying roller coasters, including the top-rated wooden Texas Giant coaster. It also

Six Flags Over Texas

In its history, Texas has been part of six countries. The flags or seals of those nations are commemorated all over the state, from the amusement park of the same name in Arlington to the mosaic tiles in the floor of the state capitol in Austin.

- **Spain:** 1519 to 1685 and 1690 to 1821
- **France:** 1685 to 1690
- **Mexico:** 1821 to 1836
- **The Republic of Texas:** 1836 to 1845
- **The United States of America:** 1845 to 1861 and 1865 to the present
- **Confederate States of America:** 1861 to 1865

features a parachute drop, a number of thrill and entertainment shows, and Looney Tunes characters roaming the grounds. One of the best attractions here is called the Right Stuff, a virtual-reality ride that creates the full sensation of supersonic flight.

Hurricane Harbor (ages 2 and up)

1800 East Lamar Boulevard, across the freeway from Six Flags, Arlington (817-530-6000; www.sixflags.com/hurricaneHarborTexas/). Open daily May through Labor Day, weekends only through mid-September. $$$–$$$$.

This huge, forty-seven-acre water park (formerly Wet 'n' Wild) is one sure way to beat the Texas heat. You'll find water slides, tube rides, lagoons, and a special area for families with small children that is like a park within a park.

Putt-Putt Fun Center (ages 4 and up)

2004 W. Pleasant Ridge Road, Arlington (817-467-6565; www.putt-puttgolf.com). Open Monday through Thursday noon to 11 p.m., Friday noon to 1:00 a.m., Saturday 9 a.m. to 1 a.m., and Sunday 11 a.m. to 11 p.m. $–$$.

There's lots of stuff to keep the kids occupied: a beautiful miniature golf course, video games, pinball, batting cages, and the top-rated go-kart track in the Metroplex area.

Dyno-Rock Indoor Climbing Gym (ages 6 and up)

608 East Front Street, Arlington (817-461-3966; www.dynorock.com). Open Monday and Tuesday 3 to 10 p.m., Wednesday through Friday 11 a.m. to 10 p.m., Saturday 3 to 11 p.m., Sunday 1 to 7 p.m. $$$.

Now here's an unusual place where your children can be entertained and get exercise at the same time. And what kid doesn't like to climb? Here they do so safely, in a controlled environment.

River Legacy Living Science Center (ages 6 and up)

703 Northwest Green Oaks Boulevard, Arlington (817-860-6752; www.riverlegacy.org). Open Tuesday through Saturday 9 a.m. to 5 p.m. $.

You'll find a wide range of interactive environmental education exhibits here, including a simulated raft ride down the Trinity River.

Where to Eat

Chuck E. Cheese. 2216 Fielder Road, Arlington (817-861-7912; www.chuckecheese.com). Food and fun with pizza and video games. $–$$

Cracker Barrel. 1251 North Watson Road, Arlington (817-633-5477; www.crackerbarrel.com). Great southern cooking, huge gift shop in lobby. $–$$

Outback Steakhouse. 1151 West I–20, Arlington (817-557-5959). People rave about the flavorful steaks, pasta dishes, shrimp, and Bloomin' Onions. $$–$$$

Rawlings All American Grille. 1000 Ballpark Way (inside Ameriquest Field), Arlington (817-277-2706). Food is good, but the view is spectacular. Open game days only—call for hours. $$

Where to Stay

La Quinta Inn. 825 North Watson Road, Arlington (817-640-4142). Outdoor pool, cable TV, **free** continental breakfast, high-speed Internet. $$–$$$

Marriott. 1500 Nolan Ryan Expressway, Arlington (817-277-2774 or 800-321-2211; www.marriott.com/hotels/travel/dalal-courtyard-dallas-arlington-by-the-ballpark). A little pricey, but it's directly adjacent to Ameriquest Field and close to Six Flags and Hurricane Harbor. $$$

Quality Inn and Suites. 1607 North Watson Road, Arlington (817-640-4444). Close to all the attractions, but out of the flow of the main traffic. Pool, whirlpool/spa, spacious rooms, high-speed Internet, **free** breakfast. Children stay **free.** $$

For More Information

Arlington Visitors Center. 1905 East Randol Road, Arlington 76011; (800) 342-4305 or (817) 461-3888; www.arlington.org.

Duncanville, Grand Prairie, Irving, and Grapevine

Whatever you do, don't miss the annual **Championship American Indian Pow-Wow** if you're in Grand Prairie in early September. Dancers from tribes across the country gather to compete for money and trophies. Try the fry bread or Navajo tacos.

Kidsville (ages 4 and up)

200 James Collins Boulevard, Duncanville (972-780-5070). Open daily 5 a.m. to 11:30 p.m. Free.

Kidsville has been rated the top children's playground in the Metroplex by Dallas Child magazine. The huge mazelike facility was built by volunteers and offers children an almost endless variety of slides, swings, and places to climb on or up or around or through. Part of Armstrong Park, which also includes a swimming pool and tennis courts.

Cedar Hill State Park (ages 4 and up)

On Farm Road 1382, 4 miles southeast of Grand Prairie (972-291-3900; www.tpwd.state.tx.us/spdest/findadest/parks/cedar_hill).

Surrounded by the largest urban area in Texas, Cedar Hill offers a quiet, rustic respite. Here you'll find wooded campsites and picnic areas. On Joe Pool Lake you can boat, fish, or swim. Or you can visit the pioneer homestead at the Penn Farm Complex.

Louis Tussaud's Palace of Wax and Ripley's Believe It or Not! Museum (ages 4 and up)

601 E. Palace Parkway, Grand Prairie (972-263-2391; www.palaceofwax.com). Open Monday through Friday 10 a.m. to 5 p.m. and Saturday and Sunday 10 a.m. to 6 p.m. $$–$$$.

That castle you see off I–30 at Beltline is the Palace of Wax and Ripley's Believe It or Not! Your family will find their favorite movie stars and historic figures portrayed in lifelike detail at the wax museum, while over at Ripley's they'll be amazed at the collection of oddities and curiosities.

National Scouting Museum (ages 5 and up)

1329 West Walnut Hill Lane, Irving (800-303-3047 or 972-580-2100; www.bsamuseum.org). $–$$.

This outstanding museum is a tribute to the history of the Boy Scouts of America. The huge state-of-the-art facility features several exhibit areas and lots of hands-on learning experiences.

Mustangs of Las Colinas (ages 2 and up)

5215 North O'Connor Road in Williams Square Plaza, Irving. Free.

Bring your camera! This group of huge, galloping mustangs is the largest equestrian sculpture in the world and took over seven years to create. After you take your pictures, go into the Williams Square West Tower building and turn left on the first floor to visit the small museum/exhibit and to watch the short film about the making of the sculpture. The museum (972-869-9047; www.mustangsoflascolinas.com) is open Wednesday through Saturday 11 a.m. to 5 p.m.

Dallas Cowboys (ages 6 and up)

I-30 at Hwy. 360, Arlington (www.dallascowboys.com). $$$$.

The Dallas Cowboys have a brand new multimillion dollar state-of-the-art stadium in 2009. It will include a Dallas Cowboys Hall of Fame gallery. No team has won more Super Bowls than the Cowboys, long called America's Team in football. The Cowboys play from September to January, and, given the popularity of the team, you'd be well advised to buy tickets many weeks, even months, in advance. The Cowboys also offer special packages that include hotel rooms, tickets for better seats than you can buy through an agent, and transportation to the stadium.

Grapevine Vintage Railroad and Heritage Center (ages 2 and up)

707 South Main Street, Grapevine (817-410-8136; www.gvrr.com). Excursion times vary seasonally (closed for maintenance in January). $$–$$$.

This steam excursion train, pulled by a restored 1896 steam locomotive, makes a 21-mile run from Grapevine's Cotton Belt Depot to the Stockyards Historic District in Fort Worth. The train runs through the Trinity River valley, following the route of the old Chisholm Cattle Trail, and across an old trestle. After a layover in the Stockyards, the train returns to Grapevine—watch it turn around on the 1927 Santa Fe turntable. Don't miss the Grapevine Heritage Center in the restored 1901 Cotton Belt Railroad train station (free admission). It houses railroad memorabilia as well as several exhibits on the history of Grapevine and casts of dinosaur tracks found nearby.

For More Information

Duncanville Chamber of Commerce. 300 East Wheatland Road, Duncanville 75116; (972) 780-4990; www.duncanvillechamber.org.

Grand Prairie Convention and Visitor Bureau. 2170 N. Belt Line Road, Grand Prairie 75050; (800)-288-8FUN; www.gptexas.com.

Grapevine Convention and Visitors Bureau. One Liberty Park Place, Grapevine 76051; (800) 457-6338 or (817) 410-3185; www.grapevinetexasusa.com.

Irving Convention and Visitors Bureau. 222 West Las Colinas Boulevard, Suite 1550, Irving 75039; (800) 2-IRVING or (972) 252-7476; www.irvingtexas.com.

Plano, Garland, and Mesquite

Plano has become known as the "Balloon Capital of Texas." On most calm mornings you'll see a colorful balloon or two floating over the city, and hot-air balloon races are scheduled the last weekend in September. The festival (www.planoballoonfest.com) features hundreds of balloons wafting through the air, an arts-and-crafts fair, and balloon rides for the adventurous. Also, the **Adventure Balloonport** at 1791 Millard Drive will take up to four passengers at sunrise and sunset every day, weather permitting. Call (972) 422-0212.

Interurban Railway Station Museum (ages 4 and up)

901 East Fifteenth Street, Plano (972-941-2117; www.plano.gov/Departments/ParksandRecreation/Parks_Facilities/Pages/interurban.aspx). Open Monday through Friday 10 a.m. to 2 p.m., Saturday 1 to 5 p.m. Free, donations welcome.

Railroad memorabilia and historic artifacts are preserved at this museum, housed in the restored train station in the midst of historic downtown. The surrounding downtown area has several nice shops, boutiques, and cafes.

Southfork Ranch (ages 6 and up)

3700 Hogge Road (Farm Road 2551), Parker (972-442-7800 or 800-989-7800; www.southfork.com). Open daily 9 a.m. to 5 p.m. $$, children 4 and under free.

If anyone in your family was a fan of the TV show Dallas, then don't miss a tour of Southfork, made famous by the program. You can tour the mansion and grounds and a museum dedicated to the show and see herds of horses and longhorn cattle. You can eat at Miss Ellie's Deli or buy western stuff at the Lincolns and Longhorns gift shop, which features the Continental that J. R. Ewing drove in the show.

Surf and Swim Wave Pool (ages 4 and up)

440 W. Oates Drive, Garland (972-205-3993). Open daily Memorial Day weekend through August 15, then weekends through Labor Day. $–$$, children 2 and under free. Open daily 11 a.m. to 7 p.m., Fridays until 9 p.m.

Surf and Swim is a city park with a wave-action pool, grass beaches, and picnic areas in the pecan groves in Audubon Park.

Celebration Station (ages 4 and up)

4040 Towne Crossing Boulevard, Mesquite (972-279-7888; www.celebrationstation.com). Open Monday through Thursday noon to 9 p.m., Friday noon to 11 p.m., Saturday 10 a.m. to 11 p.m., and Sunday 11 a.m. to 9 p.m. Each activity priced separately.

A challenging miniature golf course, bumper boats, go-karts, and a video arcade are just a few of the attractions that will entertain your family here. Kids may be drawn to the paintball arena, but only those 10 or older can play, and a parent or guardian must sign a waiver.

Mesquite Championship Rodeo (ages 4 and up)

1818 Rodeo Drive, Mesquite (972-285-8777; www.mesquiterodeo.com). Gates open at 6:30 p.m., performance at 8 p.m. $$–$$$$; parking $.

You don't have to wait for an annual event to see top-notch rodeoing. Just take the family to the Mesquite Championship for performances every Friday and Saturday night April through September. The rodeos are sanctioned by the Professional Rodeo Cowboys Association, and include Mutton Bustin' and a Calf Scramble for kids. The facility has a restaurant, pony rides, and a Kiddie Korral for youngsters.

Devil's Bowl Speedway (ages 6 and up)

1711 Lawson Road at US 80, Mesquite (972-222-2421; www.devilsbowl.com). Every Saturday evening March through November. $–$$, children 5 and under free.

The Devil's Bowl Speedway features car and motorcycle racing on its half-mile oval track.

Where to Eat

Romano's Macaroni Grill. 5005 West Park Boulevard, Plano (972-964-6676; www.macaronigrill.com). Plentiful Italian food, and the kids get to color on the tablecloth with crayons. $–$$

Ryan's Family Buffet. 909 Tripp Road, Mesquite (972-613-8826; www.ryans.com). The buffet offers nearly 100 items or you may order off the menu. $-$$

Where to Stay

Fairfield Inn. 4020 Towne Crossing, Mesquite (972-686-8286; www. marriott.com). Indoor pool, **free** breakfast, no smoking. $$–$$$

La Quinta. 1820 North Central Expressway (US 75), Plano (972-423-1300 or 800-531-5900; www.laquinta.com). Outdoor pool, **free** high-speed Internet, **free** breakfast. $$

For More Information

Garland Chamber of Commerce. 914 South Garland Avenue, Garland 75040; (972) 272-7551; www.garlandchamber.com.

Mesquite Chamber of Commerce. 617 North Ebrite Street, Mesquite 75149; (972) 285-0211; www.mesquitechamber.com.

Plano Convention and Visitors Bureau. 2000 East Spring Creek Parkway, Plano 75074; (800) 81-PLANO; www.planocvb.com.

Dallas

Dallas and San Antonio have been running neck-and-neck in terms of population since the 2002 census. Dallas is now Texas' third largest city, but certainly the most metropolitan of them all. It's the leader in the Southwest for banking and wholesale business and headquarters to many of the nation's top companies. Wholesalers flock to the Dallas Market Center complex, where items at the Home Furnishings Mart, Infomart, World Trade Center, Trade Mart, Apparel Mart, Decorative Center District, and Menswear Mart set the standards for what you'll be buying in the future. The complex isn't open to the public, but you'll notice its futuristic buildings on the north side of I–35 just before you get to downtown.

The city loves sports and culture and hosts the annual **State Fair of Texas,** one of the largest such extravaganzas in the country. Restaurants, shops, and boutiques in Dallas are second to none. You just can't be bored here.

Frontiers of Flight Museum (ages 6 and up)

6911 Lemmon Avenue, adjacent to Love Field. Dallas (214-350-3600; www.flightmuseum.com). Open Monday through Saturday 10 a.m. to 5 p.m., Sunday 1 to 5 p.m. $–$$, children under 3 free.

The Frontiers of Flight Museum chronicles the history of aviation from early balloon flights to the space program through a number of exhibits and displays.

Cavanaugh Flight Museum (ages 6 and up)

4572 Claire Chenault Drive at Addison Airport, Addison (972-380-8800; www.cavanaughflightmuseum.com). Open Monday through Saturday 9 a.m. to 5 p.m., Sunday 11 a.m. to 5 p.m. $–$$, children under 6 free.

Top Texas **Rodeos**

- **Southwestern Exposition and Fat Stock Show,** Fort Worth, January
- **San Antonio Livestock Exposition and Rodeo,** San Antonio, early February
- **Houston Livestock Show and Rodeo,** Houston, late February
- **Mesquite Rodeo,** Mesquite, Friday and Saturday April through September
- **Pecos Rodeo,** the world's first rodeo, Pecos, July 4
- **Cowtown Rodeo,** Fort Worth, weekends
- **All-Girl Rodeo,** Fort Worth, October

More than thirty planes from both world wars, the Korean War, and the Vietnam War are displayed, along with an aviation art gallery and gift shop.

Dallas Heritage Village at Old City Park (ages 4 and up)

1515 South Harwood Street, Dallas (214-421-5141; www.dallasheritagevillage.org/). Open Tuesday through Saturday 10 a.m. to 4 p.m., Sunday noon to 4 p.m. $–$$.

Take a quick step back in time into furnished log cabins, century-old shops, a Victorian bandstand, a drummer's hotel, and southern mansions.

Dallas World Aquarium (ages 2 and up)

1801 North Griffin Street, Dallas (214-720-2224; www.dwazoo.com). Open daily 10 a.m. to 5 p.m. $$–$$$, children 2 and under free.

The Dallas World Aquarium is one of two nice aquariums in Dallas. This one features sea life from the world's oceans, including corals, giant clams, sharks, and stingrays.

Dallas Zoo (ages 2 and up)

650 South R. L. Thornton Freeway, Dallas (214-670-5656; www.dallaszoo.com). Open daily 9 a.m. to 5 p.m. $$–$$$, children 2 and under free.

Your family can see thousands of animals, including the world's largest rattlesnake collection, at the Dallas Zoo. Among the highlights are the twenty-five-acre Wilds of Africa exhibit and a monorail that will take you on a bird's-eye tour. The facility also has picnic areas and a miniature train.

Cedar Ridge Preserve (formerly Dallas Nature Center) (ages 4 and up)

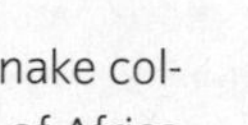

7171 Mountain Creek Parkway, Dallas (972-709-7784; www.audubondallas.org). Open November 1 to March 31 from 6:30 a.m. to 6 p.m. and April 1 to October 31 from 6:30 a.m. to 8:30 p.m.

Cedar Ridge Preserve (formerly Dallas Nature Center) is a 360-acre park with picnic areas, a butterfly garden, and 7 miles of hiking trails around Joe Pool Lake. The area is the habitat for many animals and birds, including some rare ones like the black-capped vireo. The visitor center has a number of educational exhibits.

Malibu Speedzone (ages 6 and up)

11130 Malibu Drive, Dallas (972-247-7223; www.speedzone.com). Open Monday through Thursday noon. to 11 p.m., Friday noon to 1 a.m., Saturday 10 a.m. to 1 a.m. Sunday 11 a.m. to 11 p.m. Prices vary.

See who's fastest in your family at Malibu Speedzone. The facility has differently powered racing cars for children or adults, including a two-seater. Or play the exciting video games.

Dallas Mavericks (ages 4 and up)

Administrative office at 2909 Taylor Street, Dallas (214-747-MAVS; www.nba.com/mavericks). $$–$$$$.

The ever-popular Dallas Mavericks of the National Basketball Association play in the fan-friendly American Airlines Center (www.americanairlinescenter.com) at 2500 Victory Avenue.

Dallas Stars (ages 6 and up)

2601 Avenue of the Stars, Frisco (214-387-5500, ticket line 214-GO-STARS; www.dallasstars.com). $$$$.

Always contenders in National Hockey League play, the Dallas Stars are also residents of the American Airlines Center (www.americanairlinescenter.com).

Sixth Floor Museum at Dealey Plaza (ages 10 and up)

411 Elm Street, Dallas (214-747-6660; www.jfk.org). Open Tuesday through Sunday 10 a.m. to 6 p.m., Monday noon to 6 p.m. Closed Thanksgiving and Christmas. $$$, price includes audio guide, children 5 and under free.

Unfortunately, one of the things Dallas is best known for is being the place where President John F. Kennedy was killed. The Sixth Floor Museum honors JFK with exhibits on his life and death, including photographs, artifacts, and a film. The museum is housed on the sixth floor of the former Texas Schoolbook Depository Building at Houston and Elm Streets, where Lee Harvey Oswald allegedly fired his fatal shots. Nearby, at Main and Market Streets, are a cenotaph and memorial park dedicated to Kennedy.

Fair Park (ages 2 and up)

Cullum Boulevard at Fitzhugh Avenue in the center of Dallas (214-670-8400; www.fairpark.org).

For three weeks in September and October, your family can delight in the **State Fair of Texas** (214-565-9931; www.bigtex.com), a gigantic event with livestock and food competitions, arts and crafts and food booths, a huge carnival, all sorts of entertainment, and the giant Big Tex, welcoming visitors with a hearty "Howdy!"

Constructed for the 1936 Texas Centennial Exposition and recognized as a national historic landmark for its Art Deco architecture, Fair Park features year-round attractions, including the following:

- **Museum of the American Railroad.** 1105 Washington Street in Fair Park (214-428-0101; www.dallasrailwaymuseum.com) preserves old locomotives, cars, and memorabilia. The gift shop is housed in the restored 1905 Houston and Texas Central Depot. Open Wednesday through Sunday 10 a.m. to 5 p.m. Closed major holidays. $, under 3 free.
- The **Dallas Aquarium** at Fair Park is closed for extensive remodeling and will open as a Children's Aquarium in 2010.

- The **Texas Discovery Gardens** at Fair Park. 3601 Martin Luther King Jr. Blvd. (214-428-7476; www.texasdiscoverygardens.org) is a seven-acre urban garden area with botanical collections and a special Garden for the Blind, featuring plants noted for their textures or scents. Special gardening events and classes. Open Monday through Saturday 10 a.m. to 5 p.m., closed holidays. $, children under 3 **free.**
- The **Museum of Nature and Science** (a combination of three former museums: the Dallas Museum of Natural History, the Science Place, and the Dallas Children's Museum). 3535 Grand Avenue in Fair Park (214-421-3466; www.natureandscience.org) has hundreds of hands-on exhibits and displays about natural history, science, energy, and health, as well as a 79-foot, domed IMAX theater and a planetarium show. Open Monday through Saturday 10 a.m. to 5 p.m. and Sunday noon to 5 p.m. Separate fees for exhibits, IMAX theater, and planetarium; combination tickets available. $$–$$$.

African-American Museum (ages 6 and up)

3536 Grand Avenue in Fair Park (214-565-9026; www.aamdallas.org). Open Tuesday through Friday noon to 5 p.m., Saturday 10 a.m. to 5 p.m., Sunday 1 to 5 p.m. Closed major holidays. $

The African-American Museum has one of the largest—and best—collections of African-American folk art in the country, as well as cultural and historical exhibits. The interior of the building is also impressive.

The Women's Museum (ages 6 and up)

3800 Parry Avenue in Fair Park (214-915-0860; www.thewomensmuseum.org). Open Tuesday through Sunday noon to 5 p.m., closed holidays. $, children under 5 free.

This new 70,000-square-foot museum, in association with the Smithsonian Institution, pays tribute to the contributions and achievements of women throughout history.

The Hall of State at Fair Park (ages 6 and up)

3939 Grand Avenue (214-421-4500; www.hallofstate.com). Open Monday through Saturday 9 a.m. to 5 p.m. and Sunday 1 to 5 p.m. Free.

This stately limestone building made its debut in 1936 as part of the Texas Centennial Exhibition and was the most expensive building, per square foot, in Texas at the time. Magnificent tribute to Texas.

Music Hall at Fair Park (ages 8 and up)

909 First Avenue (214-565-1116; www.liveatthemusichall.com). Show times and prices vary by performance.

The Music Hall is home to Dallas Summer Musicals, fun performances during the summer.

Dallas Firefighters Museum (ages 4 and up)

3801 Parry Avenue, near Fair Park, Dallas (214-821-1500; www.dallasfiremuseum.com). Open Wednesday through Saturday 9 a.m. to 4 p.m. $.

Everyone is fascinated with firefighters. See more than one hundred years of city history at the Dallas Firefighters Museum. The museum is housed in a restored 1907 fire station that includes an 1884 horse-drawn steamer and a 1936 ladder truck among the many historical displays and exhibits. An interesting gift shop is located in the old horse stalls.

Dallas Museum of Art (ages 10 and up)

1717 North Harwood Street, Dallas (214-922-1200; www.dallasmuseumofart.org). Open Tuesday through Sunday 11 a.m. to 5 p.m., Thursday to 9 p.m. $–$$, children under 12 free.

The Dallas Museum of Art features an extensive collection of pre-Columbian art along with American and European masters and special traveling exhibits.

Dallas Arboretum and Botanical Gardens (ages 2 and up)

8525 Garland Road, Dallas (214-515-6500; www.dallasarboretum.org). Open daily 9 a.m. to 5 p.m. except Thanksgiving, Christmas, and New Year's Day $–$$, parking $, children under 3 free.

Relax in sixty-six acres of spectacular natural beauty at the Dallas Arboretum and Botanical Gardens. The gardens have more than 2,000 varieties of azaleas among the thousands of blooming plants and ferns. Two historic mansions and scenic White Rock Lake are also on the grounds.

International Museum of Cultures (ages 4 and up)

7500 West Camp Wisdom Road, Dallas (972-708-7406; www.internationalmuseumofcultures.org). Open Monday through Friday 10 a.m. to 4 p.m. $, children 3 and under free.

Through life-size and miniature exhibits, the museum portrays cultures from around the world. The diversity here is almost overwhelming.

The Performing Arts (ages 10 and up)

Dallas is renowned for its performing-arts companies, so try to make a performance or two part of your visit.

- The **Dallas Black Dance Theatre** (214-871-2387; www.dbdt.com) performs in the Dee and Charles Wyly Theatre in the new Dallas Center for the Performing Arts, 2100 Ross Avenue.
- The **Dallas Opera** (214-443-1000; www.dallasopera.org) performs at the Margot and Bill Winspear Opera House at the new Dallas Center for the Performing Arts, 2100 Ross Avenue.
- The **Dallas Symphony** (214-692-0203; www.dallassymphony.com) plays in the Morton H. Meyerson Symphony Center, 2301 Flora Street.
- The **Dallas Theatre Center** (214-522-8499; www.dallastheatercenter.org) performsin the Dee and Charles Wyly Theatre in the new Dallas Center for the Perfoming Arts,

2100 Ross Avenue. The company presents several plays specifically for children and teenagers during the summer.

- The **Anita N. Martinez Ballet Folklorico** (214-828-0181; www.anmbf.org) performs at various venues including the restored historic Majestic Theater, 1925 Elm Street.

Where to Eat

McZoo McDonalds. 632 South R. L. Thornton Freeway, Dallas (214-946-1413; www.mcdonalds.com). Located next to the Dallas Zoo, this one-of-a-kind restaurant has rooftop characters, wildlife murals, and life-size animal statues. Kids can experience a jungle picnic with real animal sounds and safaris through the interactive playland. $

Sonny Bryan's Smokehouse. 302 North Market Street, Dallas (214-744-1610; www.sonnybryans.com). Sure the food is good, but the funky atmosphere, featuring tables made of car hoods with school-desk chairs, is what's fun. $

Extreme Pizza. 6112 Luther Lane at Preston Center West, Dallas (214-363-2464; www.extremepizza.com). The menu offers some bizarre pizzas like "Kickin' Chicken" and "Drag it Through the Garden," but you can also have a more traditional one or create your own. $$

Medieval Times Dinner & Tournament. 2021 Stemmons Freeway, Dallas (214-761-1800; www.medievaltimes.com). If you can splurge, this is a fun place for the whole family. While eating a four-course feast, you'll be entertained by knights from the eleventh century.

Where to Stay

Hyatt Place Dallas Park Central. 12411 North Central Expressway, Dallas (972-458-1224). $$–$$$

La Quinta Inn Dallas Uptown. 4440 North Central Expressway, Dallas (214-821-4220; www.laquinta.com). Outdoor pool, **free** high-speed Internet, **free** breakfast, cable TV. $$–$$$

La Quinta Inn & Suites Dallas North Central. 10001 North Central Expressway, Dallas (214-361-8200; www.laquinta.com). Outdoor pool, spa, fitness center, **free** high-speed Internet, **free** breakfast, **free** newspaper, premium cable TV. $$$

Super 8 Motel. 9229 E. John Carpenter Freeway, Dallas (214-631-6633; www.super8.com). Outdoor pool, fitness center, **free** high-speed Internet, cable TV, **free** breakfast. Convenient location in the Love Field/Market Center area. $$

For More Information

Dallas Convention and Visitors Bureau. 325 North Saint Paul, #700, Dallas 75201; (214) 571-1000 or (800) 232-5527; www.visitdallas.com.

Dallas Visitor Center. In the historic "Old Red" Courthouse, 100 South Houston Street, Dallas. Open 8 a.m. to 5 p.m. weekdays and 9 a.m. to 5 p.m. weekends.

Lewisville, Denton, and Gainesville

For a nice scenic drive with panoramic views of the rolling hills, travel on Farm Roads 372, 678, and 902 east and south of Gainesville.

Lewisville Lake (ages 4 and up)

Hackberry Road off Farm Road 423, Lewisville (972-434-1666).

This Corps of Engineers reservoir is very popular in the Metroplex area for outdoor recreation. The 23,000-acre lake is surrounded by seventeen parks, most of them administered by the Army Corps of Engineers (www.swf-wc.usace.army.mil/lewisville). You'll find marinas, boat ramps, fishing supplies, and rentals. At some of the parks you'll find campsites, screened shelters, fish-cleaning stations, picnic areas, and playgrounds.

Texas First Ladies Historic Costume Collection (ages 6 and up)

TWU Administration Tower, Second Floor, Denton (940-898-3644; www.twu.edu/firstladies). Monday through Friday 8 a.m. to 5 p.m. Free.

This Museum on the campus of Texas Women's University is a unique collection of all the inaugural gowns worn by the first ladies of Texas, either wives of presidents of the republic, wives of governors, or wives of Texans who served as U.S. president.

Annual **Area Events**

- **North Texas Farm Toy Show,** Gainesville, February
- **Denton Arts & Jazz Festival,** Denton, April
- **Cinco de Mayo,** Lewisville, May
- **Spring Fling in the Park,** Gainesville,
- **North Texas State Fair and Rodeo,** Denton, August
- **Labor Day Rodeo,** Lewisville, September
- **Depot Days,** Gainesville, October
- **Victorian Christmas and Teddy Bear Parade,** Denton, December
- **Holiday Lighting Festival,** Denton, December
- **Holiday at the Hall,** Old Town Lewisville, December

Texas Trivia

Texas celebrates both Martin Luther King Jr.'s birthday and Confederate Heroes Day as official state holidays in the same week in January.

Ray Roberts Lake State Park (ages 4 and up)

Farm Road 445 off I–35, Denton (940-686-2148 Isle du Bois or 940-637-2294 Johnson Branch; www.tpwd.state.tx.us/spdest/findadest/parks/ray_roberts_lake.

You'll find plenty of splashing and fishing at Ray Roberts Lake State Park. The park comprises two units, Isle du Bois and Johnson Branch, and several satellite parks border the 30,000-acre Ray Roberts Lake. The facilities have campsites, picnic areas, boat ramps, more than 20 miles of hiking and biking trails, and plenty of places to swim or fish.

Frank Buck Zoo (ages 4 and up)

1000 W. California Street @ I-35, Gainesville (940-668-4539; www.frankbuckzoo.com). Open daily 9 a.m. to 5 p.m. $–$$.

Unless you're traveling with your grandparents, no one in your family is likely to remember who Frank Buck was. The famous adventurer of the 1930s and 1940s made the phrase "Bring 'em back alive" a household saying as he captured hundreds of wild animals for zoos. The Frank Buck Zoo is named to honor Gainesville's famous son. The zoo is home to monkeys, zebras, flamingos, bears, elephants, and more. The facility also has shaded picnic areas.

For More Information

Denton Convention and Visitors Bureau. 414 Parkway, Denton 76201; (888) 381-1818 or (940) 382-7895; www.discoverdenton.com.

Gainesville Chamber of Commerce. 101 South Culbertson Street, Gainesville 76240; (940) 665-2831;www.gogainesville.net

Lewisville Convention & Visitors Bureau. 606 West Main Street, Lewisville 75057; (800) 657-9571 or (972) 219-3719; www.visitlewisville.com.

Denison, Sherman, and McKinney

This area, near the Texas-Oklahoma border, is a great place if you just want to relax. Small towns and lots of outdoor recreation are the order of the day here.

Dwight Eisenhower—who was born in Denison shortly before his parents moved to Kansas—was the first native Texan to become president, and two state parks in the area commemorate the World War II hero.

Eisenhower Birthplace State Historic Site (ages 10 and up)

609 South Lamar Avenue, Denison (903-465-8908; www.thc.state.tx.us/hsites/hs_eisenhower .aspx?Site=Eisenhower). Open Tuesday through Saturday 9 a.m. to 5 p.m., Sunday 1 to 5 p.m. $, children 12 and under free.

The two-story, gabled house Ike was born in has been restored to its appearance in 1890, the year Eisenhower was born. You'll see family possessions, period antiques, and hundreds of items relating to Eisenhower and his place in history. The ten-acre park also has a hiking trail following an abandoned railroad track.

Red River Railroad Museum (ages 4 and up)

101 East Main Street in the restored historic KATY Depot, Denison (903-463-KATY; www .redriverrailmuseum.org). Open Friday and Saturday 10 a.m. to 4:30 p.m., Sunday 1–4:30 p.m. Free, donations welcome.

Denison was founded in 1872 because of the railroad, specifically the Missouri, Kansas, and Texas line. That pioneer heritage has been preserved here with artifacts, pictures, MKT railroad equipment, and rolling stock.

Grayson County Frontier Village (ages 4 and up)

Loy Park at the Frontier Village exit off US 75, Denison (903-463-2487). Open daily 1 to 4 p.m.

The Grayson County Frontier Village in Denison is not a typical county museum. It's a collection of eighteen rustic buildings dating from 1840 to 1900, all restored and furnished. The museum exhibits household items, clothing, and tools from pioneer days.

Eisenhower State Park (ages 4 and up)

Park Road 20 off Farm Road 1310, 5 miles northwest of Denison (903-465-1956, www.tpwd .state.tx.us/spdest/findadest/parks/eisenhower)

Named for President Dwight David Eisenhower, this 450-acre park is perched on rocky cliffs above Lake Texoma and has a modern marina, campsites, boat rentals, screened shelters, picnic areas, hiking and biking trails, and, of course, swimming and fishing.

Annual **Area Events**

- **Livestock Show,** Sherman, March
- **Texoma Lakefest,** Denison, April
- **Hot Summer Nights Concert Series,** Sherman, June-July
- **U.S. National Aerobatic Competition,** Denison, September
- **Sherman Arts Festival,** Sherman, September
- **Grayson County Fair,** Sherman, October
- **Main Street Fall Festival,** Denison, October

Lake Texoma (ages 4 and up)

North of U.S. Highway 82, west of Denison (903-465-4990; www.laketexoma.com).

Lake Texoma is a huge, 89,000-acre reservoir, impounding the Red River in Texas and Oklahoma. It's one of the most popular places for outdoor recreation in the state. The surrounding Army Corps of Engineers parks have more than fifty campgrounds, dozens of trailer parks, more than a hundred picnic areas, more than a hundred screened shelters, and more than eighty boat ramps. Some piers even have enclosed areas where you can fish in air-conditioned comfort. Modern marinas and resorts dot the 580 miles of shoreline. The Cross Timbers Hiking Trail winds through 14 miles of woods around the lake. Fishing is considered some of the best in either state. Maps, detailed information, and exhibits on the building of Denison Dam can be found at the dam headquarters on U.S. Highway 75A, a few miles north of Denison.

Hagerman Wildlife Refuge (ages 4 and up)

On Farm Road 1417, 4 miles north of Sherman (903-786-2826; www.fws.gov/southwest/refuges/texas/hagerman/index.html).

Hagerman Wildlife Refuge surrounds the Big Mineral Arm of Lake Texoma with 12,000 acres of habitat—including 3,000 acres of marshland—that are home to 280 species of migratory waterfowl and other birds. A variety of geese spend the winter in Hagerman. The refuge has a 4-mile auto tour with roadside exhibits providing information on the area and wildlife, several hiking and biking trails, three picnic areas, an observation tower, wildlife blinds, a visitor center, and a historical exhibit depicting the old town of Hagerman, which was removed before the flooding of Lake Texoma. Camping and swimming are not permitted.

Heard Natural Science Museum and Wildlife Sanctuary

(ages 4 and up) 

On Farm Road 1378, 5 miles south of McKinney (972-562-5566; www.heardmuseum.org). Open Monday through Saturday 9 a.m. to 5 p.m., Sunday 1 to 5 p.m. $–$$, children 2 and under free.

Your family can see lots of wildlife at the Heard Natural Science Museum and Wildlife Sanctuary. Exhibits include fossils, archaeology, seashells, rocks, and live animals; there are also several nature trails through the 274-acre sanctuary and a paved trail for wheelchairs. In addition to the exhibits and nature trails, there's a native plant garden, a ropes course, and a conservation sanctuary. The gift shop has nature books, specimens, and other nature-related items. The family-friendly facility has numerous educational programs, hikes, and summer camps.

Where to Eat

Dickey's Barbecue. 529 W. Lamar Street, Sherman (903-870-2083; www.dickeys.com). A local favorite for good barbecued meat platters and sandwiches. $

Golden Corral. 900 East US 82, Sherman (903-892-3366). All-you-can-eat buffet. $–$$

The Point Restaurant. At Grandpappy Point Marina on Farm Road 84, Denison (903-463-3000 or 888-855-1972; www.grandpappy.com/the_point.asp). Good food and a great view overlooking Lake Texoma. $–$$

Where to Stay

Best Western Texoma Hotel & Suites. 810 N. US 75, Denison (903-327-8883; www.bestwestern.com). Brand new. **Free** hot breakfast, **free** WiFi high-speed Internet, pool, hot tub, fitness center, flat HD TV. $$–$$$, children 12 and under **free.**

Grandpappy Point Marina Cabins. On Farm Road 84, Denison (888-855-1972; www.grandpappy.com/cabins.asp). Nice cabins on Lake Texoma; full marina, store, restaurant, RV park. $$–$$$

La Quinta Inn. 2912 US 75 North, Sherman (903-870-1122; www.laquinta.com). Outdoor pool, fitness center, **free** WiFi high-speed Internet, **free** newspaper, **free** breakfast, premium cable TV. $$

For More Information

Denison Chamber of Commerce. 313 West Woodard Street, Denison 75020; (903) 465-1551; www.denisontexas.us.

McKinney Convention & Visitor Bureau. 321 N. Central Expressway #101, McKinney 75070; (888) 649-8499; www.visitmckinney.com.

Sherman Convention and Visitors Council. 101 South Travis Street, Sherman 75090; (903) 957-0310; www.shermantx.org.

Texas Trivia

Lake Texoma is one of 6,736 reservoirs in Texas. The Red River, at 1,360 miles, is the second longest river in the state; the Rio Grande is longest.

Wichita Falls and Jacksboro

The original falls on the Wichita River were destroyed by a flood in 1886, but the city has re-created them in a beautifully landscaped park in the middle of the city.

The **Wichita Falls Waterfall** is off I–44 on the south side of the bridge over the Wichita River. More than 3,500 gallons of water a minute are circulated through the 54-foot-high waterfall that drops in a series of steps over rocks; a stairway next to the fall goes from top to bottom. The park is cooling, relaxing, and a great place for photographs.

Lucy Park (ages 4 and up)

Sunset at Fifth Street, Wichita Falls (940-761-7490).

In a bend of the Wichita River near the waterfall, Lucy Park is a 178-acre park, a nice place for picnics and just playing around. The park has a log cabin, large swimming pool, 18-hole disc golf course, concrete vollyball court, duck pond, paved nature trail, and children's playground. The River Walk trail connects the park to the waterfall.

Railroad Museum (ages 4 and up)

500 Ninth Street, Wichita Falls (940-723-2661; www.wfrrm.com). Open Saturday noon to 4 p.m. Free.

A nice collection of railroad cars—including a diesel engine, a Pullman car, two World War II troop sleepers, a baggage car, a post office car, a coach, and several cabooses—are preserved at the museum.

The Plex Family Entertainment Center (ages 4 and up)

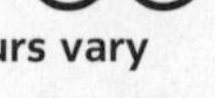

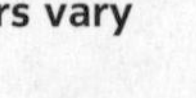

4131 Southwest Parkway, Wichita Falls (940-696-1222; www.theplexfec.com). Hours vary by season and day of the week. Prices vary by activity.

The classic kid place full of go-karts, bumper boats, video games, miniature golf courses, laser trek, batting cages, kiddie rides, and more.

Castaway Cove Waterpark (ages 5 and up)

1000 Central Freeway East, Wichita Falls (940-322-5500; www.castawaycovewaterpark.com). Hours vary seasonally. $$$–$$$$.

Slides, tubes, wave pools, fountains, and every other way to get wet you can think of.

Village Bowl (ages 6 and up)

4022½ Kemp, Wichita Falls (940-696-2695; www.villagebowl.net). Call for hours and open lane times. $.

What kid doesn't like to bowl? An outing at the lanes can make for a perfect family get-together.

Wichita Falls Museum of Art (ages 6 and up)

2 Eureka Circle, Wichita Falls (940-692-0923; www.mwsu.edu/wfma). Open Tuesday, through Friday 9:30 a.m. to 5 p.m., Thursday to 7 p.m., Saturday 10:30 a.m. to 5 p.m. Free.

The Wichita Falls Museum of Art at Midwestern State University showcases fine art and changing exhibits.

Lake Arrowhead State Park (ages 4 and up)

Off Farm Road 1954, approximately 15 miles southeast of Wichita Falls (940-528-2211, www.tpwd.state.tx.us/spdest/findadest/parks/lake_arrowhead).

Water recreation is the attraction at Lake Arrowhead State Park. You'll find campsites, restrooms with showers, a grocery store, and boat ramps. A nice place to spend the day fishing, swimming, or waterskiing. Tip: The lake is dotted with steel oil derricks, and the waters around these structures are usually great for fishing.

Fort Richardson State Historic Site (ages 6 and up)

On US 281, half a mile south of Jacksboro (940-567-3506, www.tpwd.state.tx.us/spdest/findadest/parks/fort_richardson). Historic area open 8 a.m. to 5 p.m. daily. $, children 12 and under free.

Fort Richardson has a couple of restored buildings, including an officer's quarters that serves as a visitor center, and several ruins. In addition to soaking up nineteenth-century military history, the family can enjoy camping, picnicking, fishing in the old quarry pond (stocked with rainbow trout in the winter), and hiking along the three nature trails.

Where to Eat

Casa Mañana. 609 Eighth Street, Wichita Falls (940-723-5661). A local favorite for tasty Mexican food. $

Chuck E. Cheese. 2935 Southwest Parkway, Wichita Falls (940-692-7882; www.chuckecheese.com). Fun and pasta, with video games and music. $–$$

The Feedlot Restaurant. 914 South Red River Expressway, Wichita Falls (940-569-9999; www.feedlotburk.com). Home style cooking—chicken-fried steak, chicken, pork chops, steaks, catfish, and burgers. $–$$

Where to Stay

La Quinta Airport. 1128 Central Freeway, Wichita Falls (940-322-6971). Outdoor pool, free breakfast, free high-speed Internet, cable TV. $$

Best Western Inn. 1032 Central Freeway, Wichita Falls (940-766-6881; www.bestwestern.com). Pool, fitness center, free breakfast, high-speed Internet, cable TV. $–$$

For More Information

Wichita Falls Convention and Visitors Bureau. 1000 Fifth Street, Wichita Falls 76301; (940) 716-5500; www.wichitafalls.org.

Mineral Wells and Weatherford

In this rural area of Texas, the nearby Brazos River offers the perfect chance for your family to get away from it all, enjoying beautiful scenery on a relatively calm and quiet river. Several companies rent canoes for float trips.

The area is the birthplace of the Loving-Goodnight cattle drives of the Old West, and Oliver Loving—the man Larry McMurtry based the character of Gus McCrae on in Lonesome Dove—is buried in Weatherford. Water from the Crazy Well in Mineral Wells was all the rage in the nineteenth century.

By the way, that huge castle-like structure you're bound to see at 1825 Bankhead Drive in Weatherford is the **Pythian Home,** built by the Knights of Pythias in 1907. It's private, but if you want a tour, one can be arranged through the Chamber of Commerce at (888) 594-3801.

Famous Mineral Water Company (ages 6 and up)

209 N.W. Sixth Street, Mineral Wells (940-325-8870; www.famouswater.com). Open Tuesday through Friday 8 a.m. to 5:30 p.m., Saturday 9 a.m. to 5 p.m. Tours free.

Mineral Wells was famous in the nineteenth century for water that was said to cure just about anything, including mental illness. Only one of those companies that bottled the well water, the Famous Mineral Water Company, is operating today. The company no longer makes outrageous claims for the water, however. **Free** tours take you to the drinking pavilion, well, and bottling plant.

Lake Mineral Wells State Park & Trailway (ages 4 and up)

On US 180, 4 miles east of Mineral Wells (940-328-1171, www.tpwd.state.tx.us/spdest/findadest/parks/lake_mineral_wells).

Find great outdoor recreation at Lake Mineral Wells State Park. This is another of the many parks built by the Civilian Conservation Corps in the 1930s. The chances for your kids to see wildlife like white-tailed deer and wild turkeys are excellent in this heavily wooded park surrounding Lake Mineral Wells. Facilities include boat ramps, campsites with water, picnic areas, five fishing piers, a swimming area, a recreation hall, screened shelters, and showers. More than 20 miles of hiking and equestrian trails wind through the park.

Possum Kingdom State Park (ages 4 and up)

Park Road 33, 17 miles north of Caddo (940-549-1803, www.tpwd.state.tx.us/spdest/findadest/parks/possum_kingdom).

Possum Kingdom State Park is one of the premier outdoor-recreation havens in Texas, tucked away in the rugged Palo Pinto Mountains. The 20,000-acre lake has the clearest water you'll find anywhere in the state. The kids will enjoy watching the cliff swallows, the almost-tame deer strolling through the grounds, the cattle that are part of the official State Longhorn Herd, or the opossums after which the lake is named. The park has boat

Annual **Area Events**

- **Palo Pinto County Livestock Show and Fair,** Mineral Wells, March
- **Crazy Water Festival,** Mineral Wells, October
- **Peach Festival,** Weatherford, July
- **Parker County Frontier Days Livestock Show and Rodeo,** Weatherford, June
- **PossumFest,** Possum Kingdom, October
- **Old-Fashioned Holiday Festival,** Mineral Wells, December

ramps, campsites, picnic tables, and grills. The swimming and the fishing are both great. To get there, take U.S. Highway 180 westof Mineral Wells for about 40 miles to Caddo, then go north 17 miles on Park Road 33 to the lake.

Holland Lake Park (ages 4 and up)

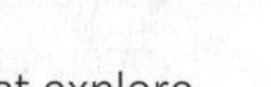

1350 Holland Lake Drive, off exit 409 from I–20, Weatherford (888-594-3801).

Holland Lake Park is a ten-acre living museum of nature with marked trails that explore three distinct ecosystems. The park also has a playground and picnic facilities.

Lake Weatherford (ages 4 and up)

On Farm Road 730, off US 180, 7 miles east of Weatherford.

Lake Weatherford is another city-owned park on the Clear Fork of the Trinity River. The area has many public and commercial swimming and fishing areas.

Weatherford City Library (ages 6 and up)

1014 Charles Street, Weatherford (817-598-4150). Open Monday through Thursday 10 a.m. to 8 p.m.; Friday and Saturday 10 a.m. to 6 p.m., Sunday 2 to 6 p.m. Free.

The kids might wonder why there's a statue of Peter Pan in front of the Weatherford City Library. You may explain to them that Weatherford was the home of Mary Martin, who created the role of Peter Pan on Broadway. The library has some costumes, music scores, and other Martin memorabilia.

For More Information

Mineral Wells Area Chamber of Commerce. 511 East Hubbard Street, Mineral Wells 76067; (940) 325-2557 or 800-252-6989; www.mineralwellstx.com.

Weatherford Visitors Center. 401 Fort Worth Highway, Weatherford 76086; (817) 596-3801 or (888) 594-3801; www.weatherford-chamber.com.

Granbury, Glen Rose, Cleburne, Meridian, and Whitney

You'll find a fair amount of history in Granbury, one of the best small towns in Texas. For example, Davy Crockett's wife and son are buried near here, and you can also visit the grave of Jesse James at the city cemetery at North Crockett and Moore Streets. Well, his family claims it's Jesse, who they say survived his wounds to retire here. Locals have heard stories about the man who claimed to be James and another who claimed to be Lincoln assassin John Wilkes Booth.

You'll find a number of nice shops and restaurants around the courthouse square with ample **free** parking in the lot inside the square. The tower clock on the magnificent courthouse still functions.

Acton State Historic Site (ages 4 and up)

On Farm Road 167, about 6 miles east of Granbury (817-463-7948; www.thc.state.tx.us/hsites/hs_acton.aspx?Site=Acton).

Davy Crockett's widow, Elizabeth, and son, Robert, are buried here. After Crockett died at the Alamo, the new Republic of Texas gave his family land nearby, so they moved from Tennessee. The entire park encompasses just the graves and monument; with just .01 acre, it is the smallest historic site in Texas.

The Brazos Drive-In Theater (ages 4 and up)

1800 West Pearl Street, Granbury (817-573-1311; www.thebrazos.com). Box Office opens at 7:15 p.m., showtime at 8:30 p.m. Friday and Saturday. $$$, carload price for up to 6.

The Brazos Drive-In is one of the few remaining old-fashioned drive-in movie theaters in the nation. Fewer than a dozen remain in Texas. Drive in, tune your radio to the movie sound, enjoy some popcorn, and relax.

Granbury Live Theater (ages 6 and up)

110 North Crockett Street, Granbury (800-989-8240 or 817-573-0303; www.granburylive.com). $$$–$$$$.

Granbury Live showcases family entertainment "within the traditional guidelines of Christian values." Their very popular nostalgia concerts are costumed and choreographed live-music productions featuring an all-professional cast with music from the golden age of rock and roll. On "Family Friday" nights, youths 15 or under are **free** with an adult (limit two youths per adult ticket).

Lake Granbury (ages 4 and up)

Lake Granbury is almost everywhere you look when you're in town. Public and commercial facilities are all along the 100 miles of shoreline, so you won't have any problem finding a place to picnic, swim, fish, or water-ski.

Annual **Area Events**

- **General Granbury's Birthday Party,** Granbury, March
- **Old-Fashioned Fourth of July,** Granbury
- **Bluegrass Festival,** Tres Rios Park, Glen Rose, September
- **Granbury Civil War Reenactment,** Granbury, September
- **Comanche County Pow-Wow,** Comanche, September
- **Harvest Moon Festival,** Granbury, October

The Promise (ages 6 and up)

Texas Amphitheatre off U.S. Highway 67, Glen Rose (800-687-2661; www.thepromise glenrose.com). Performances are Friday and Saturday evenings September and October. $$–$$$$.

Glen Rose is home to *The Promise,* a historical reenactment of the life of Jesus of Nazareth. The musical drama is presented in the 3,200-seat open-air Texas Amphitheatre.

Fossil Rim Wildlife Center (ages 4 and up)

Off US 67, 3 miles west of Glen Rose, 2299 CR 2008 (254-897-2960; www.fossilrim.org). Open daily 8:30 a.m. to 5:30 p.m., shorter hours in the winter. $$$–$$$$, children under 3 free.

Discover some the world's most endangered animals at Fossil Rim. White rhinos, zebras, and cheetahs roam free on the 2,900 acres of valleys and savannas. Facilities include a petting pasture for children, picnic areas, a restaurant, nature trails, and an educational center. For a special experience, take a family tour or a behind-the-scenes tour.

Dinosaur Valley State Park (ages 4 and up)

On Park Road 59 off Farm Road 205, 4 miles west of Glen Rose (254-897-4588; www.tpwd .state.tx.us/spdest/findadest/parks/dinosaur_valley/).

Families love Dinosaur Valley State Park. This is a very scenic park on the banks of the Paluxy River, where you can camp, have a picnic, or roam over one of the many hiking trails. But you'll also be fascinated by the dinosaurs. A couple of giant replicas overlook the grounds near the park entrance. And real footprints can be seen in the riverbed. These are the best-preserved tracks in the state and among the best in the country. Interpretive exhibits at the visitor center will give you an idea of what this area looked like a hundred million years ago.

Cleburne State Park (ages 4 and up)

On Park Road 21 off Hwy. 67, about 10 miles southwest of Cleburne (817-645-4215, www .tpwd.state.tx.us/spdest/findadest/parks/cleburne).

A real out-of-the-way place, Cleburne is a 528-acre park surrounded by white rock hills where oak, elm, mesquite, cedar, and redbud trees are almost jungle thick, and in spring bluebonnets carpet the open spaces. Your family can fish, swim, or boat on the lake that flows from three natural springs. The park has campsites and picnic areas as well. And you've got a good chance to see deer, wild turkey, ducks, geese, and armadillos.

Meridian State Park (ages 4 and up)

On Park Road 7, off Highway 22, 3 miles southwest of Meridian (254-435-2536, www.tpwd.state.tx.us/spdest/findadest/parks/meridian).

Meridian State Park is a quiet spot with 500 wooded acres and abundant plants, wildflowers, animals, and birds. Facilities include campsites, swimming, fishing, boating, 5 miles of scenic bike trails, and 6 miles of hiking trails.

Lake Whitney State Park (ages 4 and up)

On Farm Road 1244, 3 miles west of Whitney (254-694-3793, www.tpwd.state.tx.us/spdest/findadest/parks/lake_whitney).

Lake Whitney is the fourth largest lake in Texas, extending 45 miles along the Brazos River. The park itself has scattered oak groves, and in the spring bluebonnets and Indian paintbrushes cover the landscape. You can swim, ski, or fish on the lake, renowned for its trophy-size bass, or take a hike along the nature trail.

Where to Eat

Grumps Burgers. 3503 East Highway 377, Granbury (817-573-5000; www.grumpstexas.com). Local folks consistently vote Grumps the best burgers in Hood County. $–$$

Rinky-Tinks Sandwich and Ice Cream Shop. 108 North Houston Street, Granbury (817-573-4323; www.rinkytinks.com). Great ice cream and sandwiches all day. $

Ranch House BBQ. 1408 N.E. Big Bend Trail (US 67), Glen Rose (254)-897-3441. Great BBQ, great service. $

Where to Stay

Best Western Dinosaur Valley Inn & Suites. 1311 N.E. Big Bend Trail (US 67), Glen Rose (254-897-4818 or 800-280-2055; www.dinosaurvalleyinn.com). Award-winning motel, special packages, "Texas size" free hot breakfast, heated pool, spa, exercise room, arcade game room, cable TV. $$–$$$

The Lodge at Fossil Rim. Off US 67, 3 miles west of Glen Rose, 2299 CR 2008 , Glen Rose (254-897-2960 or 888-775-6742; www.fossilrim.org). Located within the Fossil Rim Wildlife Center, the lodge overlooks the wildlife preserve and pool. For more adventure choose the Safari Camp where you can stay in tented cabins nearer to the wildlife. $$$

Plantation Inn. 1451 East Pearl Street, Granbury (817-573-8846 or 800-422-2402; www.plantationinngranbury.com). Pool with children's wading pool, free continental breakfast, free high-speed Internet. $$–$$$

For More Information

Granbury Convention and Visitors Bureau. 116 West Bridge Street, Granbury 76048; (800) 950-2212 or (817) 573-5548; www.granburytx.com.

Glen Rose Convention and Visitors Bureau. 1505 N.E. Big Bend Trail, Glen Rose 76043; (254) 897-3081 or (888) DINO-CVB; www.glenrosetexas.net.

The Panhandle

The Panhandle is also known as the Llano Estacado (yah-no es-tah-cah-doe), Spanish for "staked plains." Historians believe the name originated with the famous Coronado expedition, whose members staked their route across the featureless sea of grass so they could find their way back. When you drive through the Panhandle, across many miles of almost absolutely level agricultural lands with no landmarks on any horizon, you'll see how easily a person could get lost without road signs.

But these plains are broken up, rather abruptly in places, by the Caprock Escarpment, which marks the edge of the High Plains. This escarpment creates many of the most scenic wonders in the Panhandle, like Palo Duro Canyon, Caprock Canyon, and the Red River Valley.

Getting around is remarkably easy since many of the main highways (I–27 and I–40; U.S. Highways 385, 380, 87, 84, 70, and 60; and Highway 70) travel in almost straight lines from place to place.

Brownfield and Lubbock

Several famous musicians have called Lubbock home, including rock-and-roll pioneer Buddy Holly. You can relax a while at the **Buddy Holly Statue and Walk of Fame** at Eighth Street and Avenue Q, near the Civic Center. The monument pays tribute to the many celebrities raised here. The centerpiece is a statue of Holly, guitar in hand. Plaques around the base of the statue honor Holly and his band, the Crickets; Waylon Jennings; Bob Wills; Mac Davis; Roy Orbison; Tanya Tucker; actor Barry Corbin; and others. It's a favorite place for locals to have lunch.

Coleman Park (ages 4 and up)

South of Brownfield on US 385.

This forty-four-acre recreation site has picnic areas, tent and trailer campsites, a playground, and a swimming pool.

THE PANHANDLE

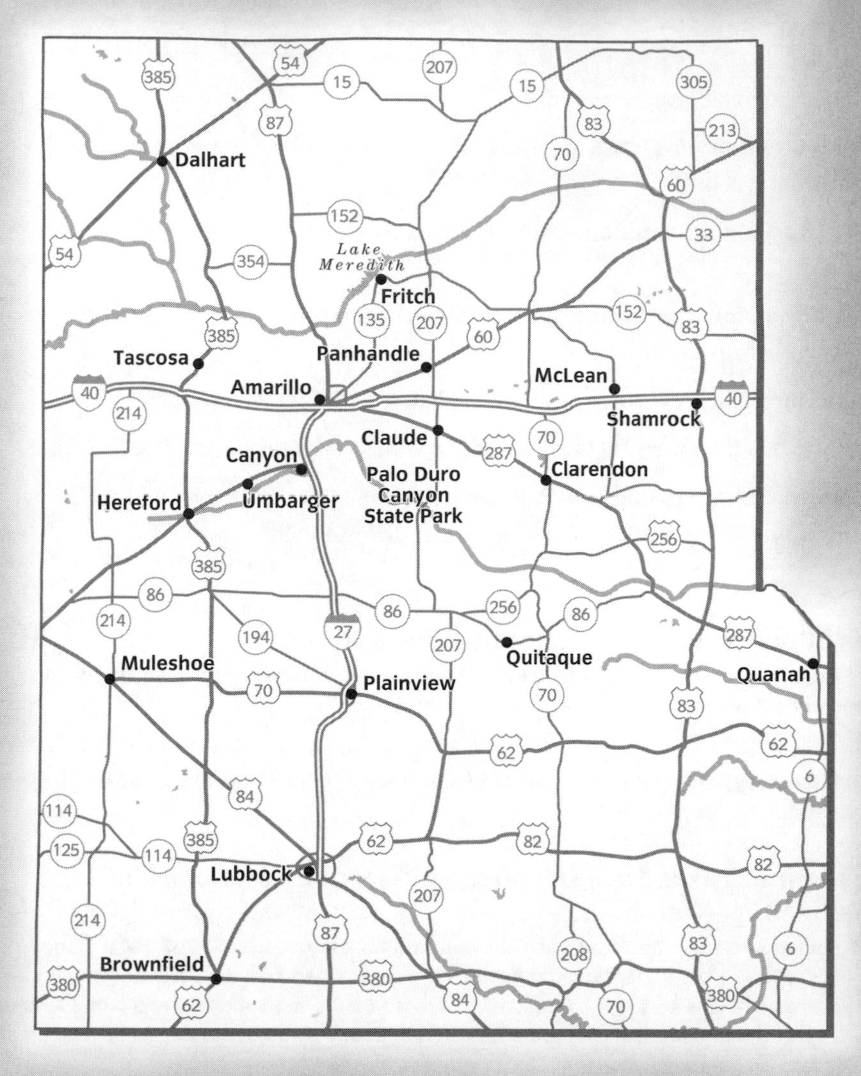

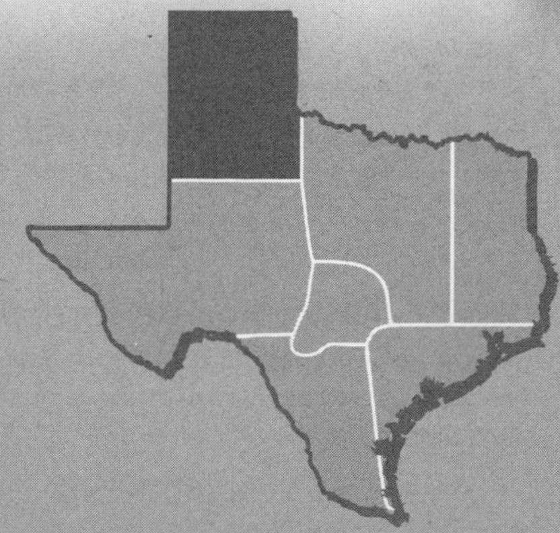

Top Annual Events in the Panhandle

- **Arts Festival,** Lubbock, May (806-744-2787)
- **Cowboy Roundup USA,** Amarillo, June (806-372-4777; www.cowboy roundupusa.org)
- **XIT Rodeo and Reunion,** Dalhart, August (806-249-5646; www.xit-rodeo .com)
- **National Cowboy Symposium,** Lubbock, September (806-798-7825; www .cowboy.org)
- **Tri-State Fair,** Amarillo, September (806-376-7767; www.tristatefair.com)
- **Texas Tech Intercollegiate Rodeo,** Lubbock, October (806-742-2455)
- **World Championship Ranch Rodeo,** Amarillo, November (806-374-9722; www.wrca.org/pages/ChampionshipRanchRodeo.php)

Terry County Historical Museum (ages 6 and up)

600 East Cardwell Street, Brownfield (806-637-2467). Open Tuesday through Friday 10 a.m. to noon and 1 to 3 p.m., Saturday noon to 4 p.m. $.

This small museum, once the home of A.M. Brownfield, has displays on area history, with an emphasis on pioneer artifacts. The first county jail and a 1917 vintage Santa Fe Railway Depot are on the grounds.

Museum of Texas Tech University and Moody Planetarium (ages 6 and up)

3301 Fourth Street on the Texas Tech campus, Lubbock (museum 806-742-2442; planetarium 806-742-2432; www.depts.ttu.edu). The museum is open Tuesday, Wednesday, Friday, and Saturday 10 a.m. to 5 p.m.; Thursday 10 a.m. to 8:30 p.m.; Sunday 1 to 5 p.m. Planetarium programs and special shows are offered Wednesday through Sunday at various times, usually late on Thursday. Museum free; planetarium $.

Lubbock is home to Texas Tech University, which could be the center of any visit. Your family could spend all day at the Museum of Texas Tech University. Museum exhibits cover the arts and humanities and the social and natural sciences, with an emphasis on area pioneer history and natural history. Moody Planetarium features astronomy programs, space exhibits, and laser shows which the kids should love.

National Ranching Heritage Center (ages 4 and up)

Fourth Street at Indiana Avenue, Lubbock (806-742-0498; www.nrhc.com). Open Monday through Saturday 10 a.m. to 5 p.m., Sunday 1 to 5 p.m. (closed major holidays). Donations welcomed.

Adjacent to the university museum is the Ranching Heritage Center. This 30-acre facility will give the kids a good idea about what pioneer life was like on the Llano Estacado. To appreciate that era of American history, wander around nearly four dozen historic structures that have been restored or relocated here. Buildings include a cowboy bunkhouse, windmills, barns, a school, and several homes.

Mackenzie Park and Prairie Dog Town (ages 2 and up)

601 Municipal Drive, Lubbock (806-775-2687). Open daily.

Frolicking prairie dogs are the main attraction at Mackenzie Park and Prairie Dog Town. The day-use park also includes two 18-hole golf courses, a 21-hole disc golf course, and a huge sports complex where you're likely to see a softball game almost anytime.

Joyland Amusement Park (ages 4 and up)

In Mackenzie Park, 601 Municipal Drive, Lubbock (806-763-2719; www.joylandpark.com). Hours vary seasonally. General admission $, unlimited rides $$$.

Joyland has lots of games, over twenty-five park rides, and a waterslide for kids.

Science Spectrum and Omni Theater (ages 2 and up)

2579 South Loop 289, Lubbock (806-745-2525; www.sciencespectrum.com). Open Monday through Friday 10 a.m. to 5 p.m., Saturday 10 a.m. to 6 p.m., Sunday 1 to 5 p.m. $–$$$, combination tickets with OMNI available.

If you want the kids to learn something and be entertained at the same time, visit the Science Spectrum. It's difficult to tell who has more fun at this place, children rushing from exhibit to exhibit or their parents watching them with delight. The Science Spectrum is a hands-on place with more than seventy exhibits on three floors encouraging children to learn about science, technology, and music. And in the OMNI Theater you can watch films much larger than life projected on the interior 58-foot dome, imparting a very real feeling of being in the film.

Lubbock Lake Landmark (ages 4 and up)

2401 Landmark Drive, Lubbock (806-742-1116; www.museum.ttu.edu). Open Tuesday through Saturday 9 a.m. to 5 p.m., Sunday 1 to 5 p.m. Free, tours for groups by prior arrangement.

On the edge of the city at US 84 (Clovis Road) and Loop 289, you'll find Lubbock Lake Landmark, where your family can relax, have a picnic, and learn about America from the

Texas Trivia

It costs Texas about $18 million each year to pick up litter from along state highways.

beginning of human occupation. Scientists have discovered evidence in Yellow House Canyon indicating that this site has been occupied since 12,000 B.C. It's the only known site in North America that contains deposits related to all of the cultures that have occupied the Southern Plains. Excavations have also revealed mammoths, extinct American camels and horses, giant bison, and a 6-foot-long armadillo. An interpretive center displays fossils and artifacts from the site and features a children's learning center. The day-use area includes picnic tables and interpretive trails.

The Maize (ages 5 and up)

About 15 miles northwest of Lubbock off FM 1294 (806-763-5994; www.cornfieldmaze.com/sites.php?ID=&username=txlubbock). Open Friday 5 to 9 p.m., Saturday 10 a.m. to 9 p.m., Sunday 2 to 9 p.m. from mid-September until the end of October. Special Thanksgiving hours. $$, children under 3 free.

What fun! Not only is this an outstanding maze, there's also a mini-maze, barnyard with farm animals, pumpkin patch, and hayrides.

Buffalo Springs Lake (ages 2 and up)

5 miles southeast of Lubbock on Farm Road 835 (806-747-3353; www.buffalospringlake.net). $-$$.

If your family likes to get wet at a more relaxed pace, head to Buffalo Springs Lake. At this spring-fed oasis in Yellow House Canyon, you can relax on the beach, camp out, or just have a picnic. You can swim, fish, hike or bike, rent a paddleboat at the marina, sharpen your skill on the archery range, or attend a performance in the outdoor amphitheater.

Where to Eat

Cattle Baron Steak and Seafood Grill. 8201 Quaker Avenue, Lubbock (806-798-7033). Steaks and seafood done up right, great salad bar. $$

J & M BBQ. 3605 Thirty-fourth Street, Lubbock (806-796-1164; www.jandmbar-b-q.com). Good Mesquite-smoked Texas barbecue since 1986. Eat in or carry out. $$

Buns Over Texas. 3402 Seventy-third Street, Lubbock (806-793-0012). Great burgers with a trimming bar where you can dress up your own. $$

Where to Stay

Comfort Suites. 5113 South Loop 289, Lubbock (806-798-0002; www.comfortsuites.com). Pool, free continental breakfast, free WiFi, no smoking, cable TV, children under 18 stay free. $$

Lubbock Inn. 3901 Nineteenth Street, Lubbock (806-792-5181 or 800-545-8226; www.lubbockinn.com). Outdoor pool, free high-speed Internet. $$–$$$

For More Information

Lubbock Convention and Visitors Bureau. 1500 Broadway, Lubbock 79401; (806) 747-5232 or (800) 692-4035; www.visitlubbock.org.

Plainview, Muleshoe, and Hereford

You'd expect to find a memorial to mules in a town called Muleshoe, wouldn't you? You won't be disappointed. The **National Mule Memorial** is at the intersection of US 70 and 84 downtown and is a popular spot to take photos of the kids.

Llano Estacado Museum (ages 6 and up)

1900 West Eighth Street, Plainview (806-291-3660). Open Monday through Thursday 9 a.m. to 5 p.m., Friday 9 a.m. to 4 p.m. year-round, also weekends April through November 1 to 5 p.m. Free.

The Llano Estacado Museum, on the campus of Wayland Baptist University, is full of intriguing items, including prehistoric artifacts dating from 8,000 B.C., a gem and mineral collection, and a prehistoric elephant skull and tusks.

Muleshoe National Wildlife Refuge (ages 4 and up)

20 miles south of Muleshoe on Texas Highway 214 (806-946-3341; www.fws.gov/southwest/refuges/texas/muleshoe). Open during daylight hours.

If you want to see live animals, head south of town to the Muleshoe Wildlife Refuge. Your children will delight in the prairie-dog town, located along the entrance road. The refuge's three lakes attract a number of birds, including rare sandhill cranes. As many as 100,000 cranes nest here at one time. Eagles can be seen during fall and winter months.

Deaf Smith County Historical Museum (ages 6 and up)

400 Sampson Street, Hereford (806-363-7070; www.deafsmithcountymuseum.org). Open Monday through Friday 10 a.m. to 5 p.m., Saturday 10 a.m. to 3 p.m. Free.

The Deaf Smith Museum presents a look at the region as it was one hundred years ago. The museum is housed in a pioneer schoolhouse. There are other restored frontier buildings on the grounds, along with a railroad caboose and an old dugout home.

Texas Trivia

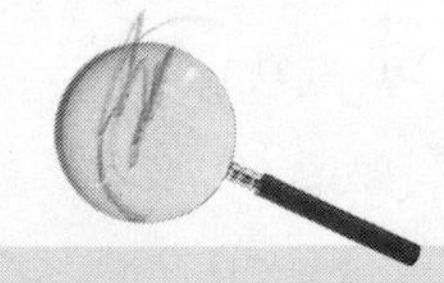

Famed area rancher and former Texas Ranger Charles Goodnight not only pioneered cattle drives, he also invented the chuckwagon.

Canyon

Canyon is a small town with some pretty big attractions, such as the impressive Palo Duro Canyon just outside of town, and is home to West Texas State University. The town figured heavily in the history of the Texas cattle business, originating as the headquarters of the huge T Anchor Ranch in 1878, and famed cattleman Charles Goodnight lived nearby. Several Native American battles also took place in the area, including the final battle that Colonel Ranald Mackenzie led against the Comanche, crushing the tribe as a serious threat to white settlers in the state.

Panhandle-Plains Historical Museum (ages 4 and up)

2401 Fourth Avenue, on the campus of West Texas A&M University, Canyon (806-651-2244; www.panhandleplains.org). Open Monday through Saturday 9 a.m. to 5 p.m. (to 6 p.m. during the summer), Sunday 1 to 6 p.m. $, children 3 and under free.

The first place to visit in Canyon has to be the Panhandle-Plains Historical Museum. This is Texas's oldest and largest state museum and is the best place in the state to learn all about the Panhandle. Your family will learn about regional ranching and petroleum-mining history and enjoy impressive natural-history exhibits. Walk through an authentic pioneer town rebuilt inside the museum. See an extensive gun collection and prehistoric

Texas **Tunes**

Texas has an incredible diversity of music, and to capture the state's true flavor you should play its music as you drive its roads, which you'll have ample opportunity for in the Panhandle. Here's a sampling of the best Texas traveling CDs:

- *After Awhile* by Jimmie Dale Gilmore (lyrical traveling music)
- *Buddy Holly: The Original Master Tapes* by Buddy Holly (no one sang it better)
- *Conjunto Aztlan* by Conjunto Aztlan (a history of Tex-Mex sounds on one disc)
- *Corridos De La Frontera* by Santiago Jimenez Jr. (authentic border music)
- *Desert Dreams* by Ben Tavera King (music meant for Big Bend)
- *Destiny's Gate* by Tish Hinojosa (folk rock with a Latina accent)
- *Ernest Tubb Live* by Ernest Tubb (no-frills country by the master)
- *Fathers and Sons* by Asleep at the Wheel (the ultimate road music)
- *Little Love Affairs* by Nanci Griffith (sweetness)

The First **Thanksgiving?**

One claim to the first Thanksgiving on what is now American soil is the one for Palo Duro Canyon on May 29, 1541, several decades before the Pilgrims broke bread with Native Americans in New England. This was a day of Thanksgiving ordered by Spanish explorer Francisco Vasquez de Coronado after leading his men up from Mexico in search of gold. Instead, nearly out of food, Coronado found the canyon oasis and a tribe of Native Americans living on the canyon floor.

fossils. If your children like dinosaurs or cowboys and Indians, they're going to love this place.

Palo Duro Canyon State Park (ages 4 and up)

12 miles east of Canyon on Highway 217 at 11450 Park Road 5 (806-488-2227; www.palo durocanyon.com and www.tpwd.state.tx.us/spdest/findadest/parks/palo_duro). Open daily at 8 a.m., closing times vary with the season.

In terms of size and grandeur, Palo Duro Canyon is second in the United States only to Arizona's Grand Canyon. Carved by the Prairie Dog Fork of the Red River, the canyon is 20 miles across at its widest point, 1,100 feet down at its deepest. Palo Duro means "hard wood," referring to the junipers in the canyon. Rock formations here date back more than 900 million years, and it's easy to find dinosaur fossils in the canyon, but leave them where you find them so others can enjoy them as well. You can rent horses or mountain bikes or drive around. You might also want to hike some of the many trails, the most famous of which is the Lighthouse Trail, a half-day trip that passes through delightful scenery but can be quite hot in summer. The park has an interpretive center, picnic and camping areas, a concession stand, and a store.

Texas (ages 4 and up)

At Pioneer Amphitheater in Palo Duro Canyon State Park (806-655-2181; www.texas-show .com). Performances are at 8:30 p.m. mid-June through mid-August. $$–$$$$.

Here's a play even the children will be thrilled to see. Thunder and lightning, horsemen carrying flags atop the 600-foot canyon wall that serves as a backdrop to the stage, and singers and dancers in western and Native American garb bring back the 1880s at the outdoor musical Texas. The play is presented in the 1,742-seat Pioneer Amphitheater and was written by Pulitzer Prize–winning author Paul Green. An optional steak dinner ($$), catered by the famous Big Texan Steak Ranch in Amarillo, is served before every performance from 6 to 8 p.m. There is a ticket office located at 1514 Fifth Avenue in downtown Canyon where you can get tickets and also pick up information on hundreds of area attractions.

The Elkins Ranch/Cowboy Mornings and Evenings

(ages 4 and up)

At the entrance to Palo Duro State Park, Canyon (806-488-2100 or 800-658-2613; www.theelkinsranch.com). Open seasonally. Fee varies with activity.

The Elkins Ranch purchased a very popular attraction at Palo Duro Canyon called "Cowboy Mornings and Evenings" and have added it to their variety of activities, which also includes jeep rides and tours of the canyon. From spring through fall you can have breakfast or supper as the cowpokes did, with a mesquite fire on the open range on the rim of Palo Duro Canyon. A scenic ride on mule-drawn wagons ends at the campsite where your family will chow down on a breakfast of Panhandle-size eggs, sausage, sourdough biscuits with country gravy, and cowboy coffee. The suppers feature huge steaks, beans, salad, more of those great biscuits, and campfire cobbler. You'll be entertained by the hands as they brand cattle, rope, or toss cow chips.

Where to Stay

Best Western Palo Duro Canyon Inn & Suites. 2801 Fourth Avenue, Canyon (806-655-1818; www.bestwestern.com). Pool, hot tub, fitness center, high-speed Internet, **free** breakfast. $$

For More Information

Canyon Chamber of Commerce. 1518 Fifth Avenue, Canyon 79015; (806) 655-7815; www.canyonchamber.org.

Amarillo

Amarillo is the economic and cultural center of the huge Panhandle region. There's so much to see and do there, but for whatever reason, folks drive out west on I–40 to see **Cadillac Ranch,** located in a field on the south side of the highway. People will ask if you've seen this sight, so you might as well get it out of the way. What you'll see here is Stanley Marsh III's outdoor sculpture of ten Cadillacs (from 1949 to 1963) planted nose down into the ground at the same angle as Cheops's pyramid. Your children might ask the inevitable question why, but no one really knows why Marsh did it, and he's never explained. It's just there. Marsh invites anyone to come out and paint graffiti all over the

Texas Trivia

Amarillo is the largest meat-producing area in the nation; 25 percent of all beef consumed in the United States and 88 percent of all beef consumed in Texas is produced in this city.

Texas Trivia

In 1893, Amarillo's population was listed as "between 500 and 600 humans and 50,000 head of cattle."

Caddys. For a preview, visit the Web site at www.roadsideamerica.com/attract/TXAMA cadillac.html.

Amarillo Museum of Art (ages 6 and up)

2200 South Van Buren Street, Amarillo (806-371-5050; www.amarilloart.org). Open Tuesday, Wednesday, and Friday 10 a.m. to 5 p.m., Thursday 10 a.m. to 9 p.m., Saturday and Sunday 1 to 5 p.m. Free.

More conventional art can be seen at the Amarillo Museum of Art, on the campus of Amarillo College. The museum houses a permanent exhibit of paintings and sculptures and hosts other exhibits during the year. Fine-arts performances, classes, and lectures are also featured.

Don Harrington Discovery Center (ages 4 and up)

1200 Streit Drive, Amarillo (806-355-9547; www.dhdc.org). Open Tuesday through Saturday 9:30 a.m. to 4:30 p.m., Sunday noon to 4:30 p.m. $–$$, children under 2 free.

The Don Harrington Discovery Center can be an exhaustive experience. There's something to delight everyone in your family here. Located in the Harrington Medical Center, in the center of a fifty-one-acre park with a lake and picnic areas, the museum's hands-on exhibits let your children learn about a wide range of natural phenomena, from the depths of the sea to outer space. The Space Theater is a digital planetarium featuring star shows and 360-degree films.

Amarillo Zoo (ages 4 and up)

In Thompson Park, 24th Avenue at U.S. Highway 287, Amarillo (806-381-7911; www.amarillozoo.org). Open 9:30 a.m. to 5:30 p.m. Tuesday through Sunday. Free.

A good place for the children to watch animals is the Amarillo Zoo, in Thompson Park near Wonderland. This is a very nice zoo with animals that appeal to youngsters, such as monkeys, bears, and big cats. There's also an emphasis on animals of the High Plains, including a herd of buffalo.

Wonderland Amusement Park (ages 4 and up)

2601 Dumas Drive at Thompson Park, Amarillo (806-383-0832 or 800-383-4712; www.wonderlandpark.com). Open daily Memorial Day through Labor Day, weekends April and May. Hours vary with the seasons. Prices vary by activity; one-price hand stamps available.

Typical kid fare is available at Wonderland Amusement Park, the largest theme park in Texas after the Six Flags behemoths in Houston, Dallas, and San Antonio. Your brood will find 25 rides, including the Texas Tornado, one of the highest-rated double loop roller coasters in the country, a log ride, and a white-water ride, along with miniature golf, video arcades, bumper cars, and a spook house.

American Quarter Horse Hall of Fame and Museum
(ages 6 and up)

2601 I–40, Amarillo (806-376-5181; www.aqha.com/foundation/halloffame). Monday through Saturday 9 a.m. to 5 p.m., Sunday noon to 5 p.m. $-$$, children 5 and under free.

If you have any horse lovers in your family, don't miss the American Quarter Horse Hall of Fame and Museum. Discover the breed's history as both a western ranch favorite and racehorse, the first American horse breed. The newly remodeled center features state-of-the-art displays, videos, interactive hands-on exhibits, a spacious theater, and a gift shop. Summer camp and special programs for kids.

Amarillo Dillas (ages 4 and up)

Office 801 S. Polk, Amarillo (806-342-0400; www.amarillodillasbaseball.com). $–$$.

For baseball lovers in the family, drive over to the Dilla Villa Stadium at 3300 S.E. Third Street to watch the Amarillo Dillas play professional minor-league ball in the Central Baseball League from May through August.

Amarillo Gorillas (ages 4 and up)

Office 901 S. Buchanan Street, , Amarillo (806-242-7825; www.amarillogorillas.com). $$–$$$.

The professional minor-league Gorillas play in the Central Hockey League. They take to the ice October through March at the Amarillo Civic Center.

Splash Amarillo (ages 4 and up)

1415 Sunrise Drive, Amarillo (806-376-4477; www.splashamarillo.com). Open daily Memorial Day to Labor Day: Monday through Saturday noon to 7 p.m., Sunday noon to 6 p.m. $$–$$$.

The Panhandle's only water park has water slides, a wave pool, children's activity area, arcade, and a snack bar.

Where to Eat

Big Texan Steak Ranch. 7701 I–40 East., Amarillo (800-657-7177 or 806-372-6000; www.bigtexan.com). If you can eat a monster seventy-two-ounce steak with all the trimmings in an hour, you get it **free.** Kids might be tempted to try some of the more exotic items on the menu, like rattlesnake or rabbit. Maybe not. Great breakfast buffet with omelet bar. $–$$

Cracker Barrel Old Country Store. 2323 I–40 East, Amarillo (806-372-2034; www.crackerbarrel.com). Great southern cooking; huge gift shop in lobby. $–$$

Ruby Tequila's Mexican Kitchen. 2108 Paramount, Amarillo (806-358-7829; www.rubytequilas.com). Authentic Tex-Mex fare, extensive menu. $

Where to Stay

Best Western Amarillo Inn. 1610 Coulter Street, Amarillo (806-358-7861 or 877-358-2256; www.bestwestern.com). Pool, hot tub, **free** high-speed Internet, cable TV, **free** breakfast, **free** newspaper. Children under 18 stay **free.** $$

Big Texan Motel. 7701 I–40 East, Amarillo (800-657-7177; www.bigtexan.com/motel.html). Adjacent to the Big Texan Steak Ranch, the motel is designed to look like a main street in an Old West town. Texas-shaped swimming pool, WiFi Internet, cable TV. $$

Comfort Inn. 2300 Soncy, Amarillo (806-457-9100 or 800-456-4000; www.comfortinn.com). Adjacent to Westgate Mall, free breakfast; indoor pool, hot tub, fitness center, **free** breakfast. $$

For More Information

Amarillo Convention and Visitors Bureau. 1000 South Polk Street, Amarillo 79101; (800) 692-1338 or (806) 374-1497; www.visitamarillotx.com.

Visitor Information Center in the Civic Center. 401 S. Buchanan, #101, Amarillo 79101; (806) 374-8474.

Tascosa and Dalhart

Head north on US 385 from I–40 after you leave Amarillo.

As you pass by the town of Tascosa on your way to Dalhart, don't blink—you might miss it. Tascosa was one of the roughest, toughest towns in Texas in the late 1800s, but it's gone now. Only ruins and a museum remain. Dalhart was, and continues to be, a center for the cattle business.

Old Tascosa and Cal Farley's Boys Ranch (ages 4 and up)

36 miles northwest of Amarillo on US 385 at Spur 233 (806-372-2341 or 800-687-3722). The Julian Bivins Museum, in the historic Oldham County Courthouse, is open daily 10 a.m. to 5 p.m. Free.

If you're traveling to the ghost town of Tascosa from Amarillo, take Farm Road 1061 to US 385, the most scenic drive in the area. Built by settlers in the 1870s, Tascosa was a shipping point for Panhandle farms and ranches, including the famous XIT Ranch near Dalhart. Your children will be able to walk in the footsteps of Billy the Kid and Kit Carson, who once strode along Tascosa's boardwalks. But, just like in the movies, the railroad bypassed old Tascosa, and the town up and died during the Depression. The Boot Hill Cemetery is maintained by youths from Cal Farley's Boys Ranch (www.calfarley.org), a 10,000-acre home for troubled youths founded in 1939.

The ranch also runs the **Julian Bivins Museum** in Tascosa. It houses pioneer, Native American, and prehistoric artifacts.

The renowned **Boys Ranch Rodeo,** is held over Labor Day weekend.

Texas Trivia

At its largest, the XIT Ranch encompassed 3,047,975 acres—roughly the size of Connecticut. In 1886 the ranch ran 150,000 head of cattle.

XIT Museum (ages 6 and up)

108 East Fifth Street, Dalhart (806-244-5390; www.XITmuseum.com). Open Tuesday through Saturday 9 a.m. to 5 p.m. Donations requested.

In the 1880s, the XIT Ranch was the largest ranch in the world, with three million acres. The north fence was 200 miles from the south fence. That impressive range has been subdivided over the years, but the XIT still operates. The XIT Ranch Museum preserves the ranch's history along with Indian artifacts.

In August the ranch and the city host the annual **XIT Rodeo and Reunion** (www.xit-rodeo.com) to honor all those who have ever worked on the ranch. The festival features a rodeo, of course, an antique car show, a fun run, a parade, and **free** barbecue and watermelon.

Lake Rita Blanca (ages 4 and up)

1.5 miles south of Dalhart on Farm Road 281 (806-244-5511).

For wildlife viewing, head to Lake Rita Blanca, where your family can see all sorts of waterfowl and maybe a few eagles during winter months.

Rita Blanca National Grassland (ages 4 and up)

12 miles east of Dalhart on Highway 296 (505-374-9652).

For more of a wilderness experience, visit the Rita Blanca National Grassland, where your family will discover a network of hiking, biking, and wildlife-watching trails where you're likely to see pronghorn antelope, coyotes, foxes, prairie dogs, owls, and hawks.

For More Information

Dalhart Chamber of Commerce. 102 East 7th Street, Dalhart 79022; (806) 244-5646; www.dalhart.org.

Fritch and Panhandle

Traveling east on US 87, take Highway 152 east and Highway 207 south to loop around Lake Meredith.

Fritch is the gateway town for Lake Meredith and the Alibates Flint Quarries, while Panhandle is a center for wheat farming, cattle ranching, and some petroleum production.

Lake Meredith National Recreation Area (ages 4 and up)

1 mile east of Fritch on Highway 136 (806-857-3151; www.nps.gov/lamr).

Lake Meredith was formed by damming the Canadian River, producing 100 miles of shoreline. If you're looking for outdoor recreation of any type, this is the place. Recreation areas surround the lake and include off-road vehicle trails, picnic and camping areas, shelters, boat ramps and docks, marinas, and fishing and swimming areas. Junior Ranger program for kids.

Lake Meredith Aquatic and Wildlife Museum (ages 4 and up)

101 North Robey Street, Fritch (806-857-2458). Open Monday through Saturday noon to 5 p.m. Free.

The Lake Meredith Museum has more than sixteen species of fish from the lake displayed in aquariums. There are also exhibits on Alibates flint and arrowhead making.

Alibates Flint Quarries National Monument (ages 6 and up)

About 7 miles south of Fritch on Highway 136 (806-857-3151; www.nps.gov/alfl/). Open Monday through Friday 8 a.m. to 4:30 p.m. Tours only by advance reservation. Free.

Alibates Flint Quarries National Monument overlooks Lake Meredith and preserves the quarries where native peoples mined and flaked flint for more than 12,000 years. An ancient Native American village, pictographs, and giant pits full of buffalo bones have been found here.

Square House Museum (ages 6 and up)

Fifth Street and Elsie Avenue (Hwy. 207), Panhandle (806-537-3524; www.squarehouse museum.org). Open Monday through Saturday 9 a.m. to 5 p.m., Sunday 1 to 5 p.m. Donations welcomed.

You might be a little surprised that such a small town has such a big museum as Panhandle's Square House Museum. The eight-structure complex in Pioneer Park chronicles

Texas Trivia

Don't spend too much time trying to figure out what language "Alibates" is or what it means. The area was named for nearby Allie Bates Creek. The creek was named for a local cowboy, Allen (Allie) Bates. The name Alibates was a recording mistake made by a geologist in 1907.

Panhandle history from the first native peoples to modern industries. The main building, the Square House, was built in the 1880s with wood brought from Dodge City, Kansas. In addition to the usual ranch and farming exhibits, you will find a railroad exhibit, a wildlife hall, a Texas flags exhibit, a pioneer windmill, a blacksmith shop, and two art galleries. Many of the exhibits are hands-on for children.

Claude and Quitaque

Continue south on Highway 207 to Claude, then on Highway 86 east to Quitaque.

Like many Texas towns, Claude was established as a railroad stop. Today you'll see grain elevators and stockyards all around, with a few antiques shops in town. Quitaque (pronounced *Kitty-kway*) has a more romantic background. It began as the site of a Native American trading post, was a major stagecoach stop, and now serves the area's farms and ranches.

Armstrong County Museum (ages 6 and up)

120 North Trice Street, Claude (806-226-2187; www.armstrongcountymuseum.org). Open Tuesday through Saturday from noon to 4 p.m. Free.

This small town museum is operated almost entirely by volunteers and does an amazing job preserving and displaying the history of the area. The museum owns and operates the Gem Theatre, one of the six historic buildings comprising the museum complex, which is used for educational and entertainment programs.

Caprock Canyons State Park (ages 4 and up)

3 miles north of Quitaque on County Road 1065 (806-455-1492; www.tpwd.state.tx.us/spdest/findadest/parks/caprock_canyons).

Caprock Canyons State Park near Quitaque covers 13,960 scenic acres of colorful cliffs and canyons and is loaded with wildlife and birds. You can take the kids hiking or

Thomas Cree's **Little Tree**

On the south side of U.S. Highway 60, about 5 miles southwest of the city of Panhandle, is the very first tree planted in the entire Panhandle region of Texas. Immense plains were once a sea of grass from horizon to horizon here. In 1888 pioneer settler Thomas Cree hauled a sapling of bois d'arc from beyond the Caprock area and planted it by his dugout home. Cree is long gone, but the tree thrived until 1969, when it was killed by an agricultural chemical. Natural seedlings from the original tree are growing at the site today.

Scenic **Drive**

When you leave Claude, take Highway 207 south for a nice scenic drive that'll surprise you. For miles, agricultural riches spread from horizon to horizon, then the highway plunges into spectacular Palo Duro and Tule Canyons, revealing several sheer buttes and a rampage of colors.

mountain biking or hire a horse and trot off on several trails. You'll find picnic areas, campsites, fishing, and swimming at Lake Theo, where you can also rent canoes.

You can access the Caprock Canyon Trailway here as well. This is a 65-mile-long system of trails that runs through three counties, across the plains, through rugged canyons, and into the Red River Valley. One of the features is an abandoned railway tunnel, one of very few in Texas.

For More Information

Quitaque Chamber of Commerce. P.O. Box 487, Quitaque 79255; (806) 455-1456; www.quitaque.org.

Clarendon

Head north on Highway 70.

Farming and ranching remain the focus in the Clarendon area, one of the oldest towns in the Panhandle. The city was founded by the Reverend L. H. Carhart in 1878 as a refuge for cowboys who weren't rowdy drinkers.

Saints' Roost Museum (ages 6 and up) 

610 East Harrington Street, Clarendon (806-874-2746; www.saintsroost.org). Open Wednesday through Saturday 1 to 5 p.m. Free.

The highest temperature ever recorded in Texas was 120 degrees in Seymour on August 12, 1936.

Clarendon was founded by a Methodist minister as a "sobriety settlement" to counteract the wide-open ways common in other cow towns. For that reason cowboys nicknamed the place "Saints' Roost," and you can find out all about its history at the Saints' Roost Museum on the main road downtown. The museum is housed in the former Adair Hospital, founded in 1910 for local cowboys, and features heirlooms from area ranches, farms, and businesses.

The city holds an annual Saints' Roost Celebration over the Fourth of July weekend, with three nights of rodeoing, a parade, an arts-and-crafts show, country music, an old-timer's reunion, children's contests and games, and a barbecue cookout. Great family fun. Call (806) 874-2421.

Bar H Dude Ranch (ages 4 and up)

3 miles west of Clarendon on Farm Road 3257, off Highway 287 (800-627-9871; www.barhduderanch.com). Lodging rates ($$–$$$) include horseback riding and all meals.

For a taste of real ranch life, check into the Bar H Dude Ranch for a night or two. Here the kids can watch cowboys work cattle, feed livestock, mend fences, move the herd, and do dozens of other ranch chores. You can climb into the saddle and join in, too, if you want. Or you can just relax on the porch, pitch horseshoes, take a stroll, try some fishing, or splash around in the pool. Mesquite-grilled food awaits at the chuck wagon when the sun comes up and when it goes down.

McLean

It might be difficult to explain to your children the almost mythical lure of old Route 66, but maybe a trip to McLean will help. In town are a restored Phillips 66 gas station dating from the 1930s and re-creations of an old Route 66 cafe and typical tourist court. You can't miss them; they're on Route 66 right in town.

Devil's Rope Museum (ages 6 and up)

Kingsley Street at Old Route 66, McLean (806-779-2225; www.barbwiremuseum.com). Open May through October, Tuesday through Saturday 10 a.m. to 4 p.m. Winter hours vary with the weather. Donations requested.

Make a stop at the Devil's Rope Museum, home not only to the world's largest collection of barbed wire ("the devil's rope" to ranchers favoring open ranges) and related artifacts but also to the largest display of old Route 66 memorabilia along Old Route 66.

Alanreed-McLean Area Museum (ages 6 and up)

117 North Main Street, McLean (806-779-2731). Open March through December, Tuesday through Friday 10 a.m. to 4 p.m. Donations welcomed.

More traditional artifacts tracing the history of area pioneers can be found at the Alanreed-McLean Area Museum. This museum also contains exhibits and records on the German prisoner-of-war camp that was located here during World War II.

Shamrock and Quanah

Traveling east on I–40 will take you to Shamrock, near the Oklahoma border. To get to Quanah, head south on U.S. Highway 83, then east on US 287, following near the border.

Shamrock was named by its founder, George Nichels, an Irish sheep rancher, and ranching was the primary business in town until oil was struck in 1926. Today agriculture, tourism, and oil and gas production are what keep the city bustling. Quanah was named for Quanah Parker, last war chief of the Comanches. Today the city is a central shipping point for cotton, dairy, and meat products.

Blarney Stone (ages 4 and up)

400 East Second Street in Elmore Park, Shamrock (806-256-2501). Free.

You say you'd like to kiss the Blarney Stone but don't want to travel all the way to Ireland to do it? Go to Shamrock. A fragment of genuine Blarney Stone from the ruins of Blarney Castle in County Cork is displayed in Elmore Park. As befits a town with this name, there's a big festival on the weekend closest to St. Patrick's Day (March 17), with barrel racing, team roping, a beard-growing contest, fun runs, water polo, a chili cook-off, dancing, and a carnival.

Pioneer West Museum (ages 6 and up)

206 North Madden Street, Shamrock (806-256-3941; www.shamrocktx.net/museum). Open Monday through Friday 10 a.m. to noon and 1 to 3 p.m. Free.

Before you leave Shamrock, wander though the Pioneer West Museum, housed in the old Reynolds Hotel, where twenty rooms are filled with an eclectic blend of exhibits on topics ranging from NASA space missions to Native American culture.

Copper Breaks State Park (ages 4 and up)

8 miles south of Quanah off Highway 6 on Park Road 62 (940-839-4331; www.tpwd.state.tx .us/spdest/findadest/parks/copper_breaks).

In these canyons and plains, you'll find a fascinating blend of natural and cultural history. The Comanche and Kiowa hunted buffalo here, and Cynthia Ann Parker was recaptured nearby. Your kids are likely to spy deer, hawks, coyotes, jackrabbits, and roadrunners all over the area. And when they tire of looking for wildlife, they can cool off in the sixty-acre lake, go fishing, or hike along one of the scenic trails.

For More Information

Quanah Chamber of Commerce. 220 South Main Street, Quanah 79252; (940) 663-2222; www.quanahnet.com.

Shamrock Chamber of Commerce. 105 East Twelfth Street, Shamrock 79079; (806) 256-2501; www.shamrocktx.net.

West Texas and Big Bend

West Texas and the Big Bend country are what most non-Texans think of when they picture Texas: vast, beautiful badlands covered in cactus with an occasional mountain lurching up like a ship from the desert sea. This area west of the Pecos River is so rugged that Apache and Comanche Indians never stayed; they just passed through. Early Spanish explorers labeled this place *el despoblado,* the uninhabited land. It remains remarkably the same today, except for the sprawling metropolis of El Paso, the twin cities of Midland and Odessa in the Permian Basin, and a few other smaller towns that grew up to support ranching and oil businesses in the nineteenth century.

The major thoroughfares here are Interstate 10, Interstate 20, and U.S. Highway 90, running east and west. Be prepared to drive long distances in this region, even if you fly

Top Annual Events in West Texas and Big Bend

- **Cowboy Poetry Gathering,** Alpine, February (432-837-2326 or 800-361-3735)
- **Western Heritage Classic Rodeo,** Abilene, May (325-677-4376 or 800-727-7704)
- **Odessa Shakespeare Festival,** Odessa, summer (432-332-1586)
- **West of the Pecos Rodeo,** Pecos, July (432-445-2406)
- **Border Folk Festival,** El Paso, September (915-534-0601)
- **Commemorative Air Force Airsho,** Midland, October (432-563-1000)
- **Terlingua International Championship Chili Cook-off,** Terlingua, November (817-251-1287)
- **Christmas at Old Fort Concho,** San Angelo, December (325-657-4444)

WEST TEXAS AND BIG BEND

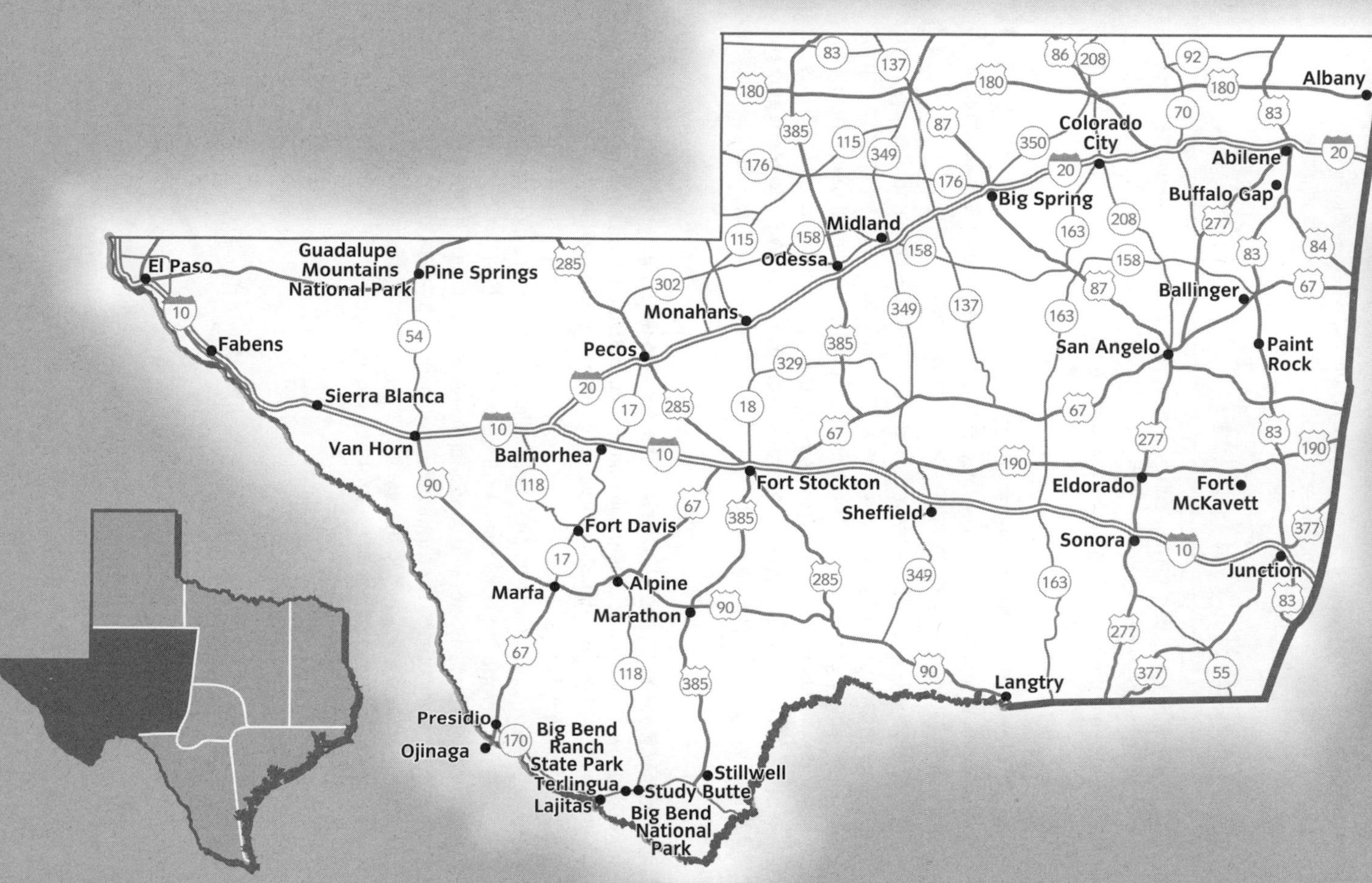

into a major population center. Cities are few and very far between, as are gas stations, so plan ahead for meals and lodging. And be prepared to have something for the kids to do in the car as you dodge tumbleweeds driving over these vast landscapes.

Junction and Fort McKavett

Driving west from Junction, I–10 becomes pretty bleak and stays that way for 450 miles until you reach the New Mexico border around El Paso. The rugged plains and hills are broken by a few buttes off in the distance. If you want variety, you'll find it only off the interstate.

South Llano River State Park (ages 4 and up)

5 miles south of Junction off U.S. Highway 377, 1927 Park Road 73 (325-446-3994; www.tpwd.state.tx.us/spdest/findadest/parks/south_llano_river).

Right where the Texas Hill Country ends and West Texas begins is Junction, a small town that is home to South Llano River State Park. The quiet, cool river is perfect for family canoeing, tubing, and swimming. Three miles of hiking trails wind through the park's pecan bottom, where you're likely to see white-tailed deer and wild turkeys. Trails from the park also lead into the adjoining 2,123-acre **Walter Buck Wildlife Management Area,** where a 2-mile hiking trail circles the oxbow lakes and the kids should be able to spot a lot of wildlife.

Fort McKavett State Historic Site (ages 6 and up)

About 35 miles northwest of Junction on Farm Road 864, off Farm Road 1674, Fort McKavett (325-396-2358; www.thc.state.tx.us/hsites/hs_mckavett.aspx?Site=McKavett). Open daily 8 a.m. to 5 p.m.

Fort McKavett, founded in 1852, has been relatively untouched by time. Constant use by civilians after the fort was closed kept many of the old post structures in near original condition. The park, overlooking the San Saba River, has fifteen restored buildings and the ruins of many others. Interpretive exhibits in the 1870 hospital ward trace the history of the region, and a self-guided trail leads to the lime kiln and Government Springs. At its peak, the fort housed 400 soldiers, most of them members of the famed Buffalo Soldiers regiments.

Texas Trivia

Although General Phillip Sheridan opined that he'd prefer living in hell to Texas, his colleague General William T. Sherman called Fort McKavett "the prettiest post in Texas."

For More Information

Kimble County Chamber of Commerce. 402 Main Street, Junction 76849; (325) 446-3190; www.junctiontexas.net.

Sonora and Eldorado

Caverns of Sonora (ages 4 and up)

8 miles west of Sonora off I–10, exit 392 to Ranch Road 1989 (325-387-3105; www.cavernsofsonora.com). Open daily March 1 to Labor Day 8 a.m. to 6 p.m., Tuesday after Labor Day to February 29 9 a.m. to 5 p.m. $$.

About 60 miles west of Junction is a nice little oasis, the town of Sonora. Eight miles farther you'll find the Caverns of Sonora. This isn't the biggest cave in Texas, but it's certainly the prettiest. The 1.5-mile walk winds down around some of the most delicate and brilliant formations found anywhere in the world, including a crystalline butterfly. On the surface, the kids will enjoy the sluice, where they can pan for unusual minerals.

Eldorado Woolens (ages 6 and up)

407 South Main Street, Eldorado (325-266-3383; www.eldoradotx.com/woolenmill.htm). Open Monday through Friday 8 a.m. to 5 p.m., Saturday 8 a.m. to 4 p.m. Free.

Along U.S. Highway 277 at 407 S. Main you'll find the oldest woolen mill in the Southwest, the first in Texas built in 1939. No longer in operation, it's now a museum and you may tour the mill by appointment only. Stroll along the village's Historic Walking Tour to see some old architecture.

Where to Stay

X-Bar Ranch. 8101 Farm Road 2129, Eldorado (325-853-2688 or 888-853-2688; www.xbarranch.com). Here's a chance to stay at a real working family ranch, participate in ranch activities, and enjoy nature at its best. $$

Best Western Sonora Inn. 270 Hwy. 277 North, Sonora (325-387-9111; www.bestwestern.com). Outdoor pool, fitness center, high-speed Internet, **free** breakfast. $$, children 12 and under **free.**

San Angelo

San Angelo is a little town full of big surprises. The biggest is probably the Concho River Pearls. Lustrous pearls in colors ranging from pink to purple are produced by one of twelve varieties of freshwater mussels in the river. (The word concha means "shell" in

Spanish.) Various shops in town sell items made from the pearls. If your family wants to gather their own, and kids love to try this, you need a permit from the Texas Parks and Wildlife Department. The pearls are celebrated with *Pearl of the Conchos,* a bronze mermaid statue grasping a huge pearl at Celebration Bridge in the historic area of town. The visitor bureau can give you more information on the permits at (325) 655-4136, or get more details from the Web site www.sanangelo.org.

Fort Concho National Historic Landmark (ages 4 and up)

630 South Oakes Street, San Angelo (325-657-4444; www.fortconcho.com). The Fort Concho Museum and the three other museums also housed at the fort are open 9 a.m. to 5 p.m. Monday through Saturday and 1 to 5 p.m. Sunday. $, children under 6 free.

Fort Concho National Historic Landmark is one of the best-preserved Indian Wars forts in the country, situated on forty acres in the heart of downtown San Angelo. Several of the fort's 23 buildings are furnished with original antiques and replicas of the furnishings used when the fort was active in the late 1800s. A number of infantry and cavalry units, including all four regiments of the Buffalo Soldiers, were stationed here between 1867 and 1889. Children will love seeing the staff and volunteers, who dress in period uniforms to lend authenticity.

One of the more fascinating museums on the Fort Concho grounds is the **E. H. Danner Museum of Telephony,** which displays telephone equipment used in the region from the invention of the device to modern days. Call (325) 653-0756.

Appropriately housed in the Fort Concho Post Hospital is the **Robert Wood Johnson Museum of Frontier Medicine,** tracing medical treatment from the founding of the fort in 1867 into the twentieth century. Your children will appreciate your family doctor more when they see some of these items from the nineteenth century.

Fort Concho is the site for celebrations throughout the year and on most holidays. If you're in town in June, the kids will love **Fort Concho Frontier Days,** a fun celebration of the area's ranching and agricultural heritage held on the Fort Concho grounds. Special exhibits, displays, arts and crafts booths, pancake breakfast, and children's activities. Call (325) 657-4441.

In early December the fort celebrates **Christmas at Old Fort Concho.** Dancers, singers, and living-history performers bring a typical 1800s holiday season to life, with an emphasis on different cultures. In addition, your family can enjoy wagon rides, cowboy poets, campfire entertainment, an arts-and-crafts show, food booths, and a special children's area with interactive programs and craft instruction. Call (325) 481-2646. $

San Angelo Museum of Fine Arts (ages 6 and up)

One Love Street, San Angelo (325-653-3333; www.SAMFA.org). Open Tuesday through Saturday 10 a.m. to 4 p.m., Sunday 1 to 4 p.m. $.

This new, 30,000-square-foot museum on the Concho River has a copper roof resembling a covered wagon. Enjoy a variety of permanent and changing exhibits and lots of events for children.

Texas Trivia

Tumbleweeds are the ghosts of the plains. When Russian thistles in West Texas die each summer, they break from their roots at ground level, and the spherical skeletons get blown around by the winds to haunt the prairie as tumbleweeds.

Children's Art Museum (ages 6 and up)

One Love Street, San Angelo (325-653-3333). Open Tuesday through Saturday 10 a.m. to 4 p.m., Sunday 1 to 4 p.m. $.

The Children's Art Museum, located in the San Angelo Museum of Fine Arts (above) features children's art and a picture-book library and a variety of programs designed to inspire kids' creativity.

Angelo State University Planetarium (ages 6 and up)

Pierce and Vanderventer Streets, San Angelo (325-942-2136; www.angelo.edu/dept/physics/planetarium.html). Call for show schedule. $.

Another surprise in tiny San Angelo is Angelo State University Planetarium, the fourth largest university planetarium in the nation. You'll find it in the Nursing and Physical Sciences Building on the ASU campus at 2601 W. Avenue N.

River Walk (ages 4 and up)

At Celebration Bridge, San Angelo (325-653-1206). River Walk is free; prices vary for activities.

If the family is looking for a little exercise, along with nice views, try the San Angelo River Walk, a 4.5 mile lighted trail that wanders by the new Visitor Center through landscaped parks and gardens, by huge pecan trees and beautiful homes, near fountains and waterfalls, a children's playground (Kid's Kingdom), and to a nine-hole city golf course and a miniature golf course. The River Walk ends at the River Stage (325-653-9577), a multipurpose facility for special events and performances including dance reviews, musicals, and concerts of all kinds. The big dates are the Fourth of July, when the San Angelo Symphony performs before the fireworks display and the annual Cactus Jazz and Blues Festival each September. Celebration Bridge links the historic downtown with the River Stage.

San Angelo Nature Center (ages 4 and up)

7409 Knickerbocker Road, off U.S. Highway 87 south of San Angelo (325-942-0121). Hours vary by season. $.

Another facility dedicated to children is the San Angelo Nature Center, on the shores of Lake Nasworthy at Mary Lee Park. The center provides interactive programs, a nature trail, and a museum.

San Angelo State Park (ages 4 and up)

West of downtown San Angelo, off US 87, on Farm Road 2288 (325-949-4757; www.tpwd.state.tx.us/spdest/findadest/parks/san_angelo).

On the shores of O. C. Fisher Reservoir are the 7,000 acres of San Angelo State Park. You can boat on the lake, fish, swim, camp, hike along developed and undeveloped trails, or watch abundant wildlife.

Where to Eat

Golden Corral. 1601 Knickerbocker Road, San Angelo (325-658-7656). Steaks and a huge buffet provide something for everyone, even picky eaters. $–$$

Mejor Que Nada. 1911 South Bryant Boulevard, San Angelo (325-655-3553). Great Mexican food, arcade room; patio, mariachi music sometimes. $

Where to Stay

Best Western Hotel. 3017 West Loop 306, San Angelo (325-223-1273; www.bestwestern.com). Pool, **free** high-speed Internet, **free** continental breakfast, children 12 and under **free.** $$

Howard Johnson Inn of the West. 415 West Beauregard Avenue, San Angelo (325-653-2995 or 800-582-9668). Pool, **free** high-speed Internet. $$

Econo Lodge. 4205 S. Bryant Blvd, San Angelo (325-653-6966; www.econolodge.com). Outdoor pool, **free** wireless Internet, children under 18 **free.** Good budget hotel in convenient location. $

For More Information

San Angelo Visitor Center. 418 West Avenue B, San Angelo 76903; (325) 655-4136; www.sanangelo.org. Open Monday through Friday 9 a.m. to 5 p.m., Saturday 10 a.m. to 5 p.m. and Sunday noon to 4 p.m.

Paint Rock, Ballinger, and Buffalo Gap

Paint Rock Excursions (ages 4 and up)

32 miles east of San Angelo on Ranch Road 380, Paint Rock (Ranch owners Fred or Kay Campbell: 325-732-4376). Tours by appointment only. $–$$.

Tiny Paint Rock is one of the largest prehistoric Native American pictograph sites in the United States. More than 1,500 paintings line a limestone bluff just north of the Concho River.

O. H. Ivie Reservoir (ages 4 and up)

20 miles southeast of Ballinger on Farm Road 1929 (325-365-5611).

Stop at Lake Ivie to cool the family off in its 25,000 acres, which include boating and fishing opportunities. The lake, created in 1992, also has several campsites.

Abilene State Park (ages 4 and up) 

4 miles southwest of Buffalo Gap on Park Road 32, Tuscola (325-572-3204; www.tpwd.state.tx.us/spdest/findadest/parks/abilene).

Take a short detour down to Abilene State Park, where you'll find overnight camping facilities ranging from tent sites to screened shelters with electricity. Or your family can picnic under giant pecan trees and swim at the pool (open Memorial Day through Labor Day). Most of the park's 490 acres have been left in their natural, semiarid state of prairie grass and wooded stream valleys. Bordering the park on the west is Lake Abilene, the water supply for Abilene, where you can fish.

Buffalo Gap Historic Village (ages 4 and up) 

133 North William Street off Farm Road 89, Buffalo Gap (325-572-3365; www.buffalogap.com). Open from 10 a.m. to 5 p.m. Monday through Saturday and noon to 5 p.m. Sunday. $, children 5 and under free.

About 4 miles north of Abilene State Park is Buffalo Gap Historic Village, where an entire frontier town is preserved, including many original buildings, most of them more than one hundred years old. You'll find a museum depicting the history of the Abilene area in the courthouse and jail building. The current town has several restaurants and unusual shops.

Abilene

Abilene is at the junction of several major highways in West Texas: I–20 and U.S. Highways 83, 84, and 277.

Founded as a shipping point for cattle, Abilene was named for Abilene, Kansas, another great cattle town. Once oil was discovered, it gave the city a double economic punch. While reveling in its past, the city also looks to its future with three universities—Abilene Christian, Hardin-Simmons, and McMurry—as well as Cisco Junior College and Texas State Technical College.

Texas Trivia

In April, most of Texas is experiencing weather much of the rest of the nation would call summer, not spring. But on April 5, 1996, Sweetwater received 18 inches of snow. The same storm dropped a record-breaking 9.3 inches of snow on Abilene.

Texas **Critters**

- **Armadillos**—A favorite of children, the nine-banded armadillo is the state small mammal and the critter you're most likely to see squished on the pavement since it's slow, has poor eyesight, and is rather stupid. Don't allow your kids to play with them; many carry serious diseases.
- **Coyotes**—The wild dogs of Texas are almost a symbol of the Old West since they always seem to be howling in the distance whenever cowpokes build a campfire in the movies. You, too, might hear them if you're camped out in an isolated area, but they are the least commonly seen of all the critters listed here.
- **Fire Ants**—They are the reason you don't want to go barefoot on a picnic. These nasty insects are everywhere, and when they bite you'll know why they call them fire ants. Watch your kids carefully because these ants will swarm up an offending foot in a flash.
- **Horny Toads**—Some folks also call them horned frogs, especially students at Texas Christian University, where they are the school mascot, but they're neither frogs nor toads despite their flat, fat appearance. They're actually lizards, as befitting the state reptile, and look quite prehistoric.
- **Jackrabbits**—You'll know one when you see one: They have huge ears, usually held bolt upright, and large, powerful hind feet. Some oldsters swear they've seen jackrabbits outrun locomotives. But then, they also say they've seen jackalopes, a mythical cross between a white-tailed deer and a jackrabbit.
- **Longhorns**—A tough, lean breed of cattle that thrived on the Texas range and was able to withstand the withering trail drives of the late 1800s. Today they are mostly trophy cattle, as modern ranchers have turned to better moneymaking breeds. Some horn spans can reach 8 feet across.
- **Roadrunners**—In West Texas you'll hear this bird called *paisano*, which means "little buddy" in Mexican slang. You'll find them racing alongside your car all over the back roads. But only your car can go "beep-beep."

Your family is certain to enjoy the **Western Heritage Classic Rodeo** in mid-May (www.westernheritageclassic.com). Unlike many rodeos, this one features working cowboys competing in ranch events, campfire cook-offs, horse racing, and a parade and western art show. Lots of family fun.

Abilene Zoo (ages 4 and up)

In Nelson Park off Highway 36 at Loop 322, Abilene (325-676-6085 or 325-673-9453; www.abilenetx.com/zoo). Open daily from 9 a.m. to 5 p.m. and until 9 p.m. on Thursday from Memorial Day to Labor Day. $, children under 3 free.

The primary family attraction in Abilene is the Abilene Zoo, an award-winning zoo that features more than 500 species of birds, mammals, reptiles, and amphibians. The thirteen-acre complex compares plants and animals of the American Southwest with similar regions in Africa, comparing the Texas plains to the African veldt. Large open areas allow different species to live together as they would in the wild. It also features aquariums, a tropical aviary, and a trail that is home to lemurs, mongooses, and ringtails. Summer camps, weekend programs for kids. Adjacent Nelson Park has a nice children's playground.

Grace Cultural Center (ages 4 and up)

102 Cypress Street, Abilene (325-673-4587; www.thegracemuseum.org). Open Tuesday through Saturday from 10 a.m. to 5 p.m., Thursday until 8 p.m. $, children 3 and under free.

The Grace Cultural Center, in the historic Grace Hotel, is now home to three museums. The Abilene Children's Museum has hands-on activities that let your youngsters experience art, science, and technology. The Historical Museum uses re-created rooms and memorabilia to showcase Abilene's history. The Art Museum displays permanent and special exhibits of folk art, sculpture, western art, and photography.

Lake Fort Phantom Hill (ages 4 and up)

14 miles north of Abilene on Farm Road 600 (325-676-6217).

Here's a place to relax, cool off in the lake, and maybe fish a little. Near the lake is Fort Phantom Hill, built in 1851 with three buildings and a dozen chimneys, which remain from the days the fort protected area settlers and travelers on the Butterfield Trail.

For More Information

Abilene Convention and Visitors Bureau. 1101 North First Street, Abilene 79601; (325) 676-2556 or (800) 727-7704; http://abilenevisitors.com.

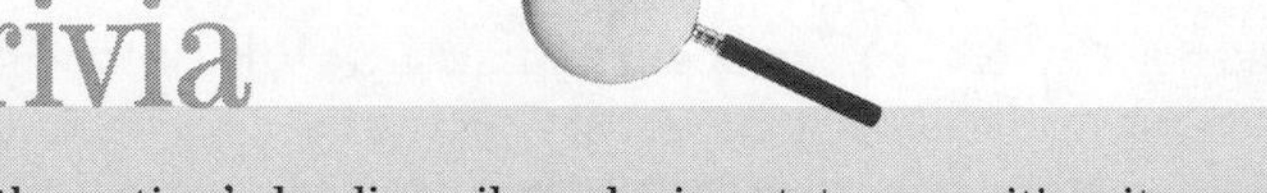

Texas Trivia

By 1928 Texas was the nation's leading oil-producing state, a position it has never relinquished. Today the state pumps out around 650 million barrels of crude oil and gas a year from more than 240,000 wells.

Albany, Colorado City, and Big Spring

Albany is on Highway 6 northeast of Abilene, while Colorado City and Big Spring are on I–20 west of Abilene.

Founded as a cattle shipping point on the Western Trail to Dodge City, Albany remains a major cattle supply center, along with its oil interests. The Fort Griffin Fandangle (www.fortgriffinfandangle.org), Texas's oldest outdoor musical production, is held the last two weekends in June ($$–$$$). Oil is a big thing in Colorado City as well. The big spring that Big Spring is named for bubbles up in the middle of the city. The spring attracted buffalo herds, antelope, wild horses, Comanches and Shawnees, and early Texas Rangers. Today, a city park surrounds the spring.

Old Jail Art Center (ages 6 and up)

201 South Second Street, Albany (325-762-2269; www.theoldjailartcenter.org). Open Tuesday through Saturday from 10 a.m. to 5 p.m., Sunday from 2 to 5 p.m., closed holidays. Free.

Don't let the name fool you. The nationally renowned Old Jail Art Center has an exceptional permanent art collection that includes the work of Picasso and Modigliani, and hosts special events throughout the year.

Fort Griffin State Historic Site (ages 4 and up)

15 miles north of Albany at 1701 N. U.S. Highway 283 (325-762-3592; www.thc.state.tx.us/hsites/hs_griffin.aspx?Site=Griffin).

At the Clear Fork of the Brazos River is Fort Griffin State Historic Site. The fort was a primary center for trail-herd cowboys and buffalo hunters. This is where Wyatt Earp met Doc Holliday. You can walk on the sidewalks they walked on and wander around the ruins of many of the buildings, seeing three restored structures and a small museum. You can also camp, fish, have a picnic, play horseshoes, or go on a nature walk. The park also has a playground for kids.

Heart of West Texas Museum (ages 6 and up)

340 East Third Street, Colorado City (325-728-8285). Open Tuesday through Saturday 10 a.m. to noon and 1 to 5 p.m. Donations welcomed.

Colorado City, on I–20, was one of the fastest growing cities in Texas before the turn of the twentieth century, but a severe drought and competition from other shipping points turned the boom into a bust from which the town has never fully recovered. The Heart of Texas Museum preserves artifacts not only from pioneer days but from modern times as well, such as the display on Operation Desert Storm.

Nearby, at Second and Chestnut Streets, is the Branding Wall in Kiwanis Park, where you can see more than 230 cattle brands that have been used in the county, making for a good backdrop in photos of the kids.

Lake Colorado City State Park (ages 4 and up)

12 miles southwest of Colorado City, at 4582 Farm Road 2836 (325-728-3931; www.tpwd.state.tx.us/spdest/findadest/parks/lake_colorado_city).

This is a 500-acre park along the banks of a 1,600-acre lake, where your family can camp, picnic, swim, water-ski, or fish.

Comanche Trail Park (ages 4 and up)

On US 87, Big Spring (432-264-2376).

The spring for which the city of Big Spring is named is in Comanche Trail Park. The park, just south of town, has a golf course and tennis courts, swimming pool, hiking and biking trails, overnight camping, sailing on Comanche Trail Lake, and Kid's Zone. The Comanche Trail Amphitheater is built of hand-cut native limestone.

Heritage Museum (ages 6 and up)

510 Scurry Street, Big Spring (432-267-8255). Open Tuesday through Friday 8:30 a.m. to 4:30 p.m., Saturday 10 a.m. to 4:00 p.m. $.

The Heritage Museum houses the world's largest collection of Texas longhorn steer horns and an exhibit of forty-six rare and unusual phonographs.

Big Spring State Park (ages 4 and up)

About 4 miles west of Big Spring on Farm Road 700, (432-263-4931; www.tpwd.state.tx.us/spdest/findadest/parks/big_spring). Open daily 8 a.m. to sunset.

Big Spring State Park is the closest thing this area of West Texas has to a mountain. A 200-foot mesa that overlooks the city west of downtown, the park has a children's playground, picnic areas, a prairie-dog town, and nature trails. Camping is available on top of Scenic Mountain.

For More Information

Big Spring Convention and Visitors Bureau. 310 Nolan Street, Big Spring 79720; (866) 430-7100 or (432) 263-8235; www.bigspring-cvb.com.

Albany Chamber of Commerce. 2 Railroad Street, Albany 76430; 325-762-2525; www.albanytexas.com.

Colorado City Chamber of Commerce. 157 West Second Street, Colorado City 79512; 325-728-3403; www.coloradocitychamberofcommerce.com.

Midland

Midway between Dallas and El Paso, about 40 miles west of Big Spring.

Permian Basin Petroleum Museum (ages 6 and up)

1500 I–20 West, Midland (432-683-4403; www.petroleummuseum.org). Open 10 a.m. to 5 p.m. Monday through Saturday and 2 to 5 p.m. Sunday. Closed Thanksgiving Day, Christmas Eve, Christmas, and New Year's Day. $–$$, children under 6 free.

Midland and its twin city, Odessa, are the centers for oil exploration in Texas, so it's appropriate that the Permian Basin Petroleum Museum is here. You can see the museum from the interstate. It's that red building at the Highway 349 exit with dozens of oil-field derricks beside it. Here your family will explore 500 million years of history, walk under a vast sea to view the Permian Basin as it was 230 million years ago, stroll through a typical boomtown, examine rock samples, learn how wells are drilled, and feel the force of an underground explosion. You'll see everything from old cable tool rigs to modern pump jacks. The kids can even play the Oil Game and might hit a gusher. In addition to the petroleum paraphernalia, the museum also focuses on the Comanche War Trail, which passed through the heart of Midland, site of the last Comanche raid in Texas.

Midland Rockhounds Baseball (ages 4 and up)

Citybank Ball Park at Hwy. 191 and Loop 250, 5514 Champions Drive, Midland (432-520-2255; www.midlandrockhounds.org). $–$$.

The Midland Rockhounds play AA minor-league baseball at Citybank Ballpark. Concessions here aren't limited to just peanuts and hot dogs; you can also get pizza, nachos, and Frito pies. The ballpark also has a special family section where beer sales aren't allowed. Good family fun. The Rockhounds play April through mid-September.

Museum of the Southwest (ages 4 and up)

1705 West Missouri Street, Midland (432-683-2882; www.museumsw.org). Open Tuesday through Saturday from 10 a.m. to 5 p.m., Sunday 2 to 5 p.m. Closed major holidays. Art Museum free; Children's Museum $, free on Sundays.

The Museum of the Southwest complex covers an entire city block. Exhibits feature southwestern painting, sculpture, and ceramics, with a crafts fair the first weekend following Labor Day. During the summer, hear pop, country, jazz, or folk music at the free Lawn Concert Series performances on Sunday evenings. In the complex are two other museums. The **Fredda Turner Durham Children's Museum** gives kids an interactive environment for exploration and learning, including a computer area. The Planetarium (432) 683-2882 is closed for renovation at this writing, but is scheduled to reopen soon.

Commemorative Air Force Headquarters and American Airpower Heritage Museum (ages 4 and up)

9600 Wright Drive, off I–20 next to the Midland International Airport, 8 miles west of the city (432-563-1000; www.commemorativeairforce.org, www.airpowermuseum.org). Open Tuesday through Saturday 9 a.m. to 5 p.m. $$, children 5 and under free.

The American Airpower Heritage Museum is one place that will fascinate both children and parents, showcasing a large number of antique aircraft. Its World War II–vintage planes fly at air shows here and around the country. About 20 of the 135 aircraft in the CAF's Ghost Squadron are on display here at any one time, and the headquarters hosts the annual Airsho (www.airsho.org) in October. The museum preserves authentic World War II artifacts and memorabilia, opening new exhibits each year. If your child is a model builder, he or she will love the gift shop, which has the largest collection of model airplanes for sale in one place.

The George W. Bush Childhood Home (ages 6 and up)

1412 W. Ohio Avenue, Midland (432-685-1112; www.bushchildhoodhome.com). Open Tuesday through Saturday 10 a.m. to 5 p.m., Sunday 2 to 5 p.m. $, children 5 and under free.

In the childhood home of the forty-third U.S. president, learn about the Bush family including two presidents and two first ladies.

Where to Eat

Luigi's. 111 N. Big Spring Street, Midland (432-683-6363). Family-owned, family-oriented, and great Italian food. $–$$

Fuddrucker's. 4511 N. Midkiff Road, Midland (432-689-0448; www.fuddruckers.com). Great burgers with a condiment bar to fix your own. $

Chuck E. Cheese. 4703 W. Loop 250 N., Midland (432-697-2322; www.chuckecheese.com). Food, games, rides, entertainment for kids. $–$$

Where to Stay

La Quinta Inn Midland. 4130 W. Wall Street, Midland (432-697-9900; www.laquinta.com). Outdoor pool, free high-speed Internet, free breakfast. $$

Americas Best Value Inn. 3904 W. Wall Stree, Midland (432-694-7774). Outdoor pool, free high-speed Internet, free breakfast. $$

For More Information

Midland Convention and Visitors Bureau. 109 North Main Street, Midland 79701; (800) 624-6435 or (432) 683-3381; http://visitmidlandtexas.com.

Texas Trivia

The county with the smallest population is Loving County in West Texas, with 96 people in 2006. Rockwall County is the smallest in land area.

Odessa

Presidential Museum (ages 6 and up)

4919 East University Drive, Odessa (432-363-PRES; www.presidentialmuseum.org). Open Tuesday through Saturday from 10 a.m. to 5 p.m. $-$$, preschool children free.

The middle of nowhere in Texas may seem like a strange place for the Presidential Museum, but it's in Odessa nonetheless. The museum houses an impressive collection of items relating to the U.S. presidency. The Hall of Presidents displays objects related to individual presidents, the Dishong Collection displays replicas of first lady inaugural gowns, and one exhibit focuses on campaigns.

Globe Theatre of the Great Southwest (ages 6 and up)

2308 Shakespeare Road, Odessa (432-332-1586; www.globesw.org). Prices vary by event.

If the idea of a Presidential Museum in Odessa isn't odd enough for you, how about a replica of Shakespeare's Globe Theatre along with a full Shakespearean library in a replica of Anne Hathaway's cottage and a summer Shakespeare festival? Call the theater for show times and special events, from Broadway musicals to country-and-western revues.

The Ellen Noel Art Museum of the Permian Basin (ages 6 and up)

4909 East University Boulevard, Odessa (432-550-9696; www.noelartmuseum.org). Open Tuesday through Saturday from 10 a.m. to 5 p.m., Sunday from 2 to 5 p.m. Free.

If art is your thing, check out the Ellen Noel Art Museum, on the campus of the University of Texas–Permian Basin, for exhibits of historic and contemporary art and photography, a sculpture garden, and art education programs.

World's Largest Jack Rabbit (ages 2 and up)

802 North Sam Houston Avenue, Odessa.

Odessa calls Jack Ben Rabbit the World's Largest. So what if it's just a statue? The 8-foot bunny in the parking lot of the Ector County Independent School District's administration building is a popular place to take photos of the kids.

Odessa Meteor Crater (ages 4 and up)

About 10 miles west of Odessa off I–20 at the Farm Road 1936 exit (432-381-0946). Museum open Tuesday through Saturday 9 a.m. to 5 p.m., Sunday 1 to 5 p.m. Free.

At 550 feet in diameter and 6 feet deep, the Odessa Meteor Crater is the second largest known meteor crater in the United States, but wind erosion has taken a heavy toll on its shape, and it really doesn't look like much. At least your family can say "been there, done that" if you go. A chunk of the meteor that crashed here is at the Permian Basin Petroleum Museum in Midland. The site has picnic tables and a barbecue grill.

Texas **Tunes**

Here are some more recommendations for good Texas traveling music:

- *Live at the Old Quarter* by Townes Van Zandt (one of the great songwriters)
- *Loco Gringo's Lament* by Ray Wylie Hubbard (the quintessential Texas outlaw matured)
- *Navajo Rug* by Jerry Jeff Walker (a country folk highlight)
- *Ocean Front Property* by George Strait (straight country)
- *The Original Texas Playboys* by Bob Wills and the Texas Playboys (they created Texas swing)
- *Piano Rags* by Scott Joplin (the ragtime master)
- *Red-Headed Stranger* by Willie Nelson (the album that made Willie a legend)
- *Road to Ensenada* by Lyle Lovett (funny and poignant; the best of the best)
- *Selena Live* by Selena (capture a moment of her magic)
- *Texas Blues* by Lightnin' Hopkins (the blues master)
- *This Is My Home* by Chris and Judy (songs written for children that adults will enjoy as well)
- *22 All-Time Favorites* by Gene Autry (the original singing cowboy, still unmatched)
- *The Wind Knows My Name* by Tim Henderson (music that's pure Texas poetry)

Where to Eat

Mama's Kitchen. 1534 E. Eighth Street, Odessa (432-332-6262; www.mamaskitchen odessa.com). Popular local place for great burgers and home cooking comfort food. $

Golden Corral. 4037 E. Forty-second Street, Odessa (432-363-8705; www.goldencorral .com). Huge buffet with lots of choices. $$

Rosa's Cafe and Tortilla Factory. 4945 East Forty-second Street, Odessa (432-362-5512) and 1310 E. Eighth Street (432-580-6648). Good, homemade Mexican food. $

Where to Stay

Comfort Inn & Suites. 801 S. JBS Parkway, Odessa (432-368-4200; www.comfortinn .com). Outdoor pool, exercise room, **free** high-speed Internet, **free** breakfast, children 18 and under **free.** $$–$$$

Day's Inn. 3075 E. Business Loop 20, Odessa (432-335-8000; www.daysinn.com). Pool, **free** high-speed Internet, **free** breakfast. $$

For More Information

Odessa Convention and Visitors Bureau. 700 North Grant Street #200, Odessa 79761; (800) 780-HOST; www.odessacvb.com.

Monahans

Monahans Sandhills State Park (ages 4 and up)

6 miles northeast of Monahans off I–20 on Park Road 41 (432-943-2092; www.tpwd.state.tx.us/spdest/findadest/parks/monahans_sandhills).

This is where kids love to surf the sand. Rent a sand-surfing disk and fly down the smooth, cream-colored sand dunes. The park is 4,000 acres of always-changing, wind-sculpted dunes that look more like the Sahara Desert than Texas. In addition to sand sliding, the park has horseback rides, hiking trails, camping and picnic sites, interpretive rides in a utility vehicle, and a museum.

Million Barrel Museum (ages 6 and up)

On the eastern edge of Monahans on US Highway 80, 400 Museum Blvd. (432-943-8401). Open Tuesday through Saturday 10 a.m. to 6 p.m., Sunday 2 to 6 p.m. Free.

The Million Barrel Museum surrounds a big hole in the ground that was once a Shell Oil tank. The museum complex includes a historic hotel, the first jail in the county, oil-field equipment, and an amphitheater.

For More Information

Monahans Chamber of Commerce. 401 South Dwight Street, Monahans 79756; (432) 943-2187; www.monahans.org.

Pecos

Pecos is where rodeos began, when several cowboys from neighboring ranches got together to prove once and for all who was best at their occupation. That was back in 1883, and the town still holds a rodeo near the Fourth of July. The **West of the Pecos Rodeo** is a four-day event that also features a parade, old-timers' reunion, and western art show. Call (432) 445-2406 or visit www.pecosrodeo.com.

Texas Trivia

The deepest well in Texas was a 29,670-foot dry hole in Pecos County.

West of the Pecos Museum and Park (ages 4 and up)

120 East First Street at Cedar Street, Pecos (432-445-5076; www.westofthepecosmuseum .com). Open Memorial Day through Labor Day Monday through Saturday 9 a.m. to 5 p.m., Sunday 1 to 4 p.m.; Labor Day through Memorial Day Tuesday through Saturday 9 a.m. to 5 p.m. $, children under 6 free.

The West of the Pecos Museum and Park occupies an old saloon and two floors of a historic hotel, full of artifacts. An adjacent park contains the first building in Pecos; the grave of Clay Allison, the "Gentleman Gunfighter"; and a replica of Judge Roy Bean's saloon (you can see the real Jersey Lilly Saloon in Langtry).

Maxey Park and Zoo (ages 4 and up)

Off I–20 at exit 40, Pecos. Open 9 a.m. to 5 p.m. Free.

The kids will enjoy seeing animals indigenous to West Texas: antelope, buffalo, deer, javelina, longhorns, mountain lions, and prairie dogs. Another feature of the park is Kid's City, a large playground that can occupy children for hours. Basketball court, sand volleyball court, and miniature golf course ($).

For More Information

Pecos Chamber of Commerce. 111 South Cedar Street, Pecos 79772; (432) 445-2406; www.pecostx.com.

Balmorhea

Head south on Highway 17 about 40 miles from Pecos to the small town of Balmorhea (Bal-moh-ray), a literal oasis in the parched West Texas landscape.

Balmorhea State Park (ages 4 and up)

On Highway 17 south of I–10, Toyahvale (432-375-2370; www.tpwd.state.tx.us/spdest/finda dest/parks/balmorhea). Open daily from 8 a.m. to dark.

Families in the area flock to this park, where historic San Solomon Springs form the world's largest spring-fed swimming pool, more than an acre large. In addition to campsites, the park features San Solomon Springs Court, a moderately priced eighteen-unit motel.

Pine Springs

Guadalupe Mountains National Park (ages 8 and up)

On U.S. Highway 62, Salt Flat, at the New Mexico border (915-828-3251; www.nps.gov/gumo/). Pine Springs Visitor Center and Museum open daily 8 a.m. to 4:30 p.m., 8 a.m. to 6 p.m. from Memorial Day to Labor Day, except Christmas.

Head north on Highway 54 from Van Horn for a nice scenic drive to Guadalupe Mountains National Park, home to Guadalupe Peak, Texas's tallest mountain at 8,749 feet. The park has majestic vistas all around and some of the best hiking in the state, especially the trail into McKittrick Canyon, which blazes with color in the fall. The rugged Guadalupe Peak trail provides breathtaking panoramas at the summit. The park is maintained as a primitive wilderness, so it has no accommodations beyond a few campsites. The closest motels, restaurants, and grocery stores are in New Mexico. If you do decide to explore some of the trails, make sure you and your family are in good shape and carry lots of water. The hikes here are long and often grueling, so they're not recommended for small children. The only paved road cuts through a tiny portion of the park at its southeastern boundary.

El Paso

El Paso sprawls at the foot of the Franklin Mountains, presenting an unusual vista with rocky hills and mountains to the north and the Rio Grande plain and Chihuahuan Desert to the south. The Mexican metropolis of Juarez is just across the river. West of the city, the borders of Texas, New Mexico, and Mexico swirl together as easily as American and Mexican cultures do here. The family attractions in El Paso are numerous, and that doesn't even include the shopping possibilities, from small arts and crafts boutiques to several new malls.

If Mexico fascinates you, head across the border into Juarez, where you'll find several shopping centers, many small boutiques, parks and museums, old missions, and a variety

Texas Trivia

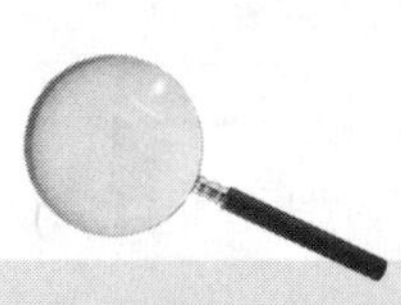

The longest river in the state is the Rio Grande (the second longest in the United States), which forms the international boundary between Texas and Mexico, extending 1,270 miles from El Paso to Brownsville. Other principal rivers are the Brazos, Colorado, Guadalupe, Neches, Nueces, Pecos, Red, Trinity, and Sabine.

of restaurants. Four international bridges cross from El Paso into Juarez. You must have a passport. For more detailed visitor information, contact the Juarez Tourist Service at (011) 52-16-11-37-07; www.juarez-mexico.com.

The best-known park area across the border is **Juarez Chamizal Park,** at the Cordova Bridge. The park has replicas of several famous sites in Mexico, such as Chichén Itzá and Teotihuacan. Adjacent to this park, on the U.S. side, is **Chamizal National Memorial** (915-532-7273; www.nps.gov/cham). Both commemorate settlement of a land dispute between the two countries.

The **Border Folk Festival** in the fall will give your family a heavy dose of what El Paso is all about. The festival features plentiful food and arts-and-crafts booths, and American, Mexican, and other international singers and dancers all day long and into the night. Call (915) 534-0601.

Hueco Tanks State Historic Site (ages 4 and up)

32 miles northeast of El Paso off Ranch Road 2775. (915-857-1135; www.tpwd.state.tx.us/spdest/findadest/parks/hueco_tanks).

Taking U.S. Highway 180 west from the Guadalupe Mountains provides a view of the salt flats before you arrive at Hueco Tanks State Historical Park, east of El Paso. *Hueco* (pronounced *Way-co*) means "hollow" in Spanish. It refers to a large number of depressions in the mountain rock that collect water and have provided refreshment to travelers for hundreds of years. The area was the site of a Butterfield Stage station and has numerous prehistoric Native American pictographs. In recent years, the rugged faces of the mountains have attracted rock climbers from around the world, and you're likely to see folks climbing up the walls on any weekend. Guided tours are available with advance reservations Wednesday through Sunday. The park has picnic areas and a few campsites.

El Paso Trolleys (ages 4 and up)

All the trolleys leave from the Civic Center Plaza at Santa Fe and San Antonio Streets, although you can board the city trolley anywhere along its route. See the following for telephone numbers and fares.

A nice way for your family to forget about traffic and still get around town is via the trolleys. **Sun Metro** offers two routes around the downtown historic district for 25 cents (915-533-1220; www.elpasotexas.gov/sunmetro) The **El Paso–Juarez Trolley** (915-544-0062) rents trolleys for private events.

Fort Bliss Museums (ages 6 and up)

Wilson Road at Highway 54, El Paso (915-568-3390; www.bliss.army.mil/museum/fort_bliss_museum.htm). Free.

Fort Bliss, bordering the El Paso airport, has been an active army base since 1848. On the base are several **free** museums, most open daily 9 a.m. to 4:30 p.m., closed Sundays and federal holidays.

- The **Fort Bliss Museum** is a replica of the original adobe fort, with several displays on frontier military life. It's at Pleasanton Road and Sheridan Drive in Building 5051.
- The **Air Defense and Artillery Museum,** in Building 5000 on Pleasanton Road, is the only one of its kind in the country, with hands-on displays and dioramas.
- The **Museum of the Noncommissioned Officer** is in Building 11331 at Barksdale and Thirty-fifth Streets. It traces the history of the NCO from the Revolutionary War to the present.
- The **Third Armored Cavalry Museum,** in Building 2407 at Forrest Road, honors the Third Cavalry that fought in the Mexican and Indian wars. Open Monday through Friday 7:30 a.m. to 4:30 p.m. Call (915) 568-1922.

Border Patrol Museum (ages 6 and up)

4315 Transmountain Road El Paso (915-759-6060; www.borderpatrolmuseum.com). Open Tuesday through Saturday 9 a.m. to 5 p.m., closed holidays. Guided tours with advance notice. Free, donations welcome.

The museum chronicles the U.S. Border Patrol from its beginnings in the Old West to the high-tech world of the present.

Museum of Archaeology at Wilderness Park (ages 4 and up)

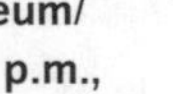

4301 Transmountain Road, El Paso (915-755-4332; www.elpasotexas.gov/arch_museum/info.asp). Open Tuesday through Saturday from 9 a.m. to 5 p.m., Sunday noon to 5 p.m., closed Mondays and holidays. Free.

Next door to the Border Patrol Museum is the Museum of Archaeology at Wilderness Park, the perfect place for your kids to get acquainted with West Texas history, geology, and plants. The museum displays collections of pottery and other prehistoric artifacts, along with several life-size dioramas, and offers a self-guided nature trail where your family can learn all about the region's plant life.

Franklin Mountains State Park (ages 4 and up)

1331 McKelligan Canyon Road, El Paso (915-566-6441; www.tpwd.state.tx.us/spdest/findadest/parks/franklin).

Continue northward on the Transmountain Road (Loop 375), the highest state highway in Texas, for some nice views of the area. Several scenic overlooks are by the side of the road. You'll also notice some parking areas that are trailheads for 100 miles of multi-use trails into Franklin Mountains State Park, which you are driving through. The park is undeveloped, so only day-use activities are allowed. A side road off the main route will take you into the picnic areas of the park. Inside Franklin Mountains State Park, Wyler Aerial Tramway (915-562-9899) will take you to the top of Ranger Peak in a Swiss gondola. Views are fabulous from the summit where you'll find an Observation Deck and a snack bar.

Wet 'n' Wild Waterworld (ages 4 and up)

At exit 0 on I–10, Anthony (915-886-2222; www.wetwild.com). Open daily May through mid-August, weekends in early May through September. Hours vary widely throughout the season. $$$.

To cool off the kids during the hot months, continue west on the interstate just a couple of miles to the last exit in Texas. Wet 'n' Wild Waterworld is on the south side of the freeway.

El Paso Centennial Museum (ages 6 and up)

University Avenue at Wiggins Road, El Paso (915-747-5565; www.utep.edu/museum). Open Tuesday through Saturday from 10 a.m. to 4:30 p.m. Free.

The Centennial Museum, on the University of Texas at El Paso campus, features photos and maps, pottery and jewelry, and other displays of the area's history and geology, focusing on the border culture of the region.

El Paso Museum of Art (ages 6 and up)

One Arts Festival Plaza, El Paso (915-532-1707; www.elpasoartmuseum.org). Open Tuesday through Saturday 9 a.m. to 5 p.m., Sunday noon to 5 p.m. Free.

The Museum of Art is renowned for its frequent exhibits of classical and contemporary Mexican and southwestern art. The new facility tripled the museum's space, so you'll now see more of its permanent collection, which used to rotate.

The First **Thanksgiving?**

Some believe that the first Thanksgiving in the United States was held in El Paso, twenty-three years before the Pilgrims' day of thanks we now celebrate nationally. In April 1598, explorer Don Juan de Oñate and his expedition reached the area after a grueling 200-mile march across the Chihuahuan Desert. Many of his men and livestock were near death. Nearby Native Americans visited Oñate's camp, shared food, and were entertained by a play written by one of the expedition captains as thanks for being delivered from their ordeal. It's said to be the first drama performed by Europeans on what would become U.S. soil.

The account of this first Thanksgiving was not translated into English until 1933, many decades after President Lincoln designated the fourth Thursday in November to commemorate the Pilgrim Thanksgiving. Of course, there are those in the Texas Panhandle who will tell you that the real first Thanksgiving took place in Palo Duro Canyon in 1541.

El Paso Museum of History (ages 6 and up)

510 N. Santa Fe Street, El Paso (915-351-3588; www.elpasotexas.gov/history/). Open Tuesday through Saturday from 10 a.m. to 5 p.m., Sunday noon to 5 p.m., closed some holidays. Free.

The Museum of History focuses on U.S. Cavalry mementos and southwestern history from the conquistadors to Pancho Villa. Its brand new facility (2008) allows more exhibits, special programs, events, and a new gift shop. Museum volunteers hold special programs for children.

Insights, El Paso Science Museum (ages 4 and up)

505 North Santa Fe, El Paso (915-534-0000; www.insightselpaso.org). Open Tuesday through Saturday 10 a.m. to 5 p.m., Sunday noon to 5 p.m., closed major holidays. $–$$, children 3 and under free.

All the exhibits at Insights, El Paso Science Center, are designed to make learning about science and technology an active experience for children and interested parents. Almost everything is hands-on.

Magoffin Home State Historic Site (ages 8 and up)

1120 Magoffin Avenue, El Paso (915-533-5147; www.thc.state.tx.us/hsites/hs_magoffin.aspx?Site=Magoffin). Open Tuesday through Sunday 9 a.m. to 5 p.m. $, ages 12 and under free.

The Magoffin Home is a perfectly preserved territorial hacienda built in 1875 by one of the prominent pioneer families in the area. Inside are many of the family's original furnishings, paintings, and artifacts.

El Paso Zoo (ages 4 and up)

4001 East Paisano Drive, El Paso (915-521-1850; www.elpasozoo.org). Open daily 9:30 a.m. to 4 p.m., until 5 p.m. on Saturday and Sunday during the summer. $, children 2 and under free.

Seems like every city of any size in Texas has a zoo, and El Paso is no exception. The El Paso Zoo is home to more than 400 exotic animals on eighteen acres. Your family will love the shaded walkways as they watch the birds, fish, mammals, and reptiles. A new "Zoo Adventure" program offers special programs and animal encounter adventures throughout the year.

El Paso Patriots Soccer (ages 6 and up)

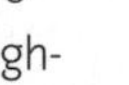

6941 Industrial Avenue, El Paso (915-771-6620; www.elpaso-patriots.com). $–$$.

This professional soccer team plays in Patriot Stadium.

Tigua Cultural Center (ages 4 and up)

305 Yaya Lane, El Paso; take the Zaragosa exit from I–10 and go south (915-859-7700). Open Wednesday through Sunday from 10 a.m. to 4 p.m. Free.

A lovely way for the family to spend part of the day is at the Tigua Cultural Center. It's the showcase for the Ysleta del Sur Pueblo, the oldest existing community in Texas, founded by Tigua Indians in 1680. The Tigua Cultural Center has a central courtyard where Tiguas demonstrate tribal dances at 11:30 a.m. and 1:30 p.m. on weekends. The courtyard is surrounded by a variety of gift shops featuring work by Tigua artists.

Nearby, at 119 South Old Pueblo Road, is **Mission Corpus Christi.** Formerly known as Ysleta Mission, it was built in 1681 and is the oldest mission in Texas. Call (915) 859-9848.

Where to Eat

Hudson's Grill. 1770 Lee Trevino (915-595-2769) and 8041 N. Mesa (915-581-3990). The classic '50s décor showcases the era of the Hudson Automobile. Jukebox rock & roll music is fun for all—varied menu includes great burgers, sandwiches, salads, sodas, and banana splits. $–$$

Casa Jurado. 226 Cincinnati Avenue (915-532-6429) and 4772 Doniphan, El Paso (915-833-1151). If you're hungry, try one of the six distinct styles of enchiladas for a real treat; the best in Texas. $–$$

Cracker Barrel. 7540 Remcon Circle, El Paso (915-581-9742; www.crackerbarrel.com). Family-style southern cooking with a huge gift shop in the lobby. $–$$

Wyngs Restaurant. 122 South Old Pueblo Road, El Paso (915-860-7777). Operated by the Tiguas, this restaurant has great portions of good food. Kids will love the hamburger served on Indian fry bread, so large it can be shared by two adults or several small children. $$

Where to Stay

Best Western Airport Inn, 7144 Gateway East (915-779-7700; www.bestwestern.com) and **Best Western Sunland Park Inn,** 1045 Sunland Park Drive (915-587-4900). Pool, fitness center, cable TV, **free** continental breakfast; children under 12 stay **free.** $$

Howard Johnson Inn. 8887 Gateway West, El Paso (915-591-9471; www.hojoelpaso.com). **Free** shuttle to airport, cable TV with HBO, outdoor pool, fitness center; children 17 and under stay **free** with parents. $$

La Quinta Inns. 7550 Remcon Circle (915-833-2522; www.laquinta.com), 11033 Gateway West (915-591-2244), and 6140 Gateway East, El Paso (915-778-9321). Perfect for families: Children under 18 stay **free**; pools and **free** continental breakfast. $$

For More Information

El Paso Convention and Tourism Department. One Civic Center Plaza, El Paso 79901-1187; (915) 534-0601 or (800) 351-6024; www.visitelpaso.com.

Fabens and Sierra Blanca

As you travel east along I–10 to Fabens and Sierra Blanca, you'll see just how desolate this area of Texas can be. Just make sure you have a full tank of gas, some snacks, and water before you leave El Paso. Sierra Blanca is historically important as the juncture of the nation's second transcontinental rail route, when the Southern Pacific and the Texas & Pacific lines met up in 1881. You'll find a historical marker commemorating that event downtown on U.S. Highway 80.

Cattleman's Steak House (ages 4 and up)

At Indian Cliffs Ranch; east on I–10 about thirty minutes from El Paso to exit 49 in Fabens, then north 4 miles to the Indian Cliffs sign (915-544-3200; www.cattlemanssteakhouse .com). Ranch playground area free, restaurant $$–$$$.

If your kids have never gotten excited about a restaurant before, they will over the Cattleman's Steak House. Although the restaurant is justly famous for items like its two-pound T-bone and the Royale ground steak, it's the ranch itself that your children will love. Sprawled over several acres around the restaurant are a small zoo, buffalo and longhorn herds, a snake pit, a frontier fort replica, a kids' playground, and a complete western town. Donkey rides and covered-wagon rides are available to other areas of the ranch. The steakhouse is renowned for its fabulous food and great views. People magazine said this was the best steak in the country.

Railroad Depot Hudspeth County Museum (ages 6 and up)

US 80, Sierra Blanca (915-369-4118). Open Wednesday 1 to 5 p.m. Free.

Near the post office is the Railroad Depot Hudspeth County Museum, where you'll find exhibits of railroad memorabilia, Native American artifacts, and county history housed in a Southern Pacific depot built in 1882.

Nearby, at US 80's intersection with Ranch Road 1111, is the **Hudspeth County Courthouse,** the only adobe structure currently in use by a government in the entire Southwest. The building is a favorite place for photos.

Fort Davis

From I-10, take Highway 118 south at Kent for one of the finest scenic drives in Texas. The road travels through the rugged Davis Mountains with a number of twists and sharp turns. The land here is almost all working ranches, and you're likely to see pronghorn antelope roaming the range by the side of the road, so have the kids keep a sharp lookout. This is where the deer and the antelope play, and the skies are not cloudy (usually) all day.

McDonald Observatory (ages 6 and up)

On Spur 78 just off Highway 118, Fort Davis (432-426-3640 or 877-984-7827; www.mcdonald observatory.org). Open daily 10 a.m. to 5:30 p.m. (later on Star Party nights), except Thanksgiving, Christmas, and New Year's Day. $–$$$.

McDonald Observatory is perched atop 6,800-foot Mount Locke. The University of Texas operates this complex of deep-space telescopes, including a new one that has the largest telescope mirror in the nation. Kids love the new visitor center, which has daily programs, films, interactive exhibits, guided tours, and solar viewing. There's an amazing number of activities available for visitors. Self-guided tours of the largest telescope are **free** during the daytime. Star Parties are held on smaller telescopes Tuesday, Friday, and Saturday evenings, so even the smallest children can enjoy the stars and planets. Twilight Programs are educational experiences and take place before the Star Parties on the same nights. Once a month, typically the Wednesday nearest the full moon, the public can peer through the "Big Eyes" of the 107-inch telescope, but reservations must be made months in advance.

Davis Mountains State Park (ages 4 and up)

On Park Road 3 off Highway 118, Fort Davis (432-426-3337; www.tpwd.state.tx.us/spdest/findadest/parks/davis_mountains).

A few miles farther south is Davis Mountains State Park. This is one of the best state parks in Texas, with picturesque campsites, picnic areas, several hiking trails, and scenic Skyline Drive, a paved road that climbs to two overlooks for magnificent views. One of the trails in the park goes over a mountain 4 miles into Fort Davis National Historical Park. Davis Mountains State Park is also the location of Indian Lodge (432-426-3254; www.tpwd.state.tx.us/spdest/findadest/parks/indian_lodge), a unique adobe pueblo-style lodging facility built during the Depression by the Civilian Conservation Corps.

Fort Davis National Historical Park (ages 4 and up)

On Highway 17, Fort Davis (432-426-3224; www.nps.gov/foda). Open daily 8 a.m. to 5 p.m., except major holidays. $, children 15 and under free.

Just north of town is Fort Davis National Historical Park, one of the best restored Indian Wars forts in the country. Officers' Row and an enlisted men's barracks are just as they were back in the 1880s. During the summer, volunteers don period uniforms and roam the fort giving living-history talks and presentations. The Junior Ranger program is **free**

Texas Trivia

The Big Bend gecko lizard (Coleonyx reticulatus) wasn't discovered until the mid-1950s, but it is now seen frequently in the Big Bend region, usually at night after a summer rain.

Texas **Indian Reservations**

Texas has three Native American reservations:

- The **Alabama-Coushatta Reservation** is near Woodville in East Texas. The Alabama-Coushattas have camping facilities—including tepee rentals—available around 26-acre Lake Tombigbee.
- The **Ysleta del Sur Pueblo,** south of El Paso in West Texas, serves as the Tigua Reservation. The Tiguas have a small gift shop and present dances. They also run an excellent restaurant nearby. The Ysleta Mission was the first Spanish settlement in Texas.
- The **Kickapoo Reserve,** south of Eagle Pass in South Texas, is small and has no tourist facilities or attractions except for a casino. Before the reservation was established in the 1980s, the Kickapoo lived in a makeshift encampment under the international bridge at Eagle Pass.

Most of the time, the Kickapoos live across the Rio Grande in Nacimiento, Coahuila.

for kids. A museum in the visitor center offers a slide show, several displays, and a gift shop with an exceptional book selection.

Overland Trail Museum (ages 6 and up)

Old Overland Trail, Fort Davis (432-426-2467). Open Tuesday, Friday, and Saturday 1 to 5 p.m. $.

The Overland Trail Museum commemorates the Overland Stage route that passed through here. The small museum is 2 blocks south of the fort and 2 blocks west of the highway at Fort and Third Streets.

Chihuahuan Desert Research Institute (ages 6 and up)

4 miles south of Fort Davis on Highway 118 (432-364-2499; www.cdri.org). Open Monday through Saturday 9 a.m. to 5 p.m., closed major holidays. $, children 12 and under free.

About 4 miles south of town is the Chihuahuan Desert Research Institute. An arboretum and desert garden display more than 500 species of plants you'll find in the area, and there is an interesting nature hike to some hidden springs, and a replica of a nineteenth century mining operation.

Where to Eat

Black Bear Restaurant. At Davis Mountains State Park, Fort Davis (432-426-3254). Good food, great view, and a nearby hill to climb afterward to work off the calories. $

Fort Davis Drugstore. On the town square, Fort Davis (432-426-3118;www.ftdavisdrugstore.com). Get a bona fide fountain Coca-Cola made from syrup and fizzy water. The marble-top counter and old-fashioned glasses should bring back memories. One of the few places in town open for breakfast. $

Hotel Limpia Dining Room. On the town square, Fort Davis (432-426-3241; www.hotellimpia.com). Considered by many to be the best food in town. The bookstore in the lobby has a great selection of books about Big Bend and the region; an adjacent gift shop is filled with unusual items. Open for dinner only. $–$$$

Where to Stay

Hotel Limpia. Main Street, Fort Davis (432-426-3237 or 800-662-5517; www.hotellimpia.com). On the town square is the Hotel Limpia, a Texas Historic Landmark whose creaking hallway boards give testament to the fact that it has been serving travelers since 1912. In addition to pleasant, low- to moderate-priced rooms, the Limpia has a new swimming pool, an herb garden, a lovely gift shop, a comprehensive bookstore, and the best restaurant in town, with moderate prices. $$

Indian Lodge. At Davis Mountains State Park, Fort Davis (432-426-3254). Rooms have hand-hewn ceiling beams and are furnished with hand-crafted cedar furniture made by the CCC. There's even a good-size pool to cool off in and a small park store. $$

For More Information

Fort Davis Chamber of Commerce. In the Union Trading Co. building near the library and the Hotel Limpia, P.O. Box 378, Fort Davis 79734; (800) 524-3015 or (432) 426-3015; www.fortdavis.com.

Alpine and Marfa

This is an area for outdoor activities—hiking, biking, horseback riding, and local rodeos. If you're lucky enough to be in Alpine during late February, don't miss the annual **Cowboy Poetry Gathering** on the campus of Sul Ross University (www.cowboy-poetry.org). This is a real family-friendly celebration of western heritage and music. Call (432) 837-2326.

Museum of the Big Bend (ages 6 and up)

At Sul Ross University, Alpine (432-837-8730; www.sulross.edu/~museum/). Open Tuesday through Saturday 9 a.m. to 5 p.m., Sunday 1 to 5 p.m. Donations welcomed.

Your family won't get a better introduction to the Big Bend area of Texas than in Alpine at Sul Ross University's Museum of the Big Bend, located on campus. The museum, in its beautiful new building, showcases area history with dioramas, paintings, photographs, and numerous artifacts, including a stagecoach full of bullet holes and a three-quarter-size replica of the largest Pterasaur ever found on earth.

Woodward Ranch (ages 6 and up)

18 miles south of Alpine on Highway 118 (432-364-2271; www.woodwardranch.net). Open daily 9 a.m. to 5 p.m.

The kids are always picking up rocks anyway, so take them to the Woodward Ranch, where they can search more than 3,000 acres for their own rainbow-hued agates and other gems to take home as souvenirs. The ranch has its own lapidary shop that will cut or polish your stones or sell you more.

Marfa Lights Viewing Area (ages 6 and up)

Off US 90, 9 miles east of Marfa. After dark.

If you head west of Alpine on US 90, you'll notice a roadside park about 9 miles before you get to Marfa. This is the prime viewing site for the famous, mysterious Marfa Lights. No one knows what the lights are, but you're likely to see them on almost any night. Some say the lights are just refractions of vehicle headlights. Look across the plain toward the base of the mountains in front of you. Unless the lights are mighty active, though, younger kids might get bored waiting for a show.

In Marfa there is a nice view of the surrounding area from the cupola at the top of the 1886 **Presidio County Courthouse,** open Monday through Friday 9 a.m. to 4:30 p.m. You can't miss the courthouse; it's the biggest, most ornate building in town.

Also check out **Marfa Gliders** at the airport (800-667-9464; www.flygliders.com), which gives gliding and soaring rides and lessons. Fun for all. $$$$

Where to Eat

Alpine City Limits. 2700 W. US 90, Alpine (432-837-9088; www.alpinecitylimits.com). Great BBQ and burgers as well as a full menu of steaks, chicken, seafood, salads, and sandwiches. Outdoor patio with panoramic view. $–$$

Longhorn Steakhouse. 801 North Fifth Street, Alpine (432-837-3217). Family dining with a varied menu. $$

Where to Stay

Best Western Alpine Classic Inn. 2401 East US 90, Alpine (432-837-1530; www.bestwestern.com). Swimming pool, cable TV, high-speed Internet, complimentary breakfast, children 12 and under **free.** $$

Thunderbird Motel. 601 West San Antonio Street, Marfa (432-729-1984; www.thunderbirdmarfa.com). Historic motor court, remodeled and updated with swimming pool, cable TV/DVD players, high-speed Internet. $$–$$$

For More Information

Alpine Chamber of Commerce. 106 North Third Street, Alpine 79830; (800) 561-3712; www.alpinetexas.com.

Marfa Chamber of Commerce. 207 N. Highland Avenue in the Paisano Hotel, Marfa 79843; (800) 650-9696 or (432) 729-4942; www.marfacc.com.

Presidio

Presidio is one of the oldest continuously inhabited places in all of North America.

Texas Trivia

Although many people think of Texas as either flat desert or beaches, the state has 91 mountains that are a mile or more high, all of them in West Texas. The top seven:

- **Guadalupe Peak,** at 8,749 feet, is the state's highest mountain.
- **Bush Mountain** is 8,631 feet.
- **Shumard Peak** is 8,615 feet.
- **Bartlett Peak** is 8,508 feet.
- **Mount Livermore** is 8,378 feet.
- **Hunter Peak** (also called Pine Top Mountain) is 8,368 feet.
- **El Capitan Peak** is 8,085 feet.

Fort Leaton State Historic Site (ages 6 and up)

4 miles east on Farm Road 170, Presidio (432-229-3613; www.tpwd.state.tx.us/spdest/findadest/parks/fort_leaton). Open daily 8 a.m. to 4:30 p.m., except Christmas. $.

Fort Leaton is a huge adobe fortress built by trader Ben Leaton in 1848. The private fort, now almost completely restored, was once the only civilized place for hundreds of miles. The visitor center includes a small museum and a slide show on the region. At various times, local high school students don costumes and present living-history programs inside the fort. Picnic areas outside overlook the Rio Grande and mountains in Mexico.

Big Bend Ranch State Park (ages 4 and up)

North of Farm Road 170, between Presidio and Lajitas (432-358-4444; www.tpwd.state.tx.us/spdest/findadest/parks/big_bend_ranch).

The largest state park is Big Bend Ranch in West Texas, sprawling over 300,000 acres. This park is so large that when the area was designated a park in 1988, it effectively doubled the amount of land in the state park system. Big Bend Ranch State Park has several scenic canyons, odd rock formations, Native American pictograph sites, and even a waterfall. The park remains relatively undeveloped, so its amenities are few. The old headquarters of the ranch at La Sauceda can be reached only after a long drive on a washboard dirt road, and only after you get the gate lock combination by paying your permit fee at either Fort Leaton or the Warnock Center in Lajitas. A couple of rooms and bunkhouse accommodations are available there. The park has a few campsites, a couple of Jeep trails, and long backpacking trails. Be sure to visit the movie set on park grounds south of the River Road (Farm Road 170) near Lajitas.

For More Information

Presidio Chamber of Commerce. On U.S. Highway 67 Business Loop, P.O. Box 2497, Presidio 79845; (432) 229-3199; www.presidiotex.com.

Lajitas

After traveling along scenic Farm Road 170, you'll arrive at the tiny village of Lajitas (La-hee-tahs). No more than a couple of shacks a few years ago, the town has been turned into an oasis in the Big Bend desert thanks to the Lajitas Resort (www.lajitas.com).

Barton Warnock Environmental Education Center

(ages 6 and up)

On Farm Road 170, just a mile east of Lajitas (432-424-3327; www.tpwd.state.tx.us/spdest/findadest/parks/barton_warnock). Open daily 8 a.m. to 4:30 p.m.

Barton Warnock Center, the Visitor Center for Big Bend Ranch State Park, has a museum focusing on the pioneer history and natural history of the area, with several dinosaur bones, a library, and a desert garden featuring all the plants you're likely to see in the area.

Scenic **Drive**

Farm Road 170 from Presidio to Lajitas is known as El Camino del Rio, the River Road, and it's one of the most scenic drives in Texas. The road runs alongside the Rio Grande for several miles, with mountains looming up on both sides. Just off the highway, 29 miles east of Presidio, is Closed Canyon, a nice, short walk into a unique canyon that offers plenty of shade as it closes in on you the farther you walk inside. Look carefully for the trailhead parking area on the south side of the road.

The scenic overlook at the top of Big Hill (don't worry, you can't miss Big Hill; it's really big) is not to be missed. Many stunning photos have been taken from this spot looking back upriver.

One of the interesting places along the drive is at Contrabando Creek on the south side of the road on the banks of the Rio Grande. It's easy to miss, so keep an eye peeled. This is the movie site, a complete border town of authentic looking, 1880s-era ruins, where many films—including the TV mini-series *Streets of Laredo*—were shot. This is an absolutely wonderful place for photos of children.

Texas Trivia

The first Texas Ranger report:
Date: August 10, 1876
Name of Offender: Bill Jones
Offense: Stealing cattle
Disposition: Mean as hell. Had to kill him.

Terlingua and Study Butte

Known primarily for the chili cook-off championships held near here the first weekend of every November, Terlingua is an old mining ghost town that probably has more activity today than it ever did. The little town, just north of Farm Road 170 (look for the sign), offers many opportunities to take cute pictures of your children. The largest, and best, gift shop and bookstore in the region is here and is called **Terlingua Trading Co.** Historic Terlingua Ghost Town (432-371-2234; www.historic-terlingua.com).

The **Terlingua Cemetery** is an interesting place, certain to give you a very real idea of what life was and is like in the midst of a true desert. If you do visit, make sure the kids show proper respect for the graves; it's not a playground.

Far Flung Outdoor Center (800-839-7238; www.farflungoutdoorcenter.com) offers half-day, full-day, or multiple-day river trips and ATV and jeep tours. Study Butte (Stew-dee Bewt), an old mercury-mining town, is just down the road at the intersection of Farm Road 170 and Highway 118. You'll find a few shops, motel rooms, gas stations, RV accommodations, a wonderfully rustic grocery store, and a restaurant or two, depending on the time of year.

Big Bend National Park (ages 4 and up)

Just east of Study Butte (432-477-2251; www.nps.gov/bibe). $$.

Big Bend National Park is remote, huge, and spectacular. The 800,000 acres encompass the Rio Grande, the Chihuahuan Desert, and the Chisos Mountains, offering three very different ecosystems and a multitude of plant and animal life for your family to marvel at. The park is as accessible as you want it to be, with paved roads to many scenic areas, dirt roads to others, four-wheel-drive routes to backcountry locations, and miles and miles of hiking trails ranging from easy walks to strenuous treks. Rangers present daily educational programs at amphitheaters at Rio Grande Village, Cottonwood Campground, and the Chisos Basin. You'll find weather forecasts and road accessibility posted at all ranger stations. The park has many campsites and picnic areas, two gas stations, three grocery stores, and motel rooms in the basin area.

Pay your entry fee at the Maverick or Persimmon Gap entrance to the park. Then stop at the park headquarters at Panther Junction to get information, peruse the bookstore,

Chili Cook-Offs

Since chili legends Frank X. Tolbert, Wick Fowler, H. Allen Smith, and Carroll Shelby started the whole chili cook-off craziness as a lark back in 1967, the Big Bend *despoblado* known as Terlingua has become the place to be on the first weekend of November. People gather from all over the country to test their chili against everyone else's in this town, whose population of just a few dusty souls inflates into the thousands for the weekend.

Why? No one is really certain why bragging rights to an eye-watering cowboy staple have such magnetism, but they do. Participants say it's the camaraderie, meeting all the other chili heads at all the other cook-offs, then gathering for the world championship in a place so desolate even the cactus seem lonely. Of course, the zany shows the various teams put on while waiting for their chili to simmer may be one big reason. It's never boring. The legendary BeBop Chili Team used to dress in dark glasses and white sport coats with pink carnations and sing dozens of 1950s and early 1960s songs with lyrics altered to impress chili judges: "It's My Chili and I'll Cry If I Want To," and "You Ain't Nothin' But a Chili Dog." Some folks will tell you that chili heads have lost their minds, but they don't seem to miss 'em none.

For more information on chili cook-offs, contact the Chili Appreciation Society International; www.chili.org.

and go outside to take the self-guided quarter-mile nature walk that will familiarize your family with the plants in the park. A post office is next to the park headquarters.

The **Lost Mine Peak Trail** is a nice half-day hike into the high Chisos Mountains that will afford you one of the best vistas in the park, a breathtaking view looking down on other mountains. You're also likely to see a lot of wildlife along this trail, especially if you begin early in the morning. And even if it's hot, your kids will want to soak in the hot springs. The Big Bend Junior Ranger program is a great way to learn about the area and have fun with an activity booklet.

Where to Eat

Chisos Mountain Lodge Restaurant. In the Chisos Basin, Big Bend National Park (432-477-2291; www.chisosmountainslodge.co). Good food; a stunning view of sunsets through the Window, an impressive V-shaped formation in the mountain walls that form the basin. Large gift shop in lobby. $–$$

La Kiva Restaurant and Bar. At Terlingua Creek on Farm Road 170, Terlingua (432-371-2250; http://lakiva.net). Funky restaurant built underground with a tree growing in the middle of it—actually more of a cave bar. Truly a unique experience. $$

Scenic **Drive**

Head south on US 67 for a scenic drive into the Big Bend. Mountains and desert surround you along the entire trip. The ghost town of Shafter, almost 40 miles from Marfa, presents an opportunity to stretch your legs and have a picnic lunch. Keep the kids away from the old silver mine because many of the shafts there are hidden and dangerous.

Starlight Theatre Restaurant. In the Ghost Town, Terlingua (432-371-2326; www.starlighttheatre.com). The best restaurant for hundreds of miles. Live entertainment fairly common. Kids will marvel at the huge cowboy campfire mural on the back wall, which is also a good place for taking photographs. $$

Where to Stay

Chisos Mountain Lodge. In the Chisos Basin, Big Bend National Park (877-386-4383; www.chisosmountainslodge.com). Many motel rooms in several buildings, from cabins built by the Civilian Conservation Corps to newer units built in the late 1980s. The cool, beautiful basin location is a prime one in Big Bend, so reservations should be made many months in advance, a year in advance for Easter, Thanksgiving, Christmas, and chili cook-off weekends. You'll also find a camping supply store and ranger station in the basin. $$$

Big Bend Resort. At the junction of FM 170 and TX Hwy. 118 near Study Butte (877-386-4383; http://foreverlodging.com/destination.cfm?PropertyKey=182&CFID=4060115&CFTOKEN=26894161). Motel, café, golf course, RV park. $$–$$$

For More Information

Superintendent, Big Bend National Park 79834; (432) 477-2251; www.nps.gov/bibe.

Area Information, www.visitbigbend.com.

Stillwell and Marathon

Just outside Big Bend National Park on U.S. Highway 385, south on Ranch Road 2627.

Hallie's Hall of Fame (ages 6 and up)

On Ranch Road 2627, Stillwell (432-376-2244).

This was the home of Hallie Stillwell, a legend in Big Bend, who died just before her one hundredth birthday. Stillwell was a teacher, ranch manager, and longtime justice of the peace in Brewster County. The Stillwell Store offers an RV park, camping, jeep tours of Maravillas Canyon, rock hunting on Hallie's ranch, a gas station, and a grocery store. You'll find Hallie's Hall of Fame next door. Inside the adobe walls, Hallie's world is preserved with a reproduction of her one-room ranch home and displays of her guns, clothing, books, awards, citations, newspaper clippings, and other memorabilia.

The **Big Bend**

You go south from Fort Davis
Until you come to the place
Where rainbows wait for rain,
And the river is kept in a stone box
And water runs uphill.
And the mountains float in the air,
Except at night when they run away to play
With other mountains.

—Anonymous Mexican vaquero

Where to Eat and Stay

Gage Hotel. On US 90, Marathon (432-386-4205 or 800-884-4243; www. gagehotel.com). Built in 1927, restored in 1987, now offering thirty-seven rooms decorated with artifacts and furnishings that represent the Native American, Mexican, and Anglo cultures of the Big Bend. The hotel has a newer area of rooms also. Most of the rooms in the main hotel do not have private baths, so it would be good to ask when making reservations. The hotel's restaurant serves good food in a great atmosphere, but is expensive. The hotel can also arrange a variety of tours and activities for your family, including Rio Grande float trips, horseback riding, and guided tours of the national park. $$–$$$

Fort Stockton and Sheffield

You'll experience more of that Big Bend desolation as you drive north from Marathon on US 385 to I–10 East and Fort Stockton. Even though you're on a main highway, it's a long and lonely drive. The city was established as an army outpost at the crossroads of the Old San Antonio Road, the Butterfield Overland Mail Route, and the Comanche War Trail. Today the town is mostly a center for oil and natural gas production, ranching, and hunting. Farther east on I–10, at the Highway 290 exit, is tiny Sheffield. Once off the interstate, the bleakness continues, broken only by an occasional oil pump jack creaking away in the desert silence.

Annie Riggs Museum (ages 6 and up)

301 South Main Street, Fort Stockton (432-336-2167). Open Monday through Saturday 10 a.m. to 5 p.m. $.

The Annie Riggs Museum in Fort Stockton is housed in a 1900 adobe hotel, featuring displays of archaeology, geology, and pioneer history in fourteen rooms and two outside areas.

Historic Fort Stockton (ages 4 and up)

At Third and Rooney Streets, Fort Stockton (432-336-2400). Open Monday through Saturday, 10 a.m. to 5 p.m. $.

Historic Fort Stockton is a reconstruction of part of the army fort that was here from 1858 to 1886, one of the main Comanche Trail forts protecting Anglo settlers along the primary raiding trail of the Comanche Indians. The fort's visitor center and museum are just east of downtown.

World's Largest Roadrunner (ages 2 and up)

U.S. Highway 290 at Main Street.

Paisano Pete's claim to be the world's largest roadrunner (statue) has recently been challenged by one in New Mexico. Nonetheless, it's a great place to take pictures of the kids.

Fort Lancaster State Historic Site (ages 4 and up)

Highway 290; take exit 343 off I–10 at Sheffield, and follow the scenic loop on Highway 290 about 8 miles east of town (432-836-4391; www.thc.state.tx.us/hsites/hs_lancaster.aspx?Site=Lancaster). Open daily 9 a.m. to 5 p.m. $, children 12 and under free.

You can walk over the old parade ground and view the cemetery. Looking at the ruins of the fort in the incredible stillness and blistering heat, your family will be amazed that people survived in this bleak frontier outpost. The park has picnic tables, a nature trail, and a museum.

For More Information

Fort Stockton Chamber of Commerce.
1000 Railroad Avenue, Fort Stockton; 432-336-2264; www.ci.fort-stockton.tx.us.

Scenic **Drive**

The best introduction to Big Bend National Park—and the best thing to do if you have only a day or two here—is the **Old Maverick Road/Ross Maxwell Scenic Drive loop.** The Old Maverick Road is a well-maintained dirt road across the desert that passes by a couple of old ruins and ends at the mouth of Santa Elena Canyon, where you can either enjoy the view or hike a mile or so upriver into the depths of the canyon.

Returning on the paved Ross Maxwell Scenic Drive, you'll pass many stunning landscapes—including Mule Ears Peak, Cerro Castellan, Tuff Canyon, Sotol Vista, Burro Mesa Pouroff—and the Castolon Store, where the kids can sit in the shade and have some ice cream.

Langtry

If you want to get a feel for what ranch life in West Texas is like, take Highway 349 south from Sheffield to Dryden; just make sure you gas up the car before you tackle this arid landscape that hasn't changed in hundreds of years. The same is true of US 90 into Langtry. Except for the paved road, old Judge Roy Bean would still recognize the area.

Judge Roy Bean Visitor Center (ages 4 and up)

On Park Road 25, Langtry (432-291-3340). Open daily from 8 a.m. to 5 p.m.; to 6 p.m. Memorial Day through Labor Day. Closed Thanksgiving, Christmas Eve, Christmas Day, and New Year's Day. Free.

The visitor center presents the history of the area in a series of dioramas and displays a few of Bean's personal items. The center is also full of travel brochures from attractions around the state. The judge's original Jersey Lilly saloon, where he dispensed his Law West of the Pecos, still stands behind the visitor center. Next to it is an impressive cactus garden that children love to roam through. The adjacent **Opera House,** which used to be Bean's residence, has been renovated into a theater. The complex is operated by the Texas Department of Transportation.

Texas Trivia

Although Judge Roy Bean believed the town of Langtry was named for the famous English actress and singer Lillie Langtry—a claim repeated in many stories, films, and in letters he wrote to Miss Langtry—Bean was mistaken. The whistle-stop village was named for George Langtry, a railroad construction foreman. Bean was so obsessed with Miss Langtry that he put a sign on his home, calling it an "Opera House," and wrote Langtry several letters in hopes she would drop in and perform there. She finally accepted but didn't arrive until 1904, several months after Bean died.

South Plains

The South Plains area is a true melting pot, a unique blend of American and Mexican cultures you won't find in any other state. No matter where you go here, you can expect to find that many folks have a good command of both Spanish and English, regardless of their native tongues; you'll also find fine Mexican restaurants and a history that predates the first Spanish missions.

It was here that cowboying began hundreds of years ago with the Spanish vaqueros and where modern-day buckaroos continue the tradition on spreads like the famous King Ranch.

Tejano music, that upbeat conglomeration of polka, pop, country, and blues set to a distinctly Latin beat, could only have originated in the unique South Plains environment.

TopAnnualEvents in the South Plains

- **San Antonio Stock Show and Rodeo,** San Antonio, February (210-225-5851)
- **Washington's Birthday Celebration,** Laredo, February (956-795-2200)
- **Poteet Strawberry Festival,** Poteet, April (830-742-8144)
- **Cinco de Mayo Celebration,** San Antonio, May (210-207-6700)
- **Texas Folklife Festival,** San Antonio, June (210-458-2330)
- **St. Louis Day Festival,** Castroville, August (830-931-2826)
- **Fiesta de Amistad,** Del Rio/Acuña, October (830-775-3551)
- **Holiday River Parade and Fiesta de las Luminarias,** San Antonio, November and December (210-227-4262)

SOUTH PLAINS

The South Plains region sprawls across vast distances between population centers, from the thriving metropolis of San Antonio to the heavily agricultural, alluvial plain along the Rio Grande that Texans call "the Valley." The population swells during the winter, when thousands of "winter Texans," many from as far away as Canada, make the Valley their home during the coldest months of the year.

When you travel the South Plains, you'll discover just how big Texas really is because you won't have the scenic attractions of West Texas or the Hill Country to distract you from those miles and miles of miles and miles.

Comstock

Seminole Canyon State Park and Historic Site

(ages 4 and up)

9 miles west of Comstock on U.S. Highway 90 (432-292-4464; www.tpwd.tx.us/spdest/findadest/parks/seminole_canyon). Guided tours to Fate Bell Shelter within the canyon: from June 1 to August 31, Wednesday through Sunday at 10 a.m. From September 1 to May 31 at 10 a.m. and 3 p.m.

Seminole Canyon State Park and Historic Site is one of the few public areas in the state where you can get a close-up look at prehistoric Native American pictographs. It's a fairly strenuous hike into the canyon and up to the natural rock shelters, especially during hot weather, and not recommended for smaller children. The visitor center has exhibits on the inhabitants of the area. The park also has many camping and picnic areas and hiking and mountain-bike trails.

Amistad National Recreation Area (ages 4 and up)

Between Comstock and Del Rio, adjacent to US 90 (830-775-7491; www.nps.gov/amis).

Amistad National Recreation Area, just west of Del Rio on US 90, is a family recreation mecca with several swimming beaches, marinas, boat ramps, and campgrounds. The 64,900-acre Lake Amistad is jointly owned by the United States and Mexico. Its waters are usually so blue as to defy description. Even if you don't stop and play in the lake or by the shore, take the drive over the international bridge that runs across the top of the dam. At

Texas Trivia

Among the pictographs you can see in the Fate Bell Shelter at Seminole Canyon State Park is one, more than 4,000 years old, that looks like a 1950s television set complete with rabbit-ears antenna.

the center of the bridge is a small visitor center showing the history and construction of the dam; there's also an interesting double-eagle monument at the borderline dedicated to amistad (friendship). At the Mexican end of the bridge is an imposing statue of Tlaloc, the rain god, and a picnic area along the beach. Both the double-eagle monument and Tlaloc make very nice backdrops for photos of the kids.

Many families like to spend a few days on a houseboat on Lake Amistad. It's a relaxing combination of recreation and accommodation. You can explore the lake's many bays, fish, bask in the sun, or boat up to Panther Cave to view more pictographs, some dating back more than 10,000 years. Call the **Lake Amistad Resort and Marina** at 800-255-5561, or visit www.lakeamistadresort.com, for more information.

For More Information

National Park Service Visitors Center.
On US 90 West, Del Rio 78840; (830) 775-7491; www.nps.gov/amis.

Del Rio

The cities of Del Rio and Ciudad Acuña, the Mexican city across the Rio Grande celebrate bi-national friendship with the **Fiesta de Amistad** in mid-October, a festival so big it's held on both sides of the border. The parade across the International Bridge is the only parade in the world that starts in one country and ends in another. Your family will be delighted by the entertainment, arts-and-crafts and food booths, and fun run. Call (830) 775-3551.

Whitehead Memorial Museum (ages 6 and up)

1308 South Main Street, Del Rio (830-774-7568; www.whiteheadmuseum.org). Open Tuesday through Saturday 9 a.m. to 4:30 p.m. Open Sunday 1 to 5 p.m. $, children under 6 free.

The Whitehead Museum is dedicated to the life and legends of this frontier region. The famed Judge Roy Bean and his son, Sam, are buried on the museum grounds, made up of several historic buildings, an old train caboose, and a replica of Bean's Jersey Lilly saloon.

San Felipe Springs and Moore Park (ages 4 and up)

About 2 miles east of Del Rio off US 90 (830-775-3551; www.edwardsaquifer.net/sanfelip.html).

San Felipe Springs and Moore Park may be just what your family is looking for if you visit here during the summer. This is a true oasis surrounded by the semiarid South Plains landscape. The springs pump ninety million gallons of pure water every day into a huge swimming pool.

Where to Eat

Luby's Cafeteria. 2211 Veterans Boulevard, Del Rio (830-768-0434). A favorite for a good selection of good food. $–$$

Applebee's Neighborhood Grill. 2205 Veterans Boulevard, Del Rio (830-768-1300; www.applebees.com). Full menu of great family fare, great burgers. $–$$

R&R's BBQ. 401 Skyline, Del Rio (830-778-2800). Great barbecue near Lake Amistad.

Where to Stay

Best Western Inn. 810 Veterans Boulevard, Del Rio (830-775-7511 or 800-336-3537). Pool, hot tub, cable TV with HBO, **free** high-speed Internet, **free** continental breakfast, children 12 and under **free.** $$

La Quinta Inn. 2005 Veterans Boulevard, Del Rio (830-775-7591 or 800-531-5900). Outdoor pool, high-speed Internet, premium cable TV, **free** continental breakfast, children under 18 **free.** $$

Amistad Lake Resort. 11207 Hwy. 90 West, Del Rio (830-775-8591 or 800-775-8591; www.amistadlakeresort.com). Year-round fishing and fun on the lake—pool, sun deck, **free** WiFi, cable TV, some rooms with kitchenette. $–$$$

For More Information

Del Rio Chamber of Commerce. 1915 Veterans Boulevard, Del Rio 78840; (830) 775-3551 or (800) 889-8149; www.drchamber.com.

Brackettville and Uvalde

At Brackettville, on US 90, your family will find one of the best places to stay in all of the South Plains (see Fort Clark Springs, below) to enjoy both real and reel western history.

In Uvalde, you can see the graves of famous westerners Pat Garrett, the man who killed Billy the Kid, and outlaw-turned-sheriff King Fisher at **Pioneer Park,** at the corner of Leona and Park Streets.

Seminole Negro Indian Scout Cemetery (ages 6 and up)

Farm Road 3348, 3 miles south of Brackettville (830-563-2466).

If your family is interested in history, don't miss visiting the Seminole Negro Indian Scout Cemetery. The scouts were runaway slaves who had assimilated into Seminole culture by the time some bands were forced out of Florida. Many of the black Seminoles were garrisoned at Fort Clark and scouted for the army, fighting in almost every major Indian War campaign. They lost not a man, and four of them won Medals of Honor. Their graves are here, along with those of other black Seminoles who fought in other American wars. The Seminole Indian Scout Cemetery was established in 1872 on the Fort Clark Reservation. You can leave a donation at the Fort Clark Museum to help maintain the cemetery.

Alamo Village (ages 4 and up)

7 miles north of Brackettville on Farm Road 674 (830-563-2580; www.alamovillage.com). Open daily 9 a.m. to 5 p.m. except Christmas week. $–$$$, children 5 and under free.

The entire family will enjoy Alamo Village, a movie set built for John Wayne's 1960 production of *The Alamo* and used for dozens of other films, television shows, and commercials since. The set, on the Shahan HV Ranch, is a complete town with jails, saloons, general stores, hotels, a blacksmith shop, a mission church, and, of course, a replica of the Alamo as it was in 1836. Several of the buildings house historic displays of either bona fide artifacts or movie memorabilia. A gift shop is also on the set. Between Memorial Day and Labor Day actors perform on the village streets with music and melodrama. You might even see a gunfight or trick roper or cowboy singer—check the event schedule on the Web site.

Fort Inge (ages 4 and up)

Located at the base of an extinct volcano on the Leona River, 2 miles south of Uvalde on Farm Road 140 (800-588-2533). Open weekends only.

At Fort Inge your family can picnic, camp, hike nature trails, or inspect the ruins of the old fort.

Where to Eat and Stay

Fort Clark Springs Resort. P.O. Box 345, U.S. 90, Brackettville 78832 (830-563-9210; www.fortclark.com). This most unusual full-service resort and leisure-living community is located in town on the grounds of historic Fort Clark, an active military fort from 1852 to 1946. Today, there's a motel, an RV park, a wilderness campground, a huge spring-fed swimming pool, tennis courts, a fine regulation 18-hole golf course and full size putting green, a health spa, and a museum displaying the history of the fort. A Youth Activity Center has basketball, tennis, arcade games, and sometimes hayrides or teen dances. Rooms are remarkably affordable. $–$$

For More Information

Brackettville/Kinney County Chamber of Commerce. (830) 563-2466.

Uvalde Chamber of Commerce. 300 East Main Street, Uvalde 78801; (800) 588-2533 or (830) 278-3363; www.visituvalde.com.

Crystal City and Laredo

If you head south on U.S. Highway 83 from Uvalde, your kids will be able to visit **Popeye the Sailor** in Crystal City, or at least they can have their picture taken in front of his statue. The town produces a prodigious amount of spinach, which is why it built the monument to the world's most famous spinach eater. The six-foot bronze statue is located on The Square downtown.

Laredo, much farther south on US 83, has a heavy Hispanic influence. In February your family will be amazed at the scale of the **George Washington's Birthday celebration** held in Laredo. It's said to be the largest anywhere, and it's been going on, on both sides of the border, every year since 1898. Two different parades feature entries from both the United States and Mexico, with one showcasing area schoolchildren. This is a birthday Washington never imagined: a jalapeño festival, a Mexican rodeo, and special Native American events. Call (956) 795-2200 for more information.

Imaginarium of South Texas (ages 4 and up)

5300 San Dario, #505 inside the Mall del Norte, Laredo (956-728-0404; www.imaginarium stx.org). Open Wednesday and Thursday 10 a.m. to 7 p.m., Friday and Saturday 10 a.m. to 8 p.m., Sunday noon to 6 p.m. $

This new facility is both a children's museum and learning center offering bicultural programs, hands-on exhibits, summer camps, special events, and loads of activities to encourage creativity.

Republic of the Rio Grande Museum (ages 8 and up)

1005 Zaragoza Street, Laredo (956-727-3480). Open Tuesday through Saturday 9 a.m. to 4 p.m. $.

The Republic of the Rio Grande Museum, across the plaza from historic San Agustin Church, is in a building that once served as the capitol for the Republic of the Rio Grande, an unsuccessful attempt in the mid-1800s to break away from Mexico. The museum has many pioneer displays.

Lake Casa Blanca International State Park (ages 4 and up)

5102 Bob Bullock Loop, east of Laredo off U.S. Highway 59 (956-725-3826; www.tpwd.state .tx.us/spdest/findadest/parks/lake_casa_blanca).

Lake Casa Blanca offers camping, screened shelters, picnic areas, a fishing pier, a boat ramp, a baseball diamond, and basketball, volleyball, and tennis courts. The lake is known for its black bass fishing.

Where to Eat

Eduardo's Mexican Food, Steak & Smokehouse. 4160 S. US 83 (956-712-3414). Everyone can find something to their liking here. Choose authentic Mexican food or great barbecue—full menu and daily lunch specials. $$

Emperor Garden. 620 West Calton Street, Laredo (956-791-4848) and 520 Shiloh (956-791-4849). Laredo has a long tradition of offering great Chinese food, and you can find the best in town here. Live music on weekends. $$

Golden Corral. 5930 San Bernardo Avenue, Laredo (956-791-3374). Steaks and an all-you-can-eat buffet make for a dining bargain. $–$$

Where to Stay

Family Gardens Inn. 5830 San Bernardo Avenue, Laredo (956-723-5300 or 800-292-4053; www.familygardeninn.com). Targeted to families, with an outdoor pool, fitness center, grills and picnic area, game room, and playground. $$

La Quinta Inn. 3610 Santa Ursula, Laredo (956-722-0511; www.laquinta.com). Outdoor pool, **free** high-speed Internet, **free** breakfast. Children under 18 **free.** $$

La Posada Hotel. 1000 Zaragoza Street, Laredo (956-722-1701; www.laposadahotel.com). Beautifully landscaped with a pool and courtyard areas and a couple of fine restaurants. $15 million makeover in 2007. Within walking distance of shopping areas in Laredo and two bridges across the Rio Grande. $$$

For More Information

Laredo Convention and Visitors Bureau. 501 San Agustin Street, Laredo 78040; (800) 361-3360 or (956) 795-2200; www.visitlaredo.com.

Roma and Rio Grande City

Taking US 83 south from Laredo will have you traveling along the Rio Grande and bring you into the area Texans call simply "the Valley," the heart of Texas agriculture. The Valley extends roughly from Rio Grande City to South Padre Island. The route from Laredo to Falcon Lake isn't quite as desolate as some of the drives in West Texas and the Big Bend, but almost. Only a few small towns and very large farms break up the landscape.

Falcon State Park (ages 4 and up)

Along the shores of the Falcon Reservoir, about 14 miles northwest of Roma via US 83, Farm Road 2098, and Park Road 46; Falcon Heights (956-848-5327; www.tpwd.state.tx.us/spdest/findadest/parks/falcon).

The park has cabins, boat docks, camping, swimming, picnicking, fishing, and RV sites. There's also a grocery store and snack bar. The 98,960-acre Falcon Lake is jointly owned by the United States and Mexico, like Lake Amistad, and is known for its abundant wildlife and black bass and catfish fishing. You can also see the old town of Guerrero, now submerged in the waters of the lake.

For More information

City of Rio Grande City. 101 S. Washington Street, Rio Grande City 78582; (956) 487-0672; www.cityofrgc.com.

Mission, McAllen, and Pharr

Continuing to follow the Rio Grande along US 83, you'll soon be in the very bustling cities of Mission, McAllen, and Pharr, heavily Hispanic in influence. The area's main business is agriculture, especially citrus farming around Mission, the home of the famous Texas Ruby Red grapefruit, a very sweet fruit. Just after Mission was founded in the early 1800s, Mexican priests planted an orange grove, the first experiment with citrus in the Valley. You'll see palm trees and lush vegetation. This is a favorite tourist location, especially with birders. Thousands of Canadians and Midwesterners spend the colder months of the year here, becoming what locals call "Winter Texans."

Across the McAllen-Hidalgo-Reynosa International Bridge on Highway 336 is the Mexican city of Reynosa, which is widely known for fine restaurants. You'll also find many crafts shops and traditional Mexican markets downtown. The largest market is **Mercado Zaragosa,** at Hidalgo and Matamoros Streets. Check out the current rules at www.travel.state.gov before you cross the border.

Tom Landry Mural (ages 4 and up)

Honoring Mission native and legendary coach of the Dallas Cowboys football team, the Tom Landry Mural depicts his life and career on the corner of N. Conway and E. Tom Landry Avenue in downtown Mission.

World Birding Center (ages 4 and up)

Headquarters at Benson-Rio Grande Valley State Park, 6 miles west of Mission off Farm Road 2062 (956-585-1107; www.worldbirdingcenter.org). Hours vary by location.

The World Birding Center is a network of nine extraordinary birding sites throughout the Lower Rio Grande Valley. Stretching over 120 miles from South Padre Island to Roma, it includes habitats ranging from dry brush to riverside thickets to freshwater marshes and coastal wetlands. All venues offer birding tours, educational events and programs, nature festivals, special events, and family fun.

Bentsen-Rio Grande Valley State Park (ages 4 and up)

6 miles west of Mission off Farm Road 2062 (956-585-1107).

Headquarters of the World Birding Center (above), Bentsen-Rio Grande Valley State Park encompasses 760 acres of woodland on the Rio Grande, preserving subtropical plants and wildlife. More than 325 species of birds and 250 species of butterflies have been documented here. An excellent visitor center has interpretive displays, a nice gift shop, and coffee bar. Visitors ride a tram through the park and can get off at nature trails, bird blinds, picnic sites, and the hawk tower.

Anzalduas County Park (ages 4 and up)

3 miles south of Mission on Farm Road 1016 (956-585-5311). Open 8:30 a.m. to dark daily.

Anzalduas County Park is located on the Rio Grande River at the site of the Anzalduas Dam. It's a lovely spot for bird and butterfly watching, boating, and having a picnic.

International Butterfly Park (ages 4 and up)

3400 South Butterfly Park Drive, 1 mile east of Bentsen-Rio Grande State Park, Mission (956-583-9009; www.naba.org). $

Stroll these gardens of native plants specifically planted to attract butterflies. The purpose is research, conservation, and education so there's lot of good information at the tiny office/visitor center. There are also butterfly gardens located throughout the city of Mission.

Los Ebanos Ferry (ages 2 and up)

14 miles west of Mission on US 83, then south on Farm Road 886 (956-485-2828). Ferry runs daily 8 a.m. to 4 p.m. $.

Even if you're not crossing the border, your kids are sure to love seeing the Los Ebanos Ferry, the only existing hand-operated ferry on the United States-Mexico border. It was once known as "Smugglers Crossing." The platform holds only three cars, and the anchor cable is tied to a 250-year-old ebony tree.

International Museum of Art and Science (ages 6 and up)

1900 Nolana Street, McAllen (956-682-1564; www.imasonline.org). Open Tuesday through Saturday 9 a.m. to 5 p.m. (Thursday until 8 p.m.), Sunday 1 to 5 p.m. $$, children 3 and under free.

This museum has permanent and rotating art exhibits, cultural events, and educational programs. KidsZone features several hands-on exhibits and activities for children. Family Fun Nights are Thursdays from 5 p.m. to 8 p.m.

Smitty's Juke Box (ages 6 and up)

116 West State Street, Pharr (956-787-0131). Open Monday through Friday 9:30 a.m. to 4 p.m. Free.

Housed in a historic building, this museum displays a large variety of restored old jukeboxes. This is probably more of a nostalgic journey for parents, but kids will enjoy seeing the old machines move and flip records to play, some with neon bright colors and animation. It's a treat to visit with the owner, son of the collector and founder of the museum, and see his workshop with restorations in progress.

Ye Old Clock Museum

929 East Preston Street, Pharr (956-787-1923). Open Monday through Friday 1 to 5 p.m. $.

This museum preserves a private collection of more than 2,000 antique clocks, some dating back to the seventeenth century.

Texas **Campgrounds**

If your family likes the outdoors, they'll love Texas. Its enormous size means there's still plenty of wide open spaces for you to explore on foot or horseback, by bicycle or canoe, and campgrounds abound.

For a complete list of Texas public campgrounds, write the Travel and Information Division of the Texas Department of Transportation, P.O. Box 5064, Austin 78763.

For a list of commercial campgrounds, contact the Texas Association of Campground Owners, www.texascampgrounds.com.

Where to Eat

El Pato. 1300 E. Tamarack, McAllen and several other locations (956-687-5227). Good Mexican food in a family setting at good prices. $–$$

Pepe's On the River. 2301 S. Conway, Mission (956-583-3092; www.pepesontheriver.net). Pepe's is an institution in the Valley. It has a full bar and features some great country-western entertainment as well as burgers, nachos, barbecue, and all-you-can-eat catfish on Fridays. $$–$$$

Taco Palenque. 3020 N. Tenth Street, McAllen (956-686-0102) and 1000 S. Tenth Street, McAllen (956-994-8950; www.tacopalenque.com). Good Mexican food and playgrounds for the kids. $–$$

Luby's Cafeteria. 2200 S. Tenth Street, McAllen (956-928-1853; www.lubys.com). Everyone can choose what they want at this good cafeteria; kids menu. $$

Red Robin. 1315 W. Polk, Pharr (956-782-7126; www.redrobin.com). Gourmet burgers prepared as you like them. Fun family fare at reasonable prices. $–$$

Rudy's Country BBQ. 209 W. Nolana Loop, Pharr (956-781-8888; www.rudys.com). Good barbecue, good prices. $–$$

Where to Stay

Texan Guest Ranch. 8301 N. Ware Road, McAllen (956-686-5425; www.texanguestranch.com). True southern hospitality in a historic setting. Pool with heated Jacuzzi, workout room, clubhouse, fully furnished suites. $$–$$$

La Quinta Inn & Suites. 805 Travis Street, Mission (956-581-7772; www.laquinta.com). Outdoor pool, **free** continental breakfast, wireless Internet, children under 18 stay **free.** $$

La Quinta Inn. 1100 South Tenth Street, McAllen (956-687-1101 or 800-531-5900; www.laquinta.com). Pool, **free** continental breakfast, high-speed Internet, and children under 18 stay **free.** $$

La Quinta Inn & Suites. 4603 N. Cage, Pharr (956-787-2900; www.laquinta.com). Outdoor pool, fitness center, **free** high-speed Internet, **free** continental breakfast, children under 18 stay **free.** $$

Drury Inn. 612West Expressway 83, McAllen (956-687-5100; www.druryhotels.com). Outdoor pool, **free** wireless high-speed Internet, exercise room, flat LCD TV with HBO, **free** hot breakfast. $$

For More Information

Rio Grande Valley Chamber of Commerce. P.O. Box 1499, Weslaco 78599; (956) 968-3141; www.ValleyChamber.com.

McAllen Convention & Visitors Bureau. 1200 Ash Avenue, McAllen 78501; (956) 682-2871; www.mcallen.org.

Mission Area Chamber of Commerce. 202 W. Tom Landry, Mission 78572; (956) 585-2727; www.missionchamber.com.

Pharr Travel Information Center. 3000 N. Cage Boulevard (inside the Pharr Convention Center), Pharr 78577; (956) 283-1385; www.cityofpharr.com.

Edinburg, Alamo, and Weslaco

Edinburg is just north of McAllen on U.S. Highway 281, while Alamo and Weslaco are just east on US 83.

Now you're in the middle of a huge citrus-, vegetable-, and cotton-producing area with hundreds of food-processing industries. Dozens of RV parks dot the landscape, home to all those "Winter Texans" in cooler months.

Edinburg Waterparks (ages 4 and up)

123 East Palm Drive, Edinburg (956-381-5631). Open April and May weekends noon to 7 p.m.; open daily June through August 15, noon to 8 or 9 p.m. $$$.

Cool off in three swimming pools at Edinburg Waterpark. The city park features an Olympic-sized pool, water slide, water basketball, beach volleyball, children's play area, barbecue grills, and picnic tables. Fountain Park, a second waterpark, is located at Twenty-second and Kuhn Streets.

Edinburg Municipal Park (ages 4 and up)

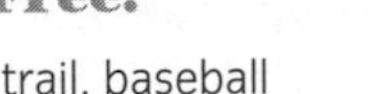

East on Hwy. 107 and south on Doolittle Road, Edinburg (956-381-5631). Free.

This huge city park has walking/jogging trails, in-line skating trail, nature trail, baseball diamonds, soccer fields, playgrounds, pavilions, picnic tables and barbecue grills, and two fishing lakes.

Edinburg Coyotes (ages 6 and up)

920 North Sugar Road, Edinburg (956-4446; www.edinburgcoyotes.com). Game prices vary, call for prices.

This professional baseball team plays in the Texas/Louisiana League in a new 4,000-seat state-of-the-art minor league stadium.

International Racetrack (ages 6 and up)

15920 North US 281, Edinburg (956-318-0355; www.edinburgracetrack.com). $–$$

This NHRA Division 4 track offers year-round drag racing, car and motorcycle racing and special performances and events, usually on Friday nights.

Museum of South Texas History (ages 6 and up)

121 East McIntyre Street on the courthouse square, Edinburg (956-383-6911; www.most history.org). Open Tuesday through Friday 9 a.m. to 5 p.m., Saturday 10 a.m. to 5 p.m., and Sunday 1 to 5 p.m. $.

The Museum of South Texas History began in the 1910 Hidalgo Country jail and has grown to a huge collection of exhibits and artifacts depicting the varied and colorful history of South Texas. The old jail is still there, incorporated into the new multimillion-dollar facility. This is a great museum for kids. Volunteers are stationed in the various areas to tell interesting tales from the past and answer questions.

Santa Ana National Wildlife Refuge (ages 4 and up)

7 miles south of Alamo via Alamo Road from Expressway 83 (956-784-7500; www.fws.gov/southwest/refuges/texas/santana.html). Visitor center open daily 8 a.m. to 4 p.m. $.

The most popular and best known wildlife refuge in the Valley, the 2,088-acre Santa Ana Wildlife Refuge preserves what the Valley looked like before agricultural development, with many species of birds nesting here during winter months. A naturalist gives interpretive tours from November through April on a 7-mile loop; you drive your own car during the other months. Or you can walk along several nature trails. A new 43-foot observation tower is one of the tallest in the Valley and affords incredible panoramic views.

Weslaco Museum (ages 6 and up)

515 South Kansas Avenue, Weslaco (956-968-9142; www.weslaco.lib.tx.us). Open Monday through Thursday 9 a.m. to 7 p.m., Friday 9 a.m. to 5 p.m., Saturday 1 to 5 p.m. Free.

The Weslaco Museum is currently housed in the Weslaco Public Library awaiting a brand new building at 500 S. Texas Boulevard downtown. It includes exhibits of all kinds.

For More Information

Edinburg Convention and Visitors Bureau. 602 W. University Drive, Edinburg (956) 383-4974 or 800-800-7214; www.edin burg.com. The Visitor Center is located in the renovated 1927 Southern Pacific Railroad depot.

Alamo Chamber of Commerce. 130 S. Eighth Street, Alamo (956) 787-2117; www .alamotexas.org.

Weslaco Area Chamber of Commerce. 301 W. Railroad Street, Weslaco (956) 968-2102; www.weslaco.com.

Brownsville and Harlingen

For an entertaining way to see all the highlights of Brownsville, hop aboard a **Historic Brownsville Trolley Tour,** beginning at the Convention and Visitors Bureau Information Center at the corner of Farm Road 802 and U.S. Highway 77/83. Call (956) 546-3721 for reservations ($–$$).

Matamoros, Mexico, is just across the river from Brownsville, and its mission for decades has been catering to U.S. visitors, with more restaurants, nightclubs, and gift shops than you could count. Bargains are still available, especially in leather goods and pottery. Take the Gateway International Bridge at East Fourteenth Street. **Mercado Juarez,** at Matamoros and Nueve Streets, is a huge, well-known market. Check out the current rules at www.travel.state.gov before you cross the border.

Harlingen is a large city with lots to see and do. Dozens of colorful murals depicting everything from tropical birds to Aztec legends decorate buildings throughout the city.

Historic Brownsville Museum (ages 6 and up)

641 East Madison Street, Brownsville (956-548-1313; www.brownsvillemuseum.org). Open from 10 a.m. to 4 p.m. Tuesday through Friday, Saturday 10 a.m.to:2 p.m. $.

Located in the 1928 Southern Pacific Depot, the Historic Brownsville Museum displays photos and memorabilia that will familiarize you with the history of Brownsville, the founding of which touched off the Mexican War in 1846. The museum building itself is a Texas Historic Landmark and listed in the National Register of Historic Places.

Children's Museum of Brownsville (toddlers and up)

501 Ringgold Street in Dean Porter Park, Brownsville (956-548-9300; www.cmofbrownsville.com). Open Tuesday through Saturday from 9 a.m. to 5 p.m. and Sunday noon to 4 p.m. $, children under one free.

This exceptional children's museum offers educational exhibits, events, and programs, as well as field trips. The learn/explore/create exhibits have such names as "On the Farm," "Weather Station," "By the Sea," and "Health Clinic."

Scenic **Drive**

For a glimpse at the unspoiled, real tropical Texas, head east from Brownsville on Farm Road 1419 to Highway 4—from the **Sabal Palm Grove Sanctuary to Boca Chica State Park,** an undeveloped beach with no facilities. The route will take your family from a native palm forest to the shores of the Gulf of Mexico at the Rio Grande delta, one of the southernmost points in the United States. By the way, don't be tempted to drive on the beach, as some do, because the sand can be very unforgiving.

Gladys Porter Zoo (ages 2 and up)

500 Ringgold Street, near the intersections of US 281 and 77, Brownsville (956-546-7187; www.gpz.org). Open Monday through Friday 9 a.m. to 5:30 p.m., Saturday and Sunday 9 a.m. to 6 p.m. $$, children under 2 free.

Your children will revel in the Gladys Porter Zoo, which has one of the world's best collections of rare animals, including lowland gorillas and specializes in breeding endangered species. The animals are in a natural setting without bars or cages, spread over 26 acres. You can get close-up views looking through one-way glass in a series of caves adjacent to animal dens. The Safari Express train ($) offers guided tours on Sunday afternoons. You can even download a zoo map and plan your visit in advance.

Iwo Jima War Memorial (ages 6 and up)

320 Iwo Jima Boulevard, Harlingen (956-412-2207 or 800-365-6006). Open Monday through Saturday 10 a.m. to 4 p.m., Sunday 1 to 4 p.m. Free.

The original, full-sized working model of the famous Iwo Jima War Memorial in Arlington National Cemetery in Washington, D.C. is on display at the Marine Military Academy, a prep school next to the Valley International Airport. The Visitor Center displays its history, along with the history of the famous WWII battle, with photographs and memorabilia. Various Texas and military souvenirs are available in an adjacent gift shop.

Rio Grande Valley Museum (ages 6 and up)

On Loop 499, 2 blocks from Valley International Airport, Harlingen (956-430-8500). Open Wednesday through Saturday 10 a.m. to 4 p.m., Sunday 1 to 4 p.m. $.

The Rio Grande Valley Museum complex in Harlingen includes a stagecoach inn from 1850, the original city hospital with vintage medical equipment on display, a pioneer home, and exhibits on the area's colorful history.

Where to Eat

Shoney's. 2344 North Expressway, Brownsville (956-504-1500). Wide variety of menu items from sandwiches to full meals. $–$$

Luby's Cafeteria. 2506 South 77 Sunshine Strip, Harlingen (956-423-4812) and 822 Dixieland Road, Harlingen (956-425-1525; www.lubys.com). Everyone loves the choices at Luby's. $–$$

Pepe's Mexican Restaurant. 117 South 77 Sunshine Strip, Harlingen (956-423-3663; www.pepes.com). Excellent Mexican food. $–$$

Where to Stay

Best Western Rose Garden Inn. 845 North Expressway 77/83, Brownsville (956-546-5501 or 800-299-9226; www.bestwestern.com). Pool, free breakfast buffet, cable TV with HBO, high-speed Internet access, children 17 and under free. $$

Country Inn & Suites. 3825 South Expressway 83, Harlingen (956-428-0043; www.countryinns.com). Outdoor pool, fitness center, high-speed Internet, $$–$$$

La Quinta Inn. 1002 South Expressway 83, Harlingen (956-428-6888 or 800-531-5900; www.laquinta.com). Pool, **free** continental breakfast, **free** WiFi, children under 18 **free.** $$

For More Information

Brownsville Convention and Visitors Bureau. 650 Farm Road 802, Brownsville 78520; (956) 546-3721 or (800) 626-2639; www.brownsville.org.

Harlingen Convention and Visitors Bureau. 311 East Tyler Street, Harlingen 78550; (800) 531-7346 or (956) 423-5440; www.visitharlingentexas.com.

Kingsville

King Ranch (ages 6 and up)

The museum is at 405 North Sixth Street, Kingsville (361-592-8055; www.king-ranch.com). Museum open Monday through Saturday 10 a.m. to 4 p.m., Sunday 1 to 5 p.m. $ The visitor center is at 2205 Highway 141 West and is open Monday through Saturday 9 a.m. to 4 p.m., Sunday noon to 4 p.m. Tour times vary, so call (361) 592-8055 for more details. Tours: $–$$, children 4 and under free.

The King Ranch is the largest ranch in the country: 825,000 acres across four counties. The ranch offers guided tours of an old cow camp, cattle pens, and the ranch headquarters. The museum is in a restored ice plant in downtown Kingsville. It showcases photos of ranch life; antique coaches, cars, and saddles; and other historic ranching items.

The King Ranch Saddle Shop, 201 East Kleberg Street, was begun by the ranch to outfit its own cowboys with riding gear. Now it outfits everyone from visiting children to presidents. A most unusual shop, it's open Monday through Saturday 10 a.m. to 6 p.m. Call (800) 282-KING or visit www.krsaddleshop.com.

John E. Conner Museum (ages 6 and up)

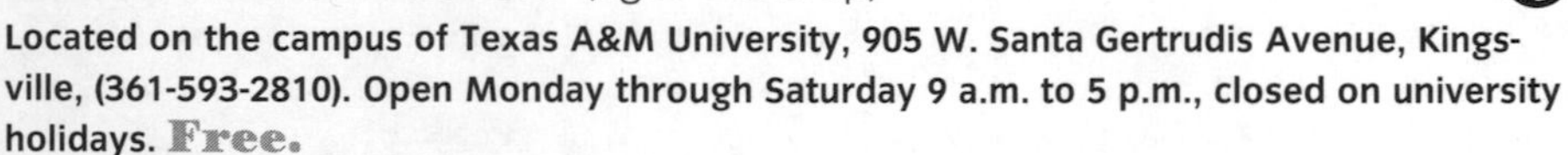

Located on the campus of Texas A&M University, 905 W. Santa Gertrudis Avenue, Kingsville, (361-593-2810). Open Monday through Saturday 9 a.m. to 5 p.m., closed on university holidays. Free.

The John E. Conner Museum displays artifacts from Native American, Spanish, Mexican, and Texan cultures. It has exhibits focusing on natural history and a Discovery Area for kids to get their hands on displays. The Peeler Hall of Horns displays 264 trophy mounts of North American game—bear, deer, moose, javalina, mountain goats, bighorn sheep, eagles, and many more.

For More Information

Kingsville Convention and Visitors Bureau. 1501 Hwy. 77, Kingsville (361-592-8516; www.kingsvilletexas.com).

Poteet and Three Rivers

Three Rivers is on US 281 at I–37. Poteet is about 40 miles south of San Antonio on Highway 16.

Poteet has the **World's Largest Strawberry,** a monument to the sweet fruit grown all around the area. You'll also discover a monument to Poteet Canyon, the Steve Canyon comic-strip character named after the city. Both are located at the Chamber of Commerce building on Farm Road 476.

In mid-April your family is certain to enjoy the **Poteet Strawberry Festival,** which features all things strawberry: ice cream, cheesecake, shortcake, parfait, and plenty of plain old strawberries. In addition to arts-and-crafts and food booths, the festival has six stages with continuous entertainment. Call (830) 742-8144 or (888) 742-8144 or visit the Web site at www.strawberryfestival.com.

Choke Canyon State Park (ages 4 and up)

West of Three Rivers off Highway 72. (Calliham unit 361-786-3868 or South Shore 361-786-3538).

You'll find very few places to swim in this region, and Choke Canyon is one of the best. Here your family can boat, swim, fish, picnic, or camp out on 26,000-acre Choke Canyon Lake. The park was designated within a wildlife management area, so spotting animals is relatively easy for kids. The park is divided into two units: South Shore is 4 miles from Three Rivers and mostly for fishing while Calliham is 12 miles. The Calliham unit has tennis and basketball courts, a baseball diamond, and a swimming pool.

For More Information

Three Rivers Chamber of Commerce. (361) 786-4330 or (888) 600-3115; www.threeriversrx.org.

Poteet Chamber of Commerce. (830) 742-8144 or (888) 742-8144.

Texas Trivia

The longest highway in Texas is US 83, stretching 899 miles from the Mexican border at Brownsville in the South Plains to the Oklahoma border in the Panhandle.

Hondo and Castroville

On US 90, west of San Antonio.

Castroville's original settlers, led by Henri Castro, came from the Alsace region between France and Germany in 1844. Today all the Alsatians come out for Castroville's **St. Louis Day Festival** in late August, and your family is certain to enjoy it as well. The celebration features an auction, bingo, children's rides and games, barbecue and Alsatian sausage, an arts and crafts show, and Flemish and Alsatian dancers. Call (830) 931-2826 or (800) 778-6775, or visit the Web site at www.castroville.com.

Medina County Museum (ages 6 and up)

2202 Eighteenth Street, Hondo (830-426-8819). Hours vary seasonally. Free.

The Medina County Museum features pioneer artifacts and exhibits about the area's history in a restored 1897 railroad depot. The depot received a Texas Historic Marker and is being updated.

Landmark Inn State Historic Site (ages 4 and up)

402 Florence Street, Castroville (830-931-2133; www.landmarkinntx.com).

The Landmark Inn in Castroville used to serve stagecoach passengers and continues to serve travelers today as a Bed and Breakfast Inn. On the site is an old water-powered gristmill. You and the kids can walk on a nature trail, fish, or picnic on the grounds. During the year, park staff conducts several interpretive tours and seminars on pioneer skills like soap making, so see what else is going on.

Castroville Regional Park (ages 4 and up)

816 Alsace Street, Castroville (830-931-4070). Open 5 a.m. to 10 p.m. daily in the summer and 6 a.m. to 9 p.m. daily in the winter. Recreational use free, $ for picnic tables and on some holidays.

Castroville Park is a nice place to picnic under a covered shelter, swim in a pool, or play tennis or volleyball. You can fish or just relax by the Medina River. The 126-acre park has camping and RV sites.

Texas Trivia

Texas has 141 species of native land animals. Only California and New Mexico have more.

Texas Trivia

In 1846 the Association for the Protection of Immigrants in Texas offered a package deal to Europeans wanting to settle in Texas. For 1,000 francs the immigrant would receive passage and meals from Bremen, Germany, to Castroville; transport of 300 pounds of luggage; a small log cabin; two oxen and yokes; two milk cows; twelve chickens and a rooster; a plow; and a "Mexican" wagon. In return, the settler agreed to live on and work the land for at least three years.

Where to Eat

Alsatian Restaurant. 1651 US 90 West. Castroville (830-931-3260). In a town known for its fine restaurants, this is one of the best, specializing in steaks and Alsatian cuisine. Many tables have a beautiful view of the Medina River Valley. $$–$$$

Haby's Alsatian Bakery. 207 US 90 East, Castroville (830-931-2118). If you're after some tasty pastries, go here. Bet you can't buy just one. $

Sammy's Restaurant. 202 US 90 East, Castroville (830-538-2204). This 1950s drive-in burger joint offered curb service until 1969. Comfortable place with a varied menu and big juicy burgers. $–$$

El Restaurante Azteca. 1708 Avenue K, Hondo (830-426-4511). Great Mexican food at good prices. $–$$

Hermann Sons Steakhouse. 577 US 90 East, Hondo (830-426-2220; www.hermannsonssteakhouse.com). Casual, family dining with full menu. Chicken-fried steak second to none. $–$$

Where to Stay

Landmark Inn. 402 Florence Street, Castroville (830-931-2133; www.landmarkinntx.com). The inn has only ten rooms to choose from, so reservations should be made well ahead of time. The inn has been restored to the 1940s era, with ceiling fans and rocking chairs but no televisions. Continental breakfasts are served in the 1849 kitchen building adjacent to the inn. $$

Best Western Hondo Inn. 301 US 90 East, Hondo (830-426-4466; www.bestwestern.com). Pool, fitness center, high-speed Internet, complimentary breakfast, children 12 and under **free.** $$

For More Information

Castroville Chamber of Commerce. 100 Karm Street, Castroville 78009; (800) 778-6775 or (830) 538-3142; www.castroville.com.

Hondo Chamber of Commerce. 1607 Avenue K, Hondo 78861; (830) 426-3037; www.hondochamber.com.

San Antonio

People always have a good time in San Antonio. It's a big, fun city with lots to see, from historic locales to modern shopping centers to family amusement parks and one of the best minor-league baseball parks in the country.

One of the best rodeos in Texas is held here every February. The **San Antonio Stock Show and Rodeo** features professional riders, a huge livestock show, a carnival, and plenty of arts and crafts and food booths. Each evening and Sunday matinee features a top-name entertainer. Call (210) 225-5851, or visit www.sarodeo.com.

San Antonio also celebrates **Cinco de Mayo** with great gusto. You'll find parades, pageants, dancing, singing, carnivals, and wonderful food in several places around the city. Call (210) 207-6700 or (800) 447-3372.

You can get to the city's famous **San Antonio River Walk** across from Alamo Plaza. The walk lines both sides of the San Antonio River for a couple of miles, and along the way you'll discover some of the city's best restaurants, specialty stores, and hotels.

The River Walk (210-227-4262; www.thesanantonioriverwalk.com) is the jewel of San Antonio. It becomes a magical place during the month of December with the **Holiday River Parade** and **Fiesta de las Luminarias** celebrations. Lights are the key—hundreds of thousands of lights that will delight kids from ages one to ninety-two. During the month, some sort of entertainment is featured almost every night. Don't miss out on the special performances on the bandstand by the River Center patio on the River Walk, or the **Las Posadas** procession through La Villita. Call (210) 207-6700 or (800) 447-3372.

Alamo (ages 6 and up)

300 Alamo Plaza, San Antonio (210-225-1391; www.thealamo.org). Open daily except Christmas Eve and Christmas Day: Monday through Saturday 9 a.m. to 5:30 p.m., Sunday 10 a.m. to 5:30 p.m. Free.

You can't talk about San Antonio without mentioning the Alamo, the mission turned into a fortress by Texans fighting for independence from Mexico in 1836. You might be

San Antonio **Tours**

You can go on a **San Antonio City Tour** (210-228-9776 or 800-868-7707) or a **Texas Trolley Tour** (210-225-8587) from the Alamo Visitor Center, between the Alamo and the Rivercenter Mall. Tours run daily 9 a.m. to 5 p.m. **Gray Line Lone Star Trolley Tours** (210-229-7200) also offers several tour options from 217 Alamo Plaza. If the family wants a guided boat tour of the river, call **Rio San Antonio Cruises** at (210) 244-5700 or (800) 417-4139, or visit their Web site at www.riosanantonio.com for more information. For great fun, ride a Segway around town with **SegCity Tours** (210) 224-0773.

Texas Trivia

While most Texans remember General Antonio López de Santa Anna as being the military dictator defeated in the fight for the state's independence, he made another lasting contribution to modern society: chewing gum. His troops used to chew chicle to relieve tension, and he introduced the idea to inventor Thomas Adams while on a visit to New York in 1869. Adams made some; it was a local hit, and the chewing gum industry was born. The Adams Gum Co. ruled the industry until Wrigleys entered the market in the 1900s. Adams's Chiclets are still popular; however, Santa Anna never got a dime of the fortune he made for Adams.

surprised at its location: right in the middle of downtown next to the Rivercenter Mall. Texans treat the Alamo as a shrine, so speak softly inside. Only the old chapel is left of the original mission; the actual battleground stretches across Alamo Plaza and into the souvenir shops on the far side of Alamo Street.

The imposing monument you see across from the Alamo in Alamo Plaza is the **Alamo Cenotaph,** which is inscribed with the names of those who died defending the mission. Some of the defenders' remains are also buried here. Craft fairs and battle reenactments often occupy the plaza. If the kids want something cold, you can almost always find raspa (snow cone) vendors here.

IMAX Theater (ages 4 and up)

Rivercenter Mall, 849 E. Commerce, San Antonio (210-247-4629 or 800-354-4629; www.imax-sa.com). Open daily 9 a.m. to 10 p.m., show times vary weekly. $$–$$$.

More Alamo history is available at the IMAX Theater. The IMAX shows a filmed account of the battle, *Alamo . . . The Price of Freedom,* on its huge, six-story screen. The sound system here is so good the explosions rattle your teeth. The theater also shows other special IMAX films and, in the evening, presents regular movies or classic films on that giant screen.

Ripley's Believe It or Not! and Plaza Wax Museum (ages 6 and up)

301 Alamo Plaza, San Antonio (210-224-9299; www.plazawaxmuseum.com). Open Monday through Thursday 9:30 a.m. to 8 p.m., Friday and Saturday 9 a.m. to 10 p.m. Sunday 9 a.m. to 8 p.m. $$–$$$.

Ripley's and the Wax Museum are quite popular with kids. Here they get to explore Ripley's Believe It or Not! with its unusual displays and famous collections of oddities and the Wax Museum with its exhibits of heroes of the battle of the Alamo and more modern celebrities, all created in wax.

Ripley's Haunted Adventure, Guinness World Records Museum, and Davy Crockett's Tall Tales Ride (ages 10 and up)

329 Alamo Plaza, San Antonio (210-226-2828; www.alamoplazaattractions.com). All open daily except Christmas; hours vary. $$–$$$.

Three exciting attractions in one—directly across from the Alamo. Folklorists say San Antonio is one of the most haunted cities in America, and this new multimillion dollar special-effects haunted house will convince you! The Guinness World Records Museum is a state-of-the-art, interactive experience to behold. Sixteen themed galleries, spread over 10,000 square feet will amaze you! The exciting Tall Tales Ride will take you on a fantastic journey through the life and times of Davy Crockett, narrated by Davy himself.

La Villita (ages 6 and up)

Alamo at Villita Street, San Antonio (210-207-8610; www.lavillita.com). Open daily 10 a.m. to 6 p.m.; individual shop hours vary widely.

Bordering the River Walk is La Villita, San Antonio's original village. The historic homes have become a diverse selection of arts and crafts shops that shouldn't be missed. Several specialize in clothes and toys for kids.

The **Mission Trail**

When the Spanish occupied Texas, they established about forty missions in the region in an attempt to convert native peoples and protect the frontier, establishing colonies and forts at each site. Although the missions ultimately did little of either, they did pave the way for later settlers. The oldest was established at El Paso. Today, ten missions or their ruins are open to the public in Texas.

San Antonio is the only city in the United States with five Spanish colonial missions within its city limits, all dating back to the early 1700s. All of them are along the San Antonio River. Missions Concepción, San José, Espada, and San Juan form the San Antonio Missions National Historic Park. The aqueduct at Mission Espada has been in continuous use since the 1730s. A series of markers showing the way along the Mission Trail begins on Alamo Street. Although the Alamo is one of the city's original missions, it is not managed by the National Park System but by the Daughters of the Republic of Texas as a state historic site. The Daughters consider the Alamo a shrine, so you should maintain hushed tones and control small children while inside, or you may be chastised. Also, show respect inside the other churches along the Mission Trail as they are all active Roman Catholic congregations.

Institute of Texan Cultures (ages 4 and up)

851 Durango Boulevard, San Antonio (210-458-2330; www.texancultures.utsa.edu). Open Tuesday through Saturday 10 a.m. to 5 p.m., Sunday noon to 5 p.m., closed major holidays. Hours are extended during the Texas Folklife Festival in June. $$, children 2 and under free.

The Institute of Texan Cultures, at Hemisfair Park downtown, is a unique museum that highlights the wide variety of cultures that have contributed to the history of Texas. The main exhibit floor allows children to touch and examine artifacts and other displays of twenty-seven ethnic groups. The gift shop has a number of products specific to each group.

The **Texas Folklife Festival** is one of the premier celebrations in the state. Vendor booths and performance stages surround the Institute of Texan Cultures for several days in early June. Your family will be overloaded with food, dancing, singing, and crafts from the state's many cultures. Many of the performers are children's groups, and there is a special Storytelling Stage for kids. You shouldn't miss this one. Call (210) 458-2330.

Market Square (ages 6 and up)

514 W. Commerce Street at I–35, San Antonio (210-207-8600; www.marketsquaresa.com). Open June through August 10 a.m. to 8 p.m. daily, September through May 10 a.m. to 6 p.m. daily.

Visit Market Square, and your family will feel like they're walking through Mexico. Three distinct shopping areas with hundreds of shops, cafes, and vendors will delight your senses with handicrafts, imports, and food.

Kiddie Park (ages 4 and up)

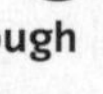

3015 Broadway, San Antonio (210-824-4351; www.kiddiepark.com). Open Monday through Saturday 10 a.m. to dark, Sunday 11 a.m. to dark. Unlimited rides with Bargain Day on Wednesday. $$.

A highlight of this old-fashioned amusement park is a 1918 Herschell-Spillman Carousel with thirty-six jumping horses and two chariots. Founded in 1925, it is the oldest original children's amusement park in the United States.

Texas Trivia

Mission Nuestra Señora de la Purisima Concepción, built in 1731, is the oldest unrestored stone church in the United States.

San Antonio Museum of Art (ages 6 and up)

200 West Jones Avenue, San Antonio (210-978-8100; www.samuseum.org). Open Tuesday 10 a.m. to 9 p.m., Wednesday through Saturday 10 a.m. to 5 p.m., Sunday noon to 6 p.m. $–$$, children 3 and under free.

The San Antonio Museum of Art is a six-building complex, formerly a renovated historic brewery, that houses excellent collections of pre-Columbian, Native American, Spanish colonial, and American paintings; photography; sculpture; and furnishings.

San Antonio Missions National Historical Park (ages 6 and up)

On the Mission Trail, beginning on Alamo Street, San Antonio (headquarters: 210-534-8833; visitor center: 210-932-1001; www.nps.gov/saan). Open daily 9 a.m. to 5 p.m. except Thanksgiving, Christmas, and New Year's Day. Free.

Give your family a sense of area history by touring San Antonio's famous missions. The driving tour to the four old churches that make up the park begins on Alamo Street. Just follow the signs south. **Mission Concepción, Mission San José, Mission Espada,** and **Mission San Juan** were built by the Spanish in the 1700s, and all are still active parish churches. Photographic possibilities at any of the missions are endless. A visitor center is located at Mission Concepción. Mission San José is justly famous for its Sunday noon mariachi mass.

Buckhorn Saloon and Museum (ages 6 and up)

318 E. Houston Street, San Antonio (210-247-4000; www.buckhornmuseum.com). Open Labor Day through Memorial Day 10 a.m. to 5 p.m., Memorial Day through Labor Day 10 a.m. to 6 p.m. $$.

The entire family will enjoy this authentic western experience that has been around for more than one hundred years. Recently relocated from an old brewery, the new two-level downtown museum offers thirteen rotating exhibits of more than 520 preserved animals and 3,300 artifacts, including horn and antler furniture, rattlesnake art, and a model church made from 50,000 matchsticks. The museum features a saloon and restaurant with cowboy entertainment, an arcade and shooting gallery, a curio shop, and the Texas History Wax Museum.

Witte Museum (ages 6 and up)

3801 Broadway, San Antonio (210-357-1900; www.wittemuseum.org). Open Monday through Saturday 10 a.m. to 5 p.m. (to 8 p.m. Tuesday), Sunday noon to 5 p.m. $$, children 3 and under are free and admission is free on Tuesday from 3 to 8 p.m.

The Witte has extensive exhibits covering Texas nature and history, including a Texas Rangers wing. Special exhibits, such as one with animated dinosaurs, are featured regularly. The Science Treehouse is a wonder of interactive fun and technology with four levels of hands-on exhibits and activities just for children, an absolute must-see.

Texas Trivia

When Spaniards first visited the area that is now San Antonio, it was a Payaya Indian camp on the banks of a gently flowing river. The Indians called it *Yanaguana*, "the clear water." The Spanish called it San Antonio because they first stopped here on the feast day of Saint Anthony.

Splashtown USA (ages 4 and up)

3600 I-35 North, San Antonio (210-227-1400; www.splashtownsa.com). Open daily in the summer until mid-August, hours vary. $$$–$$$$, children under 2 and seniors free. Nonparticipant admission ($) is available.

Splashtown USA is a sure way to cool the kids off in the Texas heat. The park has a number of water slides and other water-based attractions.

San Antonio Zoo and Aquarium (ages 2 and up)

3903 North Saint Mary's Street, San Antonio (210-734-7184; www.sazoo-aq.org). Open daily 9 a.m. to 5 p.m. (to 6 p.m. Memorial Day through Labor Day). $$.

The San Antonio Zoo and Aquarium is a family delight, fun for kids and parents alike. More than 3,000 animals, most in natural settings, are displayed here. More than 700 different species, including rare white rhinos, snow leopards, and whooping cranes, make the zoo the third largest collection in the United States. A special children's area features a tropical boat tour of animal and plant exhibits. Lots of special programs for kids.

Brackenridge Park (ages 4 and up)

3910 North St. Mary's Street, adjacent to San Antonio Zoo (210-736-9534;). Open daily 5 a.m. to 11 p.m.

Next to the zoo, Brackenridge Park and the Japanese Tea Garden provide a beautiful, tranquil setting of rustic stone bridges and winding walks by pools and flowers. This is a great place for the children and you to decompress.

Sea World San Antonio (ages 2 and up)

10500 Sea World Drive, San Antonio (800-700-7786; www.seaworld.com). Hours vary widely with the seasons. $$$$.

You might not find a better way to entertain your kids in all of the state than Sea World of Texas, the world's largest marine-life park. The park offers water slides, tube rides, beaches, surf, waterskiers, and a number of other shows featuring dolphins, killer whales, and birds. Aquariums and other exhibits teach children about marine life.

Six Flags Fiesta Texas (ages 4 and up)

17000 I–10 at Loop 1604, San Antonio (210-697-5050 or 800-473-4378; www.sixflags.com/fiestaTexas/). $$$$.

Six Flags Fiesta Texas is a 200-acre theme park with more than enough rides and shows to keep any kid entertained, from roller coasters to water slides to trains. Not only does the park put on its own themed music shows, but concerts by top-name performers are scheduled throughout the summer months. The park also brags that it is one of the most accessible theme parks in the nation for people with disabilities or hearing impairments.

Malibu Grand Prix (ages 6 and up)

3330 Cherry Ridge Drive, San Antonio (210-341-6663; www.malibugrandprix.com/park/sa). Hours vary seasonally. Prices vary by activity.

Your family can spend an entire day at Malibu Grand Prix and never get bored. Choose from a challenging miniature golf course, bumper boats, batting cages, and race cars. A snack bar, video arcade, and game room are here, too.

Monarch Collectibles (ages 4 and up)

2012 Northwest Military Highway, near the airport, San Antonio (210-341-3655 or 800-648-3655; www.dollsdolls.com). Open Monday through Saturday 10 a.m. to 5 p.m.

If you or your children like dolls, Monarch Collectibles is the place for you. Monarch is home to more than 2,500 dolls on display and hundreds of limited-edition collectors' plates. The shop also sells dolls, dollhouses, and accessories.

San Antonio Missions Baseball (ages 4 and up)

5757 US 90 West, San Antonio (210-675-7275; www.samissions.com). $–$$.

The San Antonio Missions baseball team plays in the Class AA Texas League, in the Nelson W. Wolff Stadium that will take you back to the golden age of baseball. The team caters to families, with a large picnic area and a special section that prohibits beer sales. Sure, you can get peanuts and Cracker Jack, but you can also get nachos.

Texas Trivia

Near historic San Fernando Cathedral in downtown San Antonio is the intersection of Dolorosa and Soledad Streets. That means you can stand on the corner of Sad and Lonely Streets. There is no Heartbreak Hotel at the location, however.

San Antonio Spurs Basketball (ages 6 and up)

1 AT&T Center, San Antonio (210-444-5000; www.nba.com/spurs). $$–$$$$.

The San Antonio Spurs are a class act in the National Basketball Association; they won the championship in 1999, 2003, and 2005. They play at the AT&T Center, a fan-friendly venue.

Where to Eat

Casa Rio. 430 East Commerce Street, San Antonio (210-225-6718; www.casa-rio.com). Oldest and largest Mexican restaurant on the River Walk. $–$$

Michelino's. 521 Riverwalk, San Antonio (210-223-2939; www.michelinos.us). The best Italian food in town. $$–$$$

Schilo's (Shee-lows). 424 East Commerce Street, San Antonio (210-223-6692). This excellent German-style delicatessen is a city tradition. $

Where to Stay

Comfort Inn Fiesta. 6755 North Loop 1604 West, San Antonio (210-696-4766; www.comfortinnfiesta.com). Pool, continental breakfast, convenient location to Six Flags Fiesta Texas. $$

Hill Country Inn & Suites. 2383 Northeast Loop 410, San Antonio (800-314-3424). Pool, playground, large suites. $$-$$$

La Quinta Inn Market Square. 900 Dolorosa Street, San Antonio (210-271-0001 or 866-725-1661). Pool, high-speed Internet; convenient to Market Square and much of downtown. $$–$$$

For More Information

San Antonio Convention and Visitors Bureau. 317 Alamo Plaza, San Antonio 78205; (800) 447-3372; www.SanAntonioCVB.com.

The Hill Country

The Hill Country is the heart of Texas. Although its rugged hills and hardscrabble land don't allow many folks to make a living off the land, the Hill Country draws visitors from every corner of the state to bask in its quiet and its beauty over and over and over again.

Formed by the Balcones Escarpment, the limestone ledges and steep, green hills of the Edwards Plateau are crisscrossed by spring-fed rivers and creeks, dotted with farms, scattered with arts and crafts communities, and underlaid with several spectacular caverns. For centuries the Hill Country was an Apache stronghold; it was later cultivated by German immigrants, whose influence remains substantial, and finally invaded by tourists. Except for I–35, which follows the Balcones Fault Line separating the eastern edge of the Hill Country from the Coastal Plains, and I–10, which bisects the plateau, most roads through the area are twisty, narrow, and hilly, their scenic routes unchanged for a hundred years. And except for the ever-growing metropolis of Austin, the cities in the Hill Country remain small and rustic, windows to Texas's past.

New Braunfels

New Braunfels is one of the Hill Country cities founded by German immigrants in the mid-1800s, and it still shows through the town's architecture, its street and family names, and most of the restaurants. In the summertime, Texans flock to the town for refuge in the cooling waters of the Comal and Guadalupe Rivers and one of the state's best water parks, and in the shade of the giant oak and cypress trees.

Natural Bridge Caverns (ages 4 and up)

26495 Natural Bridge Caverns Road; take exit 175 from I–35 and follow the signs (210-651-6101; www.naturalbridgecaverns.com). Open from 9 a.m. to 4 p.m., later in summer and on some weekends. $$–$$$.

THE HILL COUNTRY

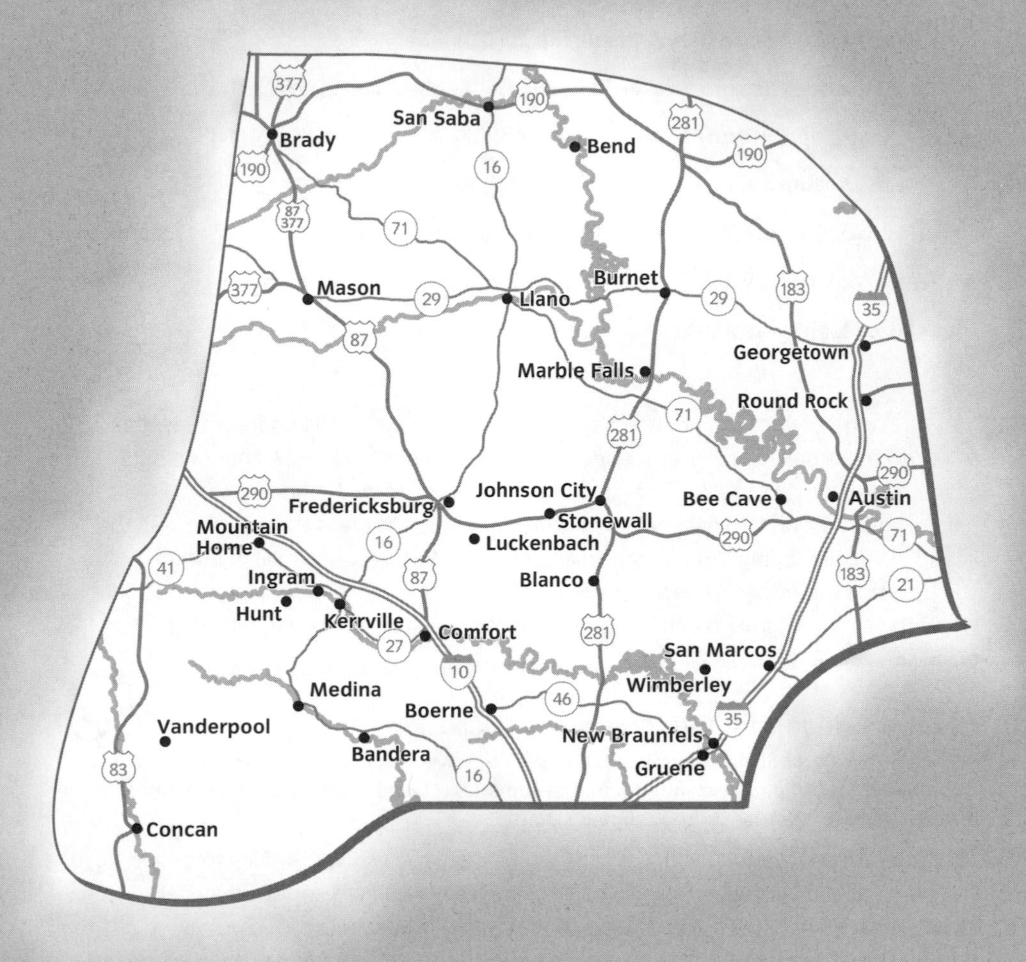

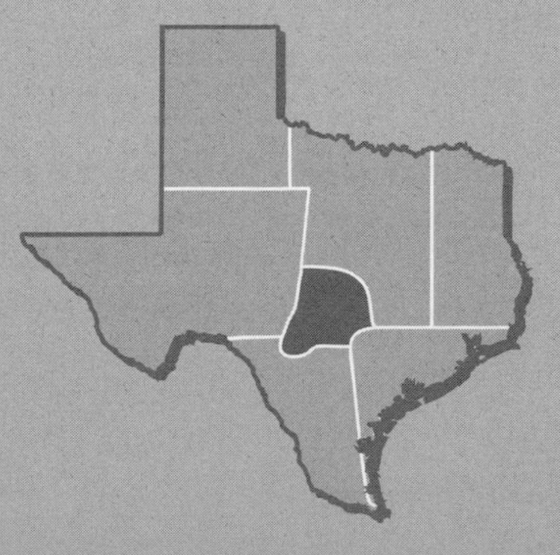

Top Annual Events in the Hill Country

- **Travis County Livestock Show and Rodeo,** Austin, March (512-919-3000)
- **Eeyore's Birthday Party,** Austin, April (512-448-5160)
- **Texas State Arts and Crafts Fair,** Kerrville, May (830-896-5711)
- **Cowboy Capital Rodeo,** Bandera, May (830-796-3045 or 800-364-3833)
- **Peach JAMboree,** Stonewall, June (830-644-2735)
- **Wimberley Gospel Music Festival,** Wimberley, October (512-847-2201)
- **The Great Turkey Escape,** Johnson City, November (830-868-7684)
- **Trail of Lights,** around the Hill Country, December (830-868-7684)

Natural Bridge Caverns is a great family adventure: You'll descend hundreds of feet into the earth to encounter the largest underground formations in Texas. All but one of the seven show caves in the state can be found in the Hill Country. Named for the 60-foot natural limestone bridge that spans its entrance, Natural Bridge is a living cave, and the sound of water dripping through the limestone to create the subterranean formations can be heard everywhere along the tour. Some formations here are huge, like the 50-foot Watchtower. Aboveground you'll find an interpretive center, snack bar, gift shop, and picnic area.

Natural Bridge Wildlife Ranch (ages 2 and up)

Adjacent to Natural Bridge Caverns (830-438-7400; www.wildliferanchtexas.com). Open daily 9 a.m. to 4:30 p.m. (extended hours in summer). Closed Thanksgiving, Christmas, and New Year's Day. $$–$$$, children under 3 free.

Next door to the cavern is Natural Bridge Wildlife Ranch, a way for the kids to get up close and personal with more than sixty-five exotic species of animals, such as rhinoceros, giraffe, wildebeest, gazelle, zebus, Cape buffalo, aoudad, and baboon. The main tour is through 200 acres of ranch land in your own vehicle. There's also a visitor center, where you can watch newborns being cared for and ostriches hatching; a children's petting zoo; a snack bar; and shaded picnic tables.

Animal World and Snake Farm (ages 4 and up)

5640 I–35 South, at the Engle Road exit, New Braunfels (830-608-9270; www.exoticanimalworld.com). Open daily 10 a.m. to 6 p.m. $$, children under 2 free.

Your kids will get an educational and slithering good time here, up close and personal with all sorts of animals. Formerly known as the Snake Farm, Animal World is now home to more than 500 animals and a petting zoo, as well as reptiles of all types, including a 275-pound constrictor. Watch snake and alligator handling and feeding and special shows and events. The farm is also home to a variety of alligators, turtles, and longhorn cattle.

McKenna Children's Museum (ages 2 and up)

801 West San Antonio Street, New Braunfels (830-606-9525; www.mckennakids.org). Open Monday through Saturday 10 a.m. to 5 p.m. (Thursday until 7 p.m.), Sunday noon to 5 p.m. Memorial Day through Labor Day; Tuesday through Saturday 10 a.m. to 5 p.m., Sunday noon to 5 p.m. Labor Day through Memorial Day. $$.

The Children's Museum gives kids the chance to explore and discover on their own with many hands-on exhibits, including a television studio and puppet palace.

Landa Park (ages 4 and up)

On Landa Park Drive, New Braunfels (830-221-4000; www.nbtexas.org/index.aspx?NID=156). Free except picnic tables. $$.

This outstanding city park is at the headwaters of the Comal River, a stream that begins and ends within the New Braunfels city limits. The towering shade trees, spring-fed swimming pools, paddle boats, hike and bike trails, golf course, miniature train tours, and picnic areas make this one of the most popular parks around. Adjacent, on Liberty Street, is **Prince Solms Park,** where you can slide down a chute from the pool in Landa Park into the Comal River.

Schlitterbahn (ages 4 and up)

Main entrance: 400 North Liberty, New Braunfels (830-625-2351; www.schlitterbahn.com/nb). Hours vary widely, so call for exact details. Water park closed from mid-September through mid-April; resort open year-round. $$$$.

Schlitterbahn means "slippery road" in German, and you'll find more than enough ways to slip and slide at the state's largest water park and resort. The park has everything from radically fast and steep chutes to leisurely floats to surf. The resort area offers more than 130 riverside rooms, cottages, and private Jacuzzi suites ($$$$). Several shops stock water fashions and accessories.

Texas Trivia

The capital of Texas has been located in more cities than capitals in any other state. The towns that have served are San Felipe, Washington-on-the-Brazos, Harrisburg, Velasco, Columbus, Houston, and Austin.

The Guadalupe River (ages 6 and up)

Along River Road, north of New Braunfels.

One of the most popular recreational activities in this part of Texas is running the Guadalupe River in an inner tube, raft, canoe, or kayak. The scenery can be spectacular, and the river has enough small rapids to keep your interest. A large number of outfitters are scattered along the river from New Braunfels almost to Sattler.

Gruene

On Gruene Road off Loop 337, or on Hunter Road off Route 306; www.gruenetexas.com.

The historic community of Gruene (pronounced *green*) is part of New Braunfels, but it maintains its century-old character with its restored old homes that are now country inns, restaurants, or boutiques. The Guadalupe River flows through, providing the most popular summer attraction in all the Hill Country: rafting, canoeing, kayaking, or tubing downstream. Two river outfitters call Gruene home: **Gruene River Co.** (1404 Gruene Road, 830-625-2800 or 888-705-2800; www.toobing.com) and **Rockin' R River Rides** (1405 Gruene Road, 830-629-9999 or 800-55-FLOAT; www.rockinr.com). Both companies' offices are just across the river from the town. If you've never been here before, taking a guided raft ride with your family is a good way to get acquainted with the area and have some safe fun at the same time.

Shopping is abundant in Gruene, where you can buy anything from T-shirts to antiques, pottery to western gifts. Kids love the store where they can get their picture taken in an Old West costume. You can also shop at **Gruene Market Days,** one of the best outdoor markets in the Hill Country, on the third weekend of each month from April through December.

Canyon Lake (ages 2 and up)

14 miles north of Gruene on Highway 306. Canyon Lake Chamber of Commerce Visitor Center, 3934 FM 2673 (830-964-2223 or 800-528-2104; www.canyonlakechamber.com).

North of Gruene is Canyon Lake, 80 miles of protected shoreline with several parks around it providing ample opportunities for boating, fishing, camping, picnicking, swimming, sunning, or just relaxing. The lake is one of the most popular in the state for scuba diving.

Where to Eat

Grist Mill Restaurant. 1287 Gruene Road, Gruene (830-625-0684; www.gristmillrestaurant.com). Laid-back atmosphere (shorts and sandals are OK) in a barely restored hundred-year-old mill on the banks of the Guadalupe River. Great food, great views, and incredible strawberry shortcake. $$

Oma's Haus Restaurant. 541 Highway 46 South, New Braunfels (830-625-3280; www.omashaus.com). Delicious, authentic German food. Special children's selections, gift shop, homemade fudge and strudel. $–$$

New Braunfels Smokehouse. 1090 North Business I-35, New Braunfels (830-625-2416; www.nbsmokehouse.com). Known for great smoked sausage, brisket, and ribs since 1952. Full menus of dinners, sandwiches, and salads.

Where to Stay

There are numerous vacation houses and cabins in the area for rent—the Chamber of Commerce Web site below has listings and more information.

Holiday Inn. 1051 I–35 East, New Braunfels (830-625-3130). Convenient to everything in New Braunfels or Gruene; pool, exercise room and hot tub. $$

La Quinta Inn & Suites. 365 Hwy. 46, New Braunfels (830-627-3333; www.laquinta.com). Outdoor pool, spa, fitness center, **free** high-speed Internet access, **free** breakfast, children under 18 **free.** $$

Howard Johnson Inn. 201 Loop 337, New Braunfels (830-629-6888; www.howardjohnsonnb.com). Convenient location, outdoor pool, **free** breakfast, **free** WiFi.

For More Information

New Braunfels Chamber of Commerce. 390 South Sequin Avenue, New Braunfels 78131; (800) 572-2626 or (830) 625-2385; www.nbcham.org.

San Marcos

Aquarena Center (ages 4 and up)

921 Aquarena Springs Drive, west of I–35 at exit 206, San Marcos (512-245-7570 or 800-999-9767; www.aquarena.txstate.edu). Free. Glass-bottom boat tours from 9:30 a.m. to 4:30 p.m. $$, children 3 and under free.

For decades San Marcos was known as the home of Ralph the Swimming Pig, who performed along with mermaids at Aquarena. Ralph and the mermaids were retired, however, when Southwest Texas State University bought the amusement park and resort, developing new programs with the Texas Parks and Wildlife Department. The park is open without charge but with few of its former attractions operating. It now specializes in education, and the always-interesting glass-bottom boat tours continue to fascinate families. A relatively new feature is the **Natural Aquarium of Texas,** showcasing several endangered species found only at Aquarena Springs.

Wonder World (ages 2 and up)

1000 Prospect Drive, off I–35 at the Wonder World Drive exit, south of downtown San Marcos (512-392–3760; www.wonderworldpark.com). Open daily Memorial Day through Labor Day 8 a.m. to 8 p.m.; September through May 9 a.m. to 5 p.m. weekdays, to 6 p.m. weekends. $$$, children 2 and under free.

Wonder World is a fun place to take younger children. It includes a wildlife park, an observation tower, an antigravity house, and a train tour. The central attraction for adults and older children here is Wonder Cave, unique because it was formed by an earthquake, so it lacks the usual cavern formations. The tour into the cave allows you to see the actual Balcones Fault Line that separates the Hill Country from the Coastal Plains.

Tube the San Marcos River (ages 6 and up)

At City Park, 170 Bobcat Drive, San Marcos (512-396-LION; www.tubesanmarcos.com). Tube rentals ($$) open 10 a.m. to 7 p.m.

When the weather is warm, the most popular family activity in San Marcos is tubin' down the San Marcos River. You can bring your own inner tube or rent one from the Lions Club facility at City Park and go on a leisurely float down the most beautiful river in the state. Most tubers take out after shooting the chute at Rio Vista Dam. The Lions Club also provides a river taxi to shuttle you from that location back to City Park. You can keep doing it until you're shriveled up. For the more experienced river runners, canoes and shuttles are available from **Spencer's Canoes** in Martindale (512-357-6113).

Where to Eat

Texas Reds Steakhouse. 120 Grove Street, San Marcos (512-754-8808; www.texasreds.com). Great food in a restored mill, and the kids get to toss peanut shells on the floor. $$

San Marcos River Pub and Grille. 701 Cheatham Street, San Marcos (512-353-3747; www.riverpubandgrill.com). Located on the banks of the San Marcos River, this is a fun place with good food: burgers, sandwiches, salads, tacos, and a nice variety of entrees.

Where to Stay

Best Western San Marcos. 917 I-35 North, San Marcos (512-754-7557; Convenient location, outdoor pool, **free** breakfast, **free** high-speed Internet access, expanded cable TV with HBO. $$

For More Information

San Marcos Convention and Visitors Bureau. 202 North C. M. Allen Parkway, San Marcos, 78667; (888) 200-5620 or (512) 393-5900; www.visitsanmarcos.com.

Wimberley

About 15 miles north of San Marcos on scenic Ranch Road 12.

Wimberley is a growing arts-and-crafts community at the confluence of the Blanco River and Cypress Creek. The village is known around Texas for its monthly **Wimberley Market Day**, held the first Saturday of each month from April through December on Ranch Road 2325 just north of downtown. This is the second largest outdoor flea market in the state, after Canton's, with more than 450 booths selling everything from junk to art to jams and jellies, from antiques to cactus to handcrafted furniture. Barbecue and live entertainment are served up at lunchtime. Call the Chamber of Commerce at (512) 847-2201 for more information.

A large number of artists call Wimberley home, and their work can be seen all over town. The town has an active arts league which hosts an Art Fest in May and other activities during the year. Around **"The Square"** and **"Old Town Plaza,"** you'll find a number of art galleries, studios, boutiques, an old-fashioned ice cream parlor, a fabulous kitchen shop, a candy company, bakery, and several eateries.

The Corral Theater (ages 6 and up)

100 Flite Acres Road at Ranch Road 3237, Wimberley (512-847-5994; www.corraltheater.com). Films begin at dark, Friday, Saturday, and Sunday, Memorial Day through Labor Day. $, children under 4 or over 85 free.

Kids love watching first-run movies under the stars at the Corral, an outdoor theater where you can either bring your own chairs, use one of the theater's, or sit in the bleachers. The films are always family fare, and the popcorn has been rated first-rate.

Wimberley Glass Works (ages 4 and up)

6469 Ranch Road 12 between Wimberley and San Marcos (800-929-6686; www.wgw.com). Open daily 10 a.m. to 5 p.m., Saturday until 6 p.m. Demonstrations Thursday through Monday from approximately 10:30 a.m. to 12:30 p.m. and 1:30 p.m. to 4:30 p.m. Free.

You and the kids will be mesmerized at the Wimberley Glass Works, the premier art glass studio in the southwest. Glassblower Tim de Jong and his staff put on public demonstrations at their modern studio, maneuvering liquid glass on long poles to create impressive art. Visitors watch from seats in an air-conditioned studio while the artists work from several white-hot vats and furnaces. Finished work is available in the adjacent showroom.

Pioneer Town (ages 6 and up)

333 Wayside Drive, Wimberley (512-847-2517; www.7aresort.com). Free; lodging $$.

Pioneer Town at 7A Ranch Resort can be a fun place for kids to roam around. An Old West village is re-created on the grounds, including an old fort, a chapel, and a popular glass-bottle house, as well as an ice cream parlor, gift shop, and video arcade. The resort also offers twenty-six rustic cottages, a half mile of Blanco River frontage for swimming and fishing, a pool, and tennis courts, at low to moderate prices.

Where to Eat

Ino'z. 14004 RR 12, Wimberley (512-847-0905). Casual dining right on Cypress Creek. Great burgers. Some live entertainment.

The Dandy Dog. 100 Oak Dr. #2, Wimberley (512-847-8101). A "to-go" place featuring gourmet hot dogs, Frito pie, soft pretzels.

Miss Mae's Bar-B-Q. 419 FM 2325, Wimberley (512-847-9808; www.missmaesbbq.com). Good barbecue and all the trimmings, to eat in or to go.

Where to Stay

The Lodge at Cypress Falls. One Woodcreek Circle, Wimberley (512-847-6595; www.thelodgeatcypressfalls.com). Newly remodeled, this lodge used to be the center of a resort on Cypress Creek. Beautiful location.

Pool, tennis courts, volleyball, shuffleboard. $$–$$$

7A Resort (see Pioneer Town, above)

Mountain View Lodge. 10600 Ranch Road 12, 3 miles south of Wimberly (512-847-2992; www.mountainviewlodge.com). Best view around, pool, nature trail, cable TV, **free** WiFi, **free** continental breakfast. Secluded yet convenient. $$

For More Information

Wimberley Chamber of Commerce. Ranch Road 12, Wimberley 78676; (512) 847-2201; www.wimberley.org.

Austin

Texas's capital city is famous for its live music scene, the number of festivals it stages throughout the year, and the hundreds of thousands of bats that live under a downtown bridge. The friendly folks at the Visitor Center will help you plan your trip, give you maps and itinerary ideas, and book tours such as the Duck tours, riverboat tours or Segway tours.

Pioneer Farm (ages 4 and up)

10621Pioneer Farm Drive, Austin (512-837-1215; www.pioneerfarms.org). Open Sunday 1 to 5 p.m., Friday 10 a.m. to 2 p.m. $$.

Aimed at teaching children what life was like for pioneer Texans more than a hundred years ago, this working farm has several hands-on exhibits, costumed interpreters, and regular programs where children can milk cows, make old-fashioned toys or candy, or harvest crops. There are also educational tours, classes and workshops offered to teach skills such as blacksmithing, candle making, Dutch oven cooking, and fiber arts.

Texas State Capitol (ages 6 and up)

Congress Avenue at Eleventh Street, Austin (512-463-0063; www.tspb.state.tx.us/spb/capitol/texcap.htm).Tours Monday through Friday 8:30 a.m. to 4:30 p.m., Saturday 9:30 a.m. to 3:30 p.m., Sunday noon to 3:30 p.m. Free.

This pink-granite building is a replica of the U.S. Capitol but just a little bit taller (of course). Portraits of the state's governors line the rotunda walls, and statues of Texas heroes crowd the foyer. The House and Senate chambers are an impressive sight. The adjacent **Capitol Complex Visitors Center** at 112 East EleventhStreet (512-305-8400) is housed in the historic Old General Land Office Building and is filled with information about local tours and attractions. Open daily 9 a.m. to 5 p.m.

Bob Bullock Texas State History Museum (ages 5 and up)

1800 N. Congress Avenue, Austin (512-936-4631; www.thestoryoftexas.com). Open Monday through Saturday 9 a.m. to 6 p.m., Sunday noon to 6 p.m. $–$$, extra fees for IMAX Theater, Texas Spirit Theater, and some special exhibits.

Three floors of interactive exhibits, an IMAX Theater, and Texas Spirit Theater tell the "Story of Texas" in this exceptional museum. There's a museum store and café, so you can spend the entire day here. All sorts of family events and programs, from story times to summer camps, are offered throughout the year.

Austin Children's Museum (ages 2 and up)

201 Colorado Street, Austin (512-472-2499; www.austinkids.org). Open Tuesday through Saturday 10 a.m. to 5 p.m.(Wednesday until 8 p.m.), Sunday noon to 5 p.m. $$, but free on Sunday 4 to 5 p.m.

The Austin Children's Museum moved into an expanded facility, showcasing a fascinating collection of hands-on exhibits where kids can climb, touch, and play to their hearts' content. The focus is on cultural diversity and science. Unique features include model cities and weather galleries.

Hill Country Flyer (ages 2 and up)

Depot: 401 E. Whitestone, Cedar Park (512-477-8468; www.austinsteamtrain.org). Schedule varies with the season. $$$–$$$$.

Everyone loves to ride an authentic steam train. The Hill Country Flyer runs between Cedar Park, about 20 miles north of Austin on Highway 183, to the city of Burnet. It's a four-hour scenic tour of the Hill Country, over creeks and through canyons, with a layover in Burnet for shopping and lunch. It's a special trip when spring wildflowers are blooming. The Bertram Flyer is a shorter trip (3 hours round trip) to and from the historic 1912 depot in Bertram. Special trips like the North Pole Flyer and a Storybook Special Flyer go occasionally.

Mexic-Arte Museum (ages 6 and up)

419 Congress Avenue, Austin (512-480-9373; www.mexic-artemuseum.org). Open Monday through Thursday 10 a.m. to 6 p.m., Friday and Saturday 10 a.m. to 5 p.m., Sunday noon to 5 p.m. $.

Exhibits include masks and photographs and other artworks highlighting Hispanic culture. Special exhibits throughout the year feature works by Latin American artists.

Texas Trivia

The capitol building was completed in 1888, covering two and a quarter acres. It's built of 4,000 carloads of Texas pink granite and 11,000 carloads of limestone, both quarried in Marble Falls and shipped to the site on a specially built railroad and by ox teams. The dome is made of iron with copper and measures 85,000 square feet.

O. Henry Home and Museum (ages 6 and up)

409 East Fifth Street, Austin (512-472-1903; www.ci.austin.tx.us/parks/ohenry.htm). Open Wednesday through Sunday noon to 5 p.m. Free.

The O. Henry Museum is where renowned short-story writer William Sydney Porter lived in 1888. A relatively small place, it houses many of the writer's personal items. The museum hosts the annual O. Henry Pun-Off in early May, an event that will delight every member of the family as hundreds of people get on stage vying to tell the punniest stories.

Zilker Park (ages 2 and up)

2100 Barton Springs Road, Austin (512-974-6700; www.ci.austin.tx.us/zilker). Open daily 7 a.m. to 10 p.m. Free. Hours for Barton Springs Pool ($) vary considerably; call (512) 476-9044 for details.

Zilker Park is where Austinites take their kids, and for good reason. The park has an impressive botanical garden, an outdoor theater, hike and bike trails, canoe rentals, picnic areas, a playscape, and the famous Barton Springs Pool. The Austin Nature Center in the park gives children the chance to learn with hands-on exhibits. The Zilker Zephyr, a miniature train, tours the park.

University of Texas (ages 8 and up)

Visitor center at Martin Luther King Jr. Boulevard and I–35, Austin (512-475-7348; www.utexas.edu). Free campus tours Monday through Saturday.

The University of Texas campus is home to three museums:

- The **Texas Natural Science Center** (formerly the Texas Memorial Museum), 2400 Trinity Street, (512-471-1604; www.utexas.edu/tmm). Open Monday through Friday 9 a.m. to 5 p.m., Saturday 10 a.m. to 5 p.m., Sunday 1 to 5 p.m., closed holidays. **Free.** This museum displays historical, archaeological, and geological collections.
- The **Harry Ransom Center,** Twenty-first and Guadalupe Streets, (512-471-8944; www.hrc.utexas.edu). Open Tuesday through Friday 9 a.m. to 5 p.m. (Thursday until 7 p.m.), Saturday and Sunday noon to 5 p.m. **Free.** This museum showcases UT's permanent collection, which features a 1455 Gutenberg Bible, western art, and Latin American art.
- The **Lyndon B. Johnson Presidential Library and Museum,** 2313 Red River Street, (512-721-0200; www.lbjlib.utexas.edu). Open daily 9 a.m. to 5 p.m. **Free.** This library and museum houses the papers and personal effects of our thirty-sixth president. A replica of Johnson's Oval Office, a Vietnam War exhibit, and gifts the president received from other heads of state are displayed. Also a nice gift shop.

Texas Trivia

More bats and more species of bats (thirty-two) make their home in Texas than in any other state. The largest urban bat colony in the world—about 1.5 million Mexican free-tailed bats—lives under the Congress Avenue Bridge in Austin.

George Washington Carver Museum (ages 6 and up)

1165 East Angelina Street, Austin (512-974-4926; www.carvermuseum.org). Open Monday, Wednesday, Friday 9:30 a.m. to 6 p.m., Tuesday and Thursday 9:30 a.m. to 8 p.m., Saturday 1 to 5 p.m. Free.

Black history and culture are showcased here, with changing exhibits displaying photographs, artifacts, and folk art.

Bat Emergence (ages 4 and up)

Congress Avenue Bridge at First Street, Austin (800-926-2282).

Don't leave downtown Austin without showing your children all the bats. The world's largest urban colony of Mexican free-tailed bats hangs out under the Congress Avenue Bridge from April to October. At dusk you can watch about 1.5 million of them take off in search of supper, one of the most unique wildlife spectacles in the United States. Best viewing areas are from the pedestrian walkway on the bridge itself, the adjacent hike and bike trail, observation decks at nearby restaurants and hotels, or the **Bat Observation Center** on the southeast shore of Town Lake at the bridge. A great photo opportunity for the kids is in front of the new 20-foot, free-swinging purple bat sculpture in the small park at Barton Creek Road and Congress Avenue.

Kiddie Acres (ages 4 and up)

4800 West Howard Lane, Austin (512-255-4131; www.kiddieacres.com). Open Tuesday through Sunday year-round, weather permitting, hours vary. $–$$.

Amusement park rides, miniature golf, pony rides, and train rides are at this Austin institution for little folk, especially under ten. Locally owned and operated since 1979.

McKinney Falls State Park (ages 4 and up)

5808 McKinney Falls Parkway, Austin (512-243-1643, www.tpwd.state.tx.us/spdest/findadest/parks/mckinney_falls).

South of Austin, at the confluence of Onion and Williamson Creeks, is McKinney Falls State Park, a quiet retreat from the nearby big city. Trails throughout the park lead to two waterfalls, a Native American rock shelter, and ruins of an old homestead and a gristmill. The park has picnic, camping, and swimming areas.

Lady Bird Johnson Wildflower Center (ages 4 and up)

4801 La Crosse Avenue, Austin (512-232-0100; www.wildflower.org). Open Tuesday through Saturday 9 a.m. to 5:30 p.m., Sunday noon to 5:30 p.m. $–$$, children 4 and under free.

Wildflowers abound at the Wildflower Center, founded by former first lady Lady Bird Johnson and recently renamed in her honor. The huge facility has several gardens, a nature trail, a visitors gallery, indoor exhibits, picnic areas, a gift shop, and a beautiful observation tower. The center also offers many classes and workshops specifically for children.

Austin Zoo (ages 2 and up)

10807 Rawhide Trail, off Highway 290 southwest of Austin (512-288-1490; www.austinzoo.org). Open daily 10 a.m. to 5 p.m. $–$$.

The Austin Zoo isn't like typical large-city zoos. This one was designed for children, giving them a chance to have a hands-on encounter with a variety of animals native to Texas. It has pony rides and a picnic area.

Where to Eat

The Texas Chili Parlor. 1409 Lavaca Avenue, Austin (512-472-2828; www.cactushill.com/TCP/). Legendary for serving up the state's official dish in the shadow of the capitol. Go for the chili pie. The cook gives you the option of three degrees of heat in your chili, and if you're not sure, start low. $

Threadgills. 6416 North Lamar Boulevard, Austin (512-451-5440; www.threadfills.com) and 301 West Riverside Drive, Austin (512-451-9304; www.threadgills.com). Threadgill's is an Austin institution with good, family-style Southern food and good music. $$

The County Line. 6500 W. Bee Cave Road, Austin (512-327-1742; www.countyline.com) and FM 2222 on the lake, Austin (512-346-3664; www.countyline.com). Legendary barbecue for more than 25 years. Always voted #1. $

Where to Stay

Days Inn Crossroads. 820 East Anderson Lane, Austin (512-835-4311). Pool, fitness center, free high-speed Internet, free breakfast. $–$$

Days Inn Downtown/University. 3105 North I-35, Austin (512-478-1631). Free breakfast, free high-speed Internet, pool. $$

La Quinta Highland Mall. 5812 North I–35, Austin (512-459-4381 or 800-531-5900; www.laquinta.com). Conveniently located just north of downtown. Free breakfast, pool, high-speed Internet, premium cable TV. $$

La Quinta Capitol. 300 East Eleventh Street, Austin (512-476-1166; www.laquinta.com). In the center of downtown. Free breakfast, high-speed Internet, outdoor pool, fitness center. $$$

For More Information

Austin Convention and Visitors Bureau. 301 Congress Avenue, Austin 78701; (800) 926-2282; www.austintexas.org.

Austin Visitors Center. 209 East Sixth Street, Austin 78701; (866) GO-AUSTIN or (512) 478-0098; www.austintexas.org/visitors/visitors_center.

Round Rock and Georgetown

History buffs will want to visit the Round Rock Cemetery on Sam Bass Road west of I–35. The bandit Sam Bass was buried here after being shot to death by Texas Rangers during an attempted bank holdup in Round Rock. Cave buffs will not want to miss Inner Space Cavern in Georgetown. It's one of the prettiest caves in Texas.

Inner Space Cavern (ages 6 and up)

4200 South I-35 at exit 259, Georgetown (512-931-CAVE; http://myinnerspacecavern.com/). Open daily 9 a.m. to 6 p.m. Memorial Day through Labor Day and 10 a.m. to 5 p.m. weekends, 9 a.m. to 4 p.m. weekdays Labor Day through Memorial Day. $$$, children 3 and under free.

Inner Space Cavern is on the outskirts of Georgetown. Texas's newest cave was discovered when construction crews were building the interstate. Visitors travel down on a cable car, then proceed on a walking tour around many impressive natural formations and by mastodon, dire wolf, and other Ice Age animal remains. The tour is enhanced with a light and sound show. More adventurous tours are available.

Round Rock Express Baseball (ages 4 and up)

3400 East Palm Valley Boulevard, Round Rock (512-255-2255; www.roundrock express .com). $$.

Texas League baseball returned to the capital area in a big way in 2000 when the Round Rock Express, owned by Hall of Famer Nolan Ryan, began play at the Dell Diamond, a small state-of-the-art ballpark. The Express was affiliated with the Houston Astros its first year.

For More Information

Georgetown Convention and Visitors Bureau. 101West Seventh Street, Georgetown 78627-0409; (800) 436-8696 or (512) 930-3545; www.visitgeorgetown.com.

Round Rock Chamber of Commerce. 212 East Main Street, Round Rock 78664; (512) 255-5805; www.roundrockchamber.org.

Burnet

If you mispronounce the name of this city, you'll be corrected by a resident very quickly: It's Burn-it, durn it! The city proclaims itself the Bluebonnet Capital of Texas. The best blooms of the state flower can be found on the rural roads all around Burnet every April, especially near Lake Buchanan.

Want to take the kids fishing? **Lake Buchanan,** 10 miles west of Burnet on Highway 29, has some of the best fishing in the Hill Country, in addition to great swimming and picnic areas. For more information or a list of fishing charter companies, contact the Lake Buchanan Chamber of Commerce at (512) 756-4297.

Historic buildings, some dating back to 1854, surround The Square in the center of town. Most house antiques and arts-and-crafts shops now. If you walk over to the train depot on Jackson Street around noon, you can welcome the Hill Country Flyer steam train, and the kids can watch a staged gunfight.

Fort Croghan Museum (ages 6 and up)

703 Buchanan Drive, on Highway 29, Burnet (512-756-8281; www.fortcroghan.org). Open April through mid-October; Thursday through Saturday 10 a.m. to 5 p.m. Free, donations appreciated.

This restored fort depicts frontier days in Texas with several buildings and more than 1,200 items of pioneer history, from musical instruments to dental instruments.

Commemorative Air Force Museum (ages 6 and up)

At Municipal Airport on U.S. Highway 281, Burnet (512-756-2226; www.highlandlakes squadron.com). Open Wednesday and Saturday 9 a.m. to 4 p.m., Sunday 1 p.m. to 5 p.m. Donations requested.

The Hill Country Squadron of the Commemorative Air Force is stationed at the airport, just south of town. See lots of World War II planes, firearms, photographs, and other memorabilia. The museum is run totally by volunteers, so call to make sure there's someone around when you want to visit.

Longhorn Cavern State Park (ages 6 and up)

On Park Road 4, six miles west of Burnet off Highway 29 (877-441-CAVE; www.longhorn caverns.com). Open daily except Christmas Eve and Christmas, tour schedule variable with season. $$$.

Most of the work on this registered natural landmark was done by the Civilian Conservation Corps during the Depression, and an exhibit honoring the CCC is on display near the visitor center. The cave is unique for the way rushing water, in addition to the usual dissolving water, carved the cavern. Some of the walls are as smooth as glass. The park also has picnic areas, two nature trails, a snack bar, and a gift shop.

Inks Lake State Park (ages 2 and up)

On Park Road 4, adjacent to Longhorn Cavern, Burnet (512-793-2223; www.tpwd.state.tx .us/spdest/findadest/parks/inks/).

So far, 153 caves have been discovered at Colorado Bend State Park.

This is one of the most popular parks in the state, a 1,200-acre panorama of cedar and oak woodlands, wildflowers, and pink granite. The park borders Inks Lake and offers 7 miles of beautiful hiking trails, camping, picnicking, swimming, canoeing, waterskiing, scuba diving, sailing, and fishing. There also are a nine-hole golf course, a playground, and a store for groceries and camping supplies. Deer, turkey, quail, and songbirds are abundant in the park. At dusk, it's common to see small children feeding deer from their hands.

Vanishing Texas River Cruise (ages 4 and up)

At Canyon of the Eagles Nature Park, 16942 Ranch Road 2341, 20 miles north of Texas Highway 29, Burnet (512-756-6986 or 800-474-8374; www.vtrc.com). Tour at 11 a.m. Wednesday through Sunday. $$$.

The Vanishing Texas River Cruise is a true delight. The two-and-a-half-hour tour will take your family through unspoiled wilderness, focusing on bald eagle nesting areas November through March, on wildflowers April through June, and on majestic scenery and wildlife July through October. By the way, Ranch Road 2341 has some of the best wildflower viewing in Texas in spring. Sunset dinner cruises, fall foliage cruises, bald eagle cruises, and customized cruises are also available.

For More Information

Burnet Chamber of Commerce. 229 South Pierce Street, Burnet 78611; (512) 756-4297; www.burnetchamber.org.

Marble Falls, San Saba, and Bend

On Ranch Road 1431 you'll drive by Lake LBJ and Lake Marble Falls, two more of the Highland Lakes chain formed by several dams on the Colorado River in this area of the Hill Country. Fishing is excellent in both, especially bass fishing. Waterskiing and sailing are also popular. Both lakes have several boat docks, marinas, and picnic areas. The land surrounding the lakes is said to be the oldest dry land on Earth.

The Lower Colorado River Authority maintains several lakeside and riverside parks with swimming and picnic areas. Call (512) 473-3200 or (800) 776-5272 for more information.

The pink granite used for the state capitol was quarried from Granite Mountain in Marble Falls. You can see the huge stone dome from a roadside picnic area on Ranch Road 1431 just north of the city. They've been cutting and carrying out granite from this mountain for more than one hundred years, but it hasn't seemed to have made a dent in it.

In San Saba your family can relax at three cooling places. **Reisen Park** is on the banks of the San Saba River east of town on U.S. Highway 190 and has picnic areas beneath large, shady pecan trees. (The city is known for its pecan crop.) **Mill Pond Park,** 5 blocks east of the courthouse, has a spring-fed lake, duck pond, waterfalls, a swimming pool, picnic areas, baseball fields, tennis courts, and a playground. **West Side Neighborhood Park** features a playground and basketball court.

Colorado Bend State Park (ages 4 and up)

6 miles south of Bend; go to Bend on Ranch Road 501 or 580, follow the signs, and take the gravel road out of town south 6 miles to the entrance (325-628-3240; www.tpwd.state .tx.us/spdest/findadest/parks/colorado_bend/).

Near Bend you'll find the most beautiful waterfall in Texas at Colorado Bend State Park.

The park, the most isolated in the Hill Country, includes 6 miles of the Colorado River before it empties into Lake Buchanan, with lots of wildlife, scenery, and solitude. You can camp, hike, fish, mountain bike, or watch the teeming bird life, including bald eagles. Rangers conduct guided tours to Gorman Falls and several caves, areas accessible only by tour.

For More Information

Marble Falls/Lake LBJ Chamber of Commerce. 916 Second Street, Marble Falls 78654; (830) 693-2815; www.marblefalls.org.

City of San Saba. P.O. Box 788, San Saba 76877; (325) 372-5144; www.sansabatexas .com.

Llano, Brady, and Mason

Llano's historic railroad district features a new depot that houses a small railroad museum and Chamber of Commerce Visitor Center.

Brady Lake, with 29 miles of shoreline, offers waterskiing, swimming, camping, and fishing. You'll also find screened shelters and picnic areas. Call (325) 597-3491.

The little town of Mason prides itself on the amount of blue topaz (the state gem) that has been found in the surrounding hills. If your kids love beautiful rocks, they'll love trudging around the brush looking for raw gems. Several area ranches allow rock hounds to search for the state gem on their lands, except during deer season. For a list of participating ranches, call (325) 347-5758.

Heart of Texas Historical Museum (ages 8 and up)

117 North High Street, Brady (325-597-0526). Open Friday and Saturday 1 to 5 p.m., Sunday 1 to 4 p.m. Free.

The imposing old county jail in Brady, in the geographical center of Texas, has been converted into a museum. It displays the typical area historical exhibits as well as jail cells and a gallows.

Texas Trivia

The geographic center of Texas is 15 miles northeast of Brady in northern McCulloch County.

Heart of Texas Country Music Museum (ages 5 and up)

1701 South Bridge Street, Brady (325-597-1895; www.hillbillyhits.com/museum.htm). Open Friday 2 p.m. to 4 p.m., Saturday 10 a.m. to 4 p.m., Sunday noon to 5 p.m. Free.

What a great tribute to country music! This assortment of instruments, costumes, autographs, and memorabilia of the best country music stars began as a private collection and is now in the hands of volunteers of the Heart of Texas Country Music Association. One of the most prized possessions is Texan Jim Reeves' tour bus.

Hill Country Wildlife Museum (ages 4 and up)

826 Ford Street, Llano (325-247-2568; www.llanotx.com/tourism/HillCountryWildlifeMuseum.htm). Open Thursday through Saturday 10 a.m. to 5 p.m. $.

Tucked into an unlikely little storefront on the main highway through town, this museum houses a renowned collection of mounted wildlife animal specimens. Well worth a visit.

Llano County Museum (ages 8 and up)

310 Bessemer, north of Llano River Bridge, Llano (325-247-3026; www.llanotx.com/tourism/LlanoCountyMuseum.htm). Open Wednesday through Saturday 11 a.m. to 5 p.m., Sunday 1 to 5 p.m. Free.

The museum is housed in an old drugstore and gives visitors a glimpse of what the area was like when it was an iron-ore boomtown.

For More Information

Llano Chamber of Commerce. The Railyard Depot, 100 Train Station Drive, Llano 78643; (325) 247-5354; www.llanochamber.org.

Brady Chamber of Commerce. 101 East First Street, Brady 76825; (325) 597-3491; www.bradytx.com.

Mason County Chamber of Commerce. P.O. Box 187, Mason 76856; (325) 347-5758; www.masontxcoc.com.

Fredericksburg and Luckenbach

Fredericksburg is another of those Hill Country towns founded by German immigrants and is well known for its German restaurants and bakeries. The town is so steeped in its heritage that many natives still speak German. You'll notice that Main Street is exceptionally wide. It was built that way by founding families so they could turn wagons around in the middle of the street. More than a hundred top-quality antiques and arts-and-crafts shops, galleries, and boutiques line the street. Fredericksburg has a new, exceptionally nice visitor center with lots of displays and brochures, a 9-minute DVD about the area, and several friendly folks who will help plan your visit and answer questions.

Near Fredericksburg is what may be the most famous small town in Texas: Luckenbach, made famous by Waylon and Willie's hit country/western song. Go 5 miles east on U.S. Highway 290 to Ranch Road 1376 and drive another 5 miles south. I'd tell you to follow the signs, but the Luckenbach signs are often stolen, so remember that if you get to the Grape Creek bridge, you've gone too far. What's left of the town is a general store and dance hall. On Sunday, singers and strummers from the famous to the obscure can often be found performing in the shade by the store near the bust of the late Hondo Crouch, a renowned storyteller who first popularized Luckenbach. Call (830) 997-3224 or visit the Web site www.luckenbachtexas.com.

Wildseed Farms (ages 4 and up)

100 Legacy Drive, 7 miles east of Fredericksburg on US 290 (800-848-0078; www.wildseedfarms.com). Open daily 9:30 a.m. to 6 p.m. Free.

This place is really something to see in the spring, when brilliant red poppies and bluebonnets blanket acres and acres just north of the highway. Walk around at any time of year, and something is always blooming. The owners have set aside special areas where you may take pictures of the family sitting among the flowers. You can shop for seeds, potted flowers, plant tools and accessories in the Pottery and Plant Nursery. Or shop for Texas wines and foods, as well as an enormous selection of gifts at the massive red-cedar-and-limestone Market Center. Grab a bite to eat and a cool drink at the adjacent Blubonnet Biergarten. The 3,000-square-foot Butterfly Haus is home to hundreds of Texas butterflies. Walk among them, enjoy them, and learn about them in a delightful atmosphere. Fun for the whole family.

Old Tunnel Wildlife Management Area (ages 4 and up)

About 11 miles south of Fredericksburgh and 13 miles north of Comfort (866-978-2287; www.tpwd.state.tx.us/huntwild/hunt/wma/find_a_wma/list/?id=17). Open May through October. Call for directions. Viewing from the upper deck free; trail to the lower viewing area $ (Thursday through Sunday).

If you have kids who like bats, they'll enjoy the bat tour at the Old Tunnel Wildlife Management Area. There's an observation deck near the parking lot where you can see hundreds

Texas Trivia

Notice the street names as you pass through Fredericksburg. The first ten streets east of the courthouse—Adams, Llano, Lincoln, Washington, Elk, Lee, Columbus, Olive, Mesquite, and Eagle—spell "All Welcome." And the streets west of the courthouse—Crockett, Orange, Milam, Edison, Bowie, Acorn, Cherry, and Kay—invite you to "Come Back."

of thousands of bats emerging from the Old Tunnel area around dusk. Directions to the area are complicated, so call for details and tour reservations.

Fort Martin Scott (ages 6 and up)

2 miles east of Fredericksburg on US 290 (830-997-9895). Hours vary. Free.

This fort was the first U.S. Army post in Texas, established to protect German settlers from Indians. You can tour the grounds and several buildings now being reconstructed, including the guardhouse, a log cabin, and officers' quarters. The visitor center displays documents and artifacts recovered from the site. Costumed volunteers are often at the fort giving living-history demonstrations.

National Museum of the Pacific War (formerly the Admiral Nimitz Museum) (ages 6 and up)

340 East Main Street, Fredericksburg (830-997-4379; www.nimitz-museum.org). Open daily 9 a.m. to 5 p.m. except Thanksgiving and Christmas. $–$$, children under 6 free.

That steamboat-looking building you see on Main Street is the National Museum of the Pacific War, formerly the Admiral Nimitz Museum. The nine-acre center is a state park honoring Chester Nimitz, a World War II hero who was born here. The park features the restored Nimitz Steamboat Hotel, the Garden of Peace (a gift from Japan), the Plaza of Presidents, a History Walk, and a Memorial Courtyard. There is also a gallery dedicated to former president George H. W. Bush's war service.

Pioneer Museum and Vereins Kirche Museum (ages 6 and up)

Two fine museums are operated by the Gillespie County Historical Society. Pioneer Museum. 325 West Main Street, Fredericksburg. (830-990-8441; www.pioneermuseum.com) open Monday through Saturday 10 a.m. to 5 p.m., Sunday 1 to 5 p.m. $, children 5 and under free. Vereins Kirche. 100 W. Main, center of Marktplatz, Fredericksburg (830-997-7832) open Monday through Saturday 10 a.m. to 4 p.m., $, children 5 and under free.

The Pioneer Museum complex preserves several old buildings, vintage photos, and pioneer artifacts. The adjacent Volunteer Fire Department Museum has items from the earliest days of organized firefighting. Across the street is the Vereins Kirche, a uniquely shaped old church that's now a museum detailing the history of the area.

Texas **Wildflowers**

Texas has more than 5,000 wildflower species. Visitors flock from all over in the spring to see blooming bluebonnets, Indian paintbrush, and Indian blankets coloring the fields blue, red, white, and yellow. But yucca, ocotillos, and cactus also burst forth with colors.

Each region of Texas has its own special places to see the wildflowers, and they are all connected by the state's highway system. In the 1930s, Texas became the first state to develop a plan for beautification of roadsides with flowers and plants. Along the roads are more than 700,000 acres of right-of-way that the Texas Department of Transportation carefully grooms and maintains so that each spring highway medians and roadsides burst into color all around the state. The department plants about 60,000 pounds of wildflower seeds a year along the roadways. In addition, cultivated varieties are planted along highways, like the miles of crape myrtles on U.S. Highway 271 north of Paris.

You can get a **free,** full-color wildflower booklet from any of the Texas Travel Visitor Centers.

Enchanted Rock State Natural Area (ages 4 and up) 

18 miles north of Fredericksburg on Ranch Road 965 (830-685-3636; www.tpwd.state.tx.us/spdest/findadest/parks/enchanted_rock).

Straddling Llano and Gillespie Counties is massive Enchanted Rock. The landscape here is dominated by an immense, smooth pink-granite dome more than one billion years old, the oldest exposed rock in North America. The rock, sacred to Native Americans, is surrounded with legends and was the site of a battle between Texas Rangers and Native Americans. Visitors love walking to the top of the rock, or trying to, but other trails in the park also offer unusual rock formations for sightseeing and photo opportunities. Enchanted Rock has a couple of fissure caves children love to scramble around. The park also has picnic and camping facilities. Be advised to arrive early on weekends between May and October, because rangers close the park once capacity is reached.

Where to Eat

Altdorf Biergarten and Restaurant. 301 West Main Street, Fredericksburg (830-997-7865; www.altdorfbiergarten-fbg.com). Famous German dinners and homemade desserts make this a popular café. $$

Auslander Biergarten and Restaurant. 323 East Main Street, Fredericksburg (830-997-7714; www.theauslander.com). International menu; children's specials. $–$$

Cranky Frank's BBQ. 1679 US 87 South, Fredericksburg (830-997-2353). Great barbecue and all the fixin's. Casual, reasonable prices. $

Where to Stay

Bed-and-breakfast inns are plentiful in the Fredericksburg area, either in town or out in the countryside, and offer a different experience than a motel. **Gasthaus Schmidt Reservation Service** will help you connect with one that suits your family. Call (830) 997-5612 or (866) 427-8374; or visit www.fbglodging.com. $$–$$$

Fredericksburg Inn and Suites. 201 South Washington, Fredericksburg (830-997-0202 or 800-446-0202; www.fredericksburg-inn.com). Comfortable, convenient location; heated pool, picnic tables and grills. $$–$$$

Sunday House Inn. 501 East Main, Fredericksburg (830-997-4484; www.sundayhouseinn.com). In-town location, large rooms, outdoor pool **free** continental breakfast. $$

For More Information

Fredericksburg Convention and Visitors Bureau. 302 East Austin Street, Fredericksburg 78624; (830) 997-6523 or (888) 997-3600; www.fredericksburg-texas.com.

Scenic **Drive**

In springtime when the bluebonnets, coreopsis, Indian blankets and paintbrushes, and wine cups are in bloom, the Willow City Loop is ablaze in blues, yellows, and reds against the most rustic and scenic backgrounds you will find anywhere.

Begin the drive by taking Ranch Road 965 northeast from Enchanted Rock, then turning south onto Highway 16. Go about 5 miles to the Willow City Loop sign and turn east, following the county road to the small village of Willow City, where you turn west onto Ranch Road 1323 and return to Highway 16. If you don't want to make the drive a complete loop, turn east onto Ranch Road 1323 at Willow City, traveling through more scenic hills, past the village of Sandy, until you reach US 281 about 5 miles north of Johnson City.

The narrow, winding back road is extremely popular, so drive carefully and respect private property. Be aware that on weekends during peak blooms, sheriff's deputies patrol the road and ticket every car illegally parked or trespassing flower peepers.

Mountain Home

Y.O. Ranch (ages 4 and up)

15 miles west of Mountain Home on Texas Highway 41 (830-640-3222 or 800-967-2624; www.yoranch.com). Tours by reservation only. $$$$.

The Y.O. Ranch in Mountain Home was founded more than 125 years ago and is still going strong. In addition to longhorn cattle, the ranch is home to fifty-eight exotic species of animals. A tour of the ranch includes visiting a pioneer cabin, an old schoolhouse, and a Wells Fargo office. In addition to the regular tour, the ranch offers overnight guest packages, photo safaris, hiking, mountain biking, and horseback and hayrides.

Hunt

On Highway 39.

Just south of Hunt is a roadside picnic area at a low-water crossing over the Guadalupe River where families seem to gather. The area has several shaded picnic tables, great fishing, and a beautiful series of waterfalls just upriver from the bridge.

Two miles west of Hunt on Farm Road 1340 you'll discover Stonehenge. Well, it's **Stonehenge II,** an exact three-quarter-scale replica of the famous stone circle plopped down in an open field. There are also several Easter Island statue replicas.

Kerrville and Ingram

The **Kerrville Folk Festival** is held at Quiet Valley Ranch, 9 miles south of Kerrville on Highway 16. The event features more than twenty straight days of the best music from singer-songwriters and folklife activities at the end of May and the first week of June. There's a special children's area with music just for kids. Most visitors camp out on the grounds, since impromptu performances occur regularly around almost every campfire. Call (830) 257-3600; www.kerrvillefolkfestival.com.

The city also hosts the official **Texas State Arts and Crafts Fair** at the end of May, the largest and best such event in the state. Call (830) 896-5711; www.tacef.com/.

Museum of Western Art (ages 6 and up)

1550 Bandera Highway, Kerrville (830-896-2553; www.museumofwesternart.org). Open Tuesday through Saturday 9 a.m. to 5 p.m. $–$$, children 8 and under free.

The Museum of Western Art has an international reputation for collecting the best in contemporary and classic western paintings and sculpture. The museum features special shows, traveling exhibits, and workshops. There's a Journey West Children's Gallery that's great fun. The grounds and building are as beautiful as the art, and the museum store is first-rate.

Riverside Nature Center (ages 4 and up)

150 Francisco Lemos Street, Kerrville (830-257-4837; www.riversidenaturecenter.org). Visitor center open Monday through Friday 9 a.m. to 4 p.m., Saturday and Sunday 10 a.m. to 3 p.m. Self-guided trails open daily dawn to dusk. Free.

The Riverside Nature Center has special programs for children, blending cultural history with the area's natural history. The center includes a wildflower meadow, walking paths, and butterfly gardens.

Kerrville-Schreiner Park (ages 4 and up)

2385 Bandera Highway, Kerrville (830-257-5392). $.

Kerrville-Schreiner Park is nestled on the cypress-shaded, sloping banks of the Guadalupe River. The 517-acre park has ample opportunities to view wildlife up close and offers campsites, shelters, picnic tables, and hiking trails.

Hill Country Arts Foundation (ages 6 and up)

507 West Highway 39, Ingram (830-367-5121 or 800-459-4223; www.hcaf.com). Gallery admission is free. Performance tickets vary with event.

The Hill Country Arts Foundation is a combination of operations: the **Alice Naylor Art Library,** full of information on art instruction and history; the **Duncan-McAshan Visual Arts Center,** with exhibition space for fine arts and a regular schedule of workshops; and the **Smith-Ritch Point Theatre,** which has two venues for the performing arts. Summer plays such as Peter Pan are geared for children. And it's all tucked away on the banks of the scenic Guadalupe River.

Where to Eat

Cracker Barrel Old Country Store. 2110 Sidney Baker Boulevard, Kerrville (830-896-7808; www.crackerbarrel.com). A nice variety of country cooking, huge gift shop in lobby. $–$$

Mamacita's Restaurant and Cantina. 215 Junction Highway, Kerrville (830-895-2441; http://mamacitas.com/). Good Mexican food in a fun setting. Watch folks make flour tortillas and watch "Davy Crockett" sing Happy Birthday on cue. $–$$

Where to Stay

Inn of the Hills. 1001 Junction Highway, Kerrville (830-895-5000 or 800-292-5690; www.innofthehills.com). Play tennis, putt some golf balls, swim in one of two indoor or three outdoor pools, work out in the gym, play racquetball or basketball, or take a hike. Some rooms overlook the Guadalupe River. $$–$$$

Y.O. Ranch Resort Hotel. 2033 Sidney Baker Boulevard, Kerrville (830-257-4440 or 877-YO-RESORT; www.yoresort.com). Kid-friendly hotel with bunk beds, video games, pool, free high-speed Internet access. $$–$$$

For More Information

Kerrville Convention and Visitors Bureau. 2108 Sidney Baker Street, Kerrville 78028; (800) 221-7958 or (830) 792-3535; www.kerrvilletexascvb.com.

Medina, Vanderpool, and Concan

The Apple Store (ages 6 and up)

Main Street (Highway 16), Medina (800-449-0882; www.lovecreekorchards.com). Open Monday through Saturday 9 a.m. to 5 p.m. and Sunday 10 a.m. to 5 p.m.

Medina bills itself as the Apple Capital of Texas and celebrates the harvest with special events in the summer and fall. The store offers a huge variety of apple gifts and goodies from baked goods to apple coffee and the popular apple ice cream. The Patio Cafe serves great burgers and sandwiches, and yummy apple desserts, for lunch.

Lost Maples State Natural Area (ages 4 and up)

5 miles north of Vanderpool on Ranch Road 187, Vanderpool (830-966-3413, www.tpwd.state.tx.us/spdest/findadest/parks/lost_maples).

Just north of Vanderpool, hidden in a remote canyon, hides a fall color display that rivals any found in New England. If the weather has been kind, bigtooth maples at Lost Maples blaze red, yellow, and orange and attract thousands of Texans in late October and early November. It's still a fairly obscure park, however. Lost Maples is great at other times of the year, too. Its 10 miles of hiking trails are mostly shaded, and you can cool off in a nice small lake. The park has camping and picnic facilities, an interpretive center, a gift shop, and rewarding bird-watching in the spring.

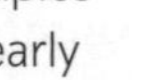

Garner State Park (ages 4 and up)

234 Ranch Road 1050, 7 miles north of Concan off US Highway 83(830-232-6132; www.tpwd.state.tx.us/spdest/findadest/parks/garner/).

Garner State Park is so popular among Texans that B.J. Thomas wrote a popular rock song about it in the sixties. Generation after generation of folks return so often that the park is a family tradition among many. Your family can admire the scenic Hill Country; splash in the sparkling cool Frio River; canoe; hike; mountain bike; camp; picnic; relax in the shade of cypress, elm, oak, or pecan trees; or stay in rustic cabins built by the Civilian Conservation Corps in the 1930s. The park also has an eighteen-hole miniature golf course and a store.

Lone Star Motorcycle Museum (ages 4 and up)

4 miles north of Vanderpool on Ranch Road 187 (830-966-6103; www.lonestarmotorcyclemuseum.com). Open Friday through Sunday 10 a.m. to 5 p.m. $.

The museum exhibits a collection of motorcycles from around the world, mostly British and early American machines dating from the early 1900s. A small cafe in the back offers Australian meat pies, gourmet burgers, and homemade desserts from 11 a.m. to 3 p.m. (admission fee not required to access café only).

Scenic **Drive**

Ranch Road 337 is an attraction in itself. This stretch of road between Medina and Camp Wood is one of the most scenic highways in the state, rolling over spectacular, pristine Hill Country and through secluded valleys. The hills are higher and steeper than in the rest of the area, the towns smaller, the traffic very light.

For a lovely scenic loop, start in Bandera going west on Highway 16 to Medina, then west on Ranch Road 337 to Vanderpool, south on Ranch Road 187 to the junction with Ranch Road 470 just north of Utopia. Turn east and return to Bandera. This is also a convenient route if you wish to visit either Lost Maples State Natural Area or Hill Country State Natural Area.

Bandera

Bandera calls itself the "Cowboy Capital of the World" with good reason: It was the staging area for the great cattle drives of the late 1800s, many champion rodeo cowboys call the city home, and dozens of dude ranches surround the city. For a list of which ranches are operating guest facilities, contact the **Bandera Visitors Center** (830-796-3045 or 800-364-3833; www.banderacowboycapital.com). Rates run moderate to high and usually include some if not all meals, horseback riding, hayrides, hiking trails, and sometimes pools.

Frontier Times Museum (ages 6 and up)

510 Thirteenth Street, Bandera (830-796-3864; www.frontiertimesmuseum.org). Open Monday through Saturday 10 a.m. to 4:30 p.m., $, children under 6 free.

This rustic building, once the editorial offices of *Frontier Times* magazine, now houses hundreds of western artifacts, art and antiques, Native American items, and Wild West Show posters.

Hill Country State Natural Area (ages 4 and up)

10 miles west of Bandera at 10600 Bandera Creek Road (830-796-4413; www.tpwd.state.tx.us/spdest/findadest/parks/hill_country).

Hill Country State Natural Area is a 5,369-acre park maintained in its primitive state. You'll find a number of equestrian, hiking, and mountain-bike trails over rugged Hill Country. Through a local ranch, the park also occasionally offers guided horseback tours.

The Camel Experiment

Camels used to be seen all over Texas in the mid-1800s, thanks to then Secretary of War Jefferson Davis. Davis talked Congress out of $30,000 so the Army could determine if camels would be better than mules as beasts of burden in the desolate areas of the western states. The camel training headquarters was at Camp Verde, Texas, and before the Civil War camel caravans went west from there through the Big Bend of Texas all the way to California.

Although the camels proved to be a success, the experiment was never reactivated after the Civil War, probably because the idea had been the brainchild of Davis, who served as president of the Confederacy. The camels were subsequently abandoned by soldiers, and many were sighted roaming the Texas hills and deserts until well into the 1920s.

Camp Verde was destroyed by a fire in 1919, but the foundation of the post remains near the current Camp Verde General Store, about 16 miles north of Bandera on Highway 173.

Boerne and Comfort

Located at the junction of Highway 46 and I–10, Boerne is another town settled by German pioneers, Boerne (pronounced *Bur-nee*) has a downtown area full of quaint shops, restaurants, and historic buildings and offers more than enough outdoor activities for anyone. About 15 miles west of Boerne at the junction of Texas Highway 27 off I-10 is Comfort, yet another village settled by German immigrants. Its downtown area is full of historic buildings, antique shops, and eateries.

Agricultural Heritage Center and Cibolo Nature Center (ages 4 and up)

In City Park on Highway 46, Boerne (830-249-6007, www.agmuseum.org; 830-249-4616, www.cibolo.org). Hours vary. Blacksmith demonstrations on Saturday. Free.

The Agricultural Heritage Center and Cibolo Nature Center combine education and recreation. The heritage center includes indoor and outdoor exhibits of antique farm machinery and implements and an operating blacksmith shop. The nature trail covers a sixty-five-acre greenbelt that crosses three distinct ecosystems within the town.

Cascade Caverns (ages 6 and up)

226 Cascade Caverns Road, Boerne (830-755-8080; www.cascadecaverns.com). Take exit 543 off I–10, then follow the signs. Open daily10 a.m. to 5 p.m. Memorial Day to Labor Day. Open 10 a.m. to 4 p.m. from Labor Day to Memorial Day. Tours leave every thirty minutes. $$–$$$.

At the end of the one-hour tour of Cascade Caverns, your family will see the 90-foot underground waterfall that gives the cavern its name. The cave has many large rooms, crystal pools, and growing formations. Above ground are a swimming pool, camping facilities, a store, and a dance hall.

Cave Without a Name (ages 6 and up)

325 Kreutzberg Road, Boerne (830-537-4212 or 888-TEX-CAVE; www.cavewithoutaname.com). Summer hours 9 a.m. to 6 p.m. daily; winter hours 10 a.m. to 5 p.m. $$–$$$, children under 6 free.

Cave Without a Name can be difficult to find, but it's worth it. Travel northeast on Farm Road 474, go right on Kreutzberg Road for about 4.5 miles, then follow the signs. The huge cave system has some beautiful formations and is said to be 98 percent active—meaning the formations are still growing. The hour-long tour visits six magnificent underground rooms.

Guadalupe River State Park and Honey Creek State Natural Area (ages 4 and up)

3350 Park Road 31, Spring Branch (830-438-2656, www.tpwd.state.tx.us/spdest/findadest/parks/guadalupe_river).

Bisected by the river from which it takes its name, the park is noted for its rugged beauty. You can enjoy hiking, swimming, canoeing, tubing, fishing, picnicking, camping, or watching wildlife. Adjacent is Honey Creek State Natural Area, a park kept so primitive that the public is allowed in only once a week, on Saturday, on **free** guided tours. The 9 a.m. tour passes through Honey Creek Canyon, a true wilderness.

Where to Eat

The Hungry Horse. 109 South Saunders Street, Boerne (830-816-8989). Huge variety of choices from salads and burgers to full meals and most everything comes in small, medium, or large portions. $–$$

Po Po Family Restaurant. At exit 533 off I–10, Welfare (830-537-4194). Between Boerne and Comfort, this is one of the nicest kid-friendly restaurants in the region. Admire the more than 2,000 commemorative plates covering the walls. The "Texas Tradition since 1929" serves comfort food like fried chicken and meatloaf. Often has all-you-can-eat dinner specials. $$

Where to Stay

America's Best Value Inn. 35150 I–10, Boerne (830-249-9791). Conveniently located, outdoor pool, **free** continental breakfast, children 12 and under stay **free.** $$

Meyer Bed and Breakfast. 845 High Street, Comfort (830-995-2304 or 888-995-6100). Extensively remodeled units, most dating back to the late 1800s when this was a stagecoach stop. Some units are large enough to house a large family; two have kitchenettes. Swim in the oversized pool or fish in Cypress Creek, just a stone's throw from the lodge. Includes full breakfast. $–$$

For More Information

Boerne Convention and Visitors Bureau. Visitor Center 1407 South Main Street, Boerne 78006; (830) 249-7277 or (888) 842-8080; www.visitboerne.org.

Comfort Chamber of Commerce. 630 Highway 27, Comfort 78013; (830) 995-3131; www.comfort-texas.com.

Blanco

On US 281, south of Johnson City.

Blanco's restored courthouse on the town square is now open as a visitor center and gift shop. On the third Saturday of each month from April through November, dozens of vendors set up around the Courthouse Square for the city's **Market Day.** On streets surrounding the square you'll discover antiques and arts and crafts shops and restaurants. By the way, the city and the river are pronounced *Blank-oh* by locals.

Blanco State Park (ages 4 and up)

US 281, at the Blanco River, Blanco (830-833-4333; www.tpwd.state.tx.us/spdest/findadest/parks/blanco).

Blanco State Park is an unpretentious little park offering great fishing (rainbow trout, perch, catfish, and bass), swimming, hiking trails, camping, and picnic facilities.

Texas **Snacks**

The most popular snack foods in Texas:

- Frito pie
- Peanuts in Dr Pepper
- Beef jerky
- Jalapeños (fresh or pickled)
- Corn dogs

Frito pies are simple to make. You tear open a bag of corn chips, pour in some chili, sprinkle chopped onions and shredded cheese on top, and eat it straight from the bag. Some restaurants now serve this concoction in a bowl, but in-the-bag is the only true Texan way.

Where to Eat

Blanco Bowling Club. 310 Fourth Street, Blanco (830-833-4416). You can bowl here, but the BBC is best known for its good eats. Home cooked food and some of the best pies in the Hill Country. $–$$

Johnson City and Stonewall

Johnson City was home to President Lyndon B. Johnson, and several parks in the area honor the former president. The downtown area has also been recently rejuvenated with boutiques, antiques shops, and restaurants.

Lyndon B. Johnson National Historical Park (ages 6 and up)

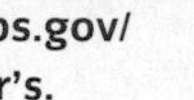

100 Lady Bird Lane, 2 blocks south of US 290, Johnson City (830-868-7128; www.nps.gov/lyjo/). Open daily 8:45 a.m. to 5 p.m. except Thanksgiving, Christmas and New Year's. Free.

The park has an impressive visitor center, complete with an audiovisual program and a full bookstore and gift shop. Across the street is LBJ's boyhood home, furnished with Johnson family household items and period furniture. Connected by a footpath is the nearby Old Johnson Settlement, a ranch complex owned by LBJ's grandfather and great uncle. Many of the old buildings have been restored.

Lyndon B. Johnson State and National Historical Park (ages 4 and up)

On Park Road 52, Stonewall (830-644-2252; www.tpwd.state.tx.us/park/lbj/lbj.htm). Visitor center open 8 a.m. to 5 p.m. Free.

This park has several distinct areas, all along or near US 290 between Johnson City and Stonewall. Ranger-guided bus tours of the LBJ Ranch ($–$$), just across the Pedernales (LBJ pronounced it *Purrrr-din-alice*) River from the state park area, depart from the visitor center 10 a.m. to 4 p.m. daily. The center features exhibits on Lyndon Johnson and on the history and wildlife of the Hill Country. A nature trail winds past wildlife enclosures with buffalo, deer, turkey, and longhorn cattle, and through beautiful wildflower fields. LBJ's gravesite is also located here.

In addition, the state park facility caters to families by providing tennis courts, a swimming pool, picnic areas, a baseball field, and fishing opportunities along the Pedernales.

Also part of the park is the Sauer-Beckmann Living History Farm, a place children love. Costumed interpreters carry out the day-to-day activities of a typical turn-of-the-twentieth-century Hill Country farm. Kids can see the hogs get slopped, the livestock fed, eggs collected, butter churned, and cheese made. They might see a farmer plowing the garden with a team of horses or catch a meal being made from scratch.

Pedernales Falls State Park (ages 4 and up)

6 miles north of US 290 off Farm Road 3232, Johnson City (830-868-7304, www.tpwd.state .tx.us/spdest/findadest/parks/pedernales_falls).

More than 20 miles of meandering trails and a wide, gently rolling waterfall make Pedernales Falls State Park a nice getaway place. Your family can have a picnic or camp out; fish, swim, or canoe the river; and hike or bike along challenging or easy trails. During wet springs, the falls are truly impressive. During drier months, kids scramble around the rocks separating the pools. Get to the park from Farm Road 2766 about 9 miles south of US 281 in Johnson City or from Farm Road 3232 about 6 miles north of US 290 between Johnson City and Dripping Springs.

Bee Cave

On Highway 71, west of Austin.

Two beautiful examples of collapsed grottoes can be found about 18 miles west of the small community of Bee Cave. Your kids can enjoy themselves swimming and hiking at one and go on a scenic informative walk at the other.

Hamilton Pool Nature Preserve (ages 4 and up)

On Farm Road 3238, 13 miles south of Highway 71 (830-264-2740). Open 9 a.m. to 6:30 p.m. daily. $$.

Gorgeous Hamilton Pool Preserve has been a popular swimming hole with Hill Country residents for many decades. Its 60-foot travertine waterfall spills into a deep jade-green pool. The park has picnic areas and a nice nature trail that follows Hamilton Creek through a heavily wooded canyon to the Pedernales River. Rangers close the park when the parking lot is full, so plan on arriving early on weekends during hot weather.

West Cave Preserve (ages 4 and up)

On Farm Road 3238, 1 mile from Hamilton Pool, first gate on the right after crossing Pedernales River (830-825-3442; www.westcave.org). Tours at 10 a.m., noon, 2 p.m., and 4 p.m. weekends only. $.

If you think Hamilton Pool is lovely, and it is, wait until you see the exquisite West Cave Preserve. This private thirty-acre natural preserve is home to many rare and endangered plants and birds, so access is by guided tour only. The tour crosses a grassland savanna with wildflower meadows and stands of ashe juniper, then descends sharply into a narrow, riverine canyon to the collapsed grotto and cave at the end of the tour. The travertine waterfall into the crystal-clear pool surrounded by ferns is one of the most spectacular yet rarely seen sights in Texas. Tour groups are limited to thirty people, and no reservations are taken.

Where to Eat and Stay

For restaurants and lodgings see listings under Austin.

Coastal Plains

All Texans pride themselves on their friendliness and informality, but coastal Texans crank those traits up a few notches. If you want laid-back times, the Texas coast is where to find them. Pirates used to love this place, especially the famous Jean Lafitte, who, legends say, buried treasure around Galveston. Today, most of the gold found along the coast comes from fishing or tourism.

U.S. Highways 77 and 59 and I–37 are the main thoroughfares in this region. US 77 is the only way to get from the South Padre Island area to North Padre Island by car, but it doesn't come very close to the coast. You should also be warned that the stretch of US 77 through Kenedy County is very long, with no facilities of any kind, so fill up both your car and your kids before you set out. The road that most closely connects with the coast itself is Highway 35, a worthy scenic attraction in its own right, especially if you wander off on the many farm roads that snake out to coastal towns. This is a route that demands that you take your time. Highway 35 is also the only road that will take you all the way from the Corpus Christi area directly to the Galveston area.

Port Isabel

About 25 miles east of Brownsville on Highway 48.

Port Isabel, a small, picturesque village on the Laguna Madre, the body of water between the Texas mainland and South Padre Island, is a distinctly seaside community where marinas abound and the sport fishing is spectacular.

Port Isabel Lighthouse State Historic Site (ages 4 and up)

421 East Queen Isabella Boulevard, at the causeway, Port Isabel (956-943-2262; www.tpwd.state.tx.us/spdest/findadest/parks/port_isabel_lighthouse). Summer hours: Sunday through Thursday 10 a.m. to 6 p.m., Friday and Saturday 11 a.m. to 8 p.m. Winter hours: daily 9 a.m. to 5 p.m. $.

COASTAL PLAINS

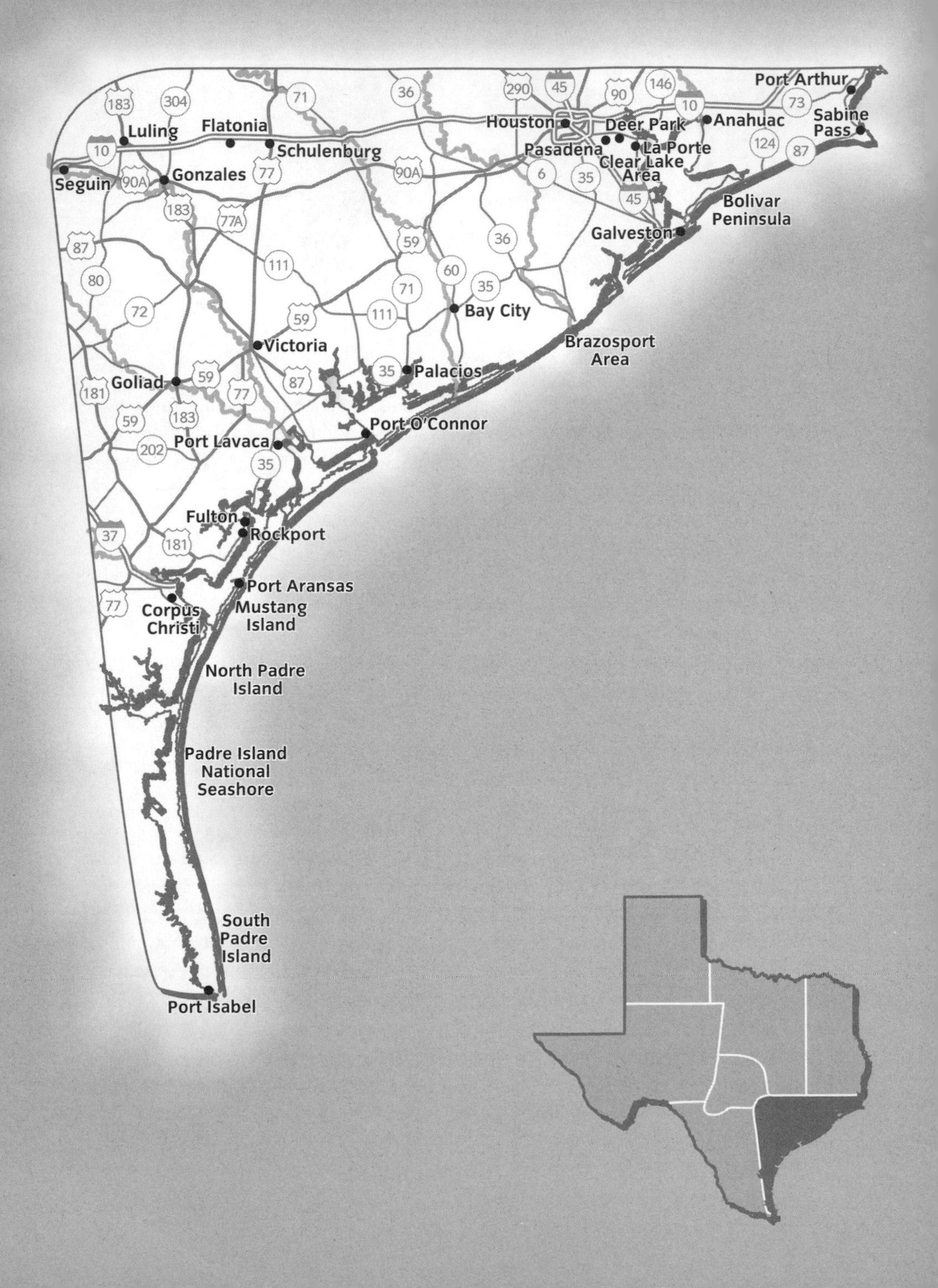

TopAnnualEvents in the Coastal Plains

- **Houston Livestock Show and Rodeo,** Houston, March (832-667-1000; www.hlsr.com)
- **Houston International Festival,** Houston, April (713-654-8808; www.ifest.org)
- **Texas Crab Festival,** Crystal Beach, May (409-684-5940)
- **Luling Watermelon Thump,** Luling, June (830-875-3214; www.watermelonthump.com)
- **Rockport Art Festival,** Rockport, July (361-729-5519)
- **Buccaneer Days,** Corpus Christi, April-May (361-882-3242; www.bucdays.com)
- **Pasadena Livestock Show and Rodeo,** Pasadena, October (281-487-0240; www.pasadenarodeo.com)
- **Bayfest,** Corpus Christi, September (361-887-0868; www.bayfesttexas.com)
- **Czhilispiel,** Flatonia, October (361-865-3920; www.czhilispielfestival.com)
- **Dickens on the Strand,** Galveston, December (409-765-7834; www.dickensonthestrand.org

Port Isabel is at the southernmost end of the Texas coast. You can see one of the few remaining lighthouses in the state here. Built in 1853, the lighthouse was used until 1905. You can climb the stairs inside for a panoramic view of the Coastal Plains. It's also a great place for photos of the kids.

Laguna Atascosa National Wildlife Refuge

At the intersection of Farm Roads 106 and 1847, Port Isabel (956-748-3607; www.fws.gov/southwest/refuges/texas/laguna.html). Visitor center open 10 a.m. to 4 p.m. daily October through April, on weekends in May. Closed June through September.

North of Port Isabel, on the shores of the Laguna Madre, is the Laguna Atascosa National Wildlife Refuge. The refuge includes 46,000 acres of habitat for wintering waterfowl and many area birds and mammals. You can walk or drive over several routes. The visitor center has exhibits, lists, and picnic areas.

Within the boundaries of Laguna Atascosa is **Adolph Thomas Jr. County Park,** which offers fishing piers, a boat ramp, picnic areas, a playground, a nature trail, and RV sites.

The Texas **Coast**

From Port Isabel to Sabine Pass, the coast curves gently for 367 miles (624 if you count the bay areas), its many cities hiding behind barrier islands.

With such a large coast, Texas is frequently hit by hurricanes, a fact you should be aware of if you travel between June and November. One of the largest hurricanes ever to hit the state in recorded history was the Great Storm of 1900 that killed 6,000 people and nearly destroyed all of Galveston. Houston took advantage of its neighbor's misfortune and built itself a giant ship channel and more oil refineries than you can count to turn itself into the nation's fourth largest city, a metropolitan area with roughly two million people.

South Padre Island

Connecting the mainland to South Padre Island is the Queen Isabella Causeway. At 2.6 miles long, this is Texas's longest bridge, and it offers a breathtaking view.

South Padre Island is a mecca for tourists year-round, although it hits its peak in late spring and summer. Your family can do it all here: bask in the sun, dive, swim, boat, sail, parasail, fish, ride horses, or frolic with dolphins.

The island is at the tropical tip of Texas, with the tranquil waters of Laguna Madre Bay on the west side and the vast beauty of the Gulf of Mexico on the east side. South Padre has 34 miles of white-sand beaches, windswept dunes, and balmy weather. And it's close to both Brownsville and Mexico.

An exciting event, certain to delight children, is the **South Padre Island Windsurfing Blowout,** held in early May. The waters are filled with colorful windsurfers ripping across waves and flying in the wind. Call (800) 767-2373 for details and schedule information.

You might want to avoid South Padre during spring break in March, when thousands upon thousands of college students descend on the area, turning the beaches into one giant party.

Island Equestrian Center (ages 8 and up)

On South Padre Boulevard, 1 mile north of the Convention Center, South Padre Island (800-761-HOSS; www.horsesonthebeach.com). Prices vary by activity.

One way your children are certain to enjoy the beaches of South Padre Island is trotting over them on horseback. The Island Equestrian Center has horses available for all levels and ages of riders, including pony rides for kids under six. The company offers guides and instruction at no extra cost. You can also enjoy carriage rides and hayrides.

Schlitterbahn Beach (ages 4 and up)

33261 Park Road 100, South Padre Island (956-772-7873; www.schlitterbahn.com/spi). Open daily during the summer, on weekends spring and fall, hours vary. $$$$.

Schlitterbahn, which runs the country's largest water park in New Braunfels, expanded to South Padre Island, with sixty-five acres of cool water fun including miles of tubing adventures, a surfing pool, playgrounds, and even an uphill water coaster. For toddlers there's the Kiddie Corner, a shaded water play area with pint-size slides and spray fountains.

Where to Eat

Dirty Al's. One Padre Boulevard, South Padre Island (956-761-4901). Local favorite for good food and reasonable prices. Try the fried shrimp or fish tacos. $$–$$$

Palmetto Inn. 1817 Padre Boulevard, South Padre Island (956-761-4325; www.palmettoinnspi.com). Authentic Mexican food since 1945. $$

Where to Stay

Accommodations are plentiful around South Padre Island. Smart families opt for a condo, giving them plenty of living space and the option of cooking many or all of their own meals. Prices range from very affordable to very expensive.

On the gulf side check out:

La Playa. 2308 Gulf Boulevard, South Padre Island (956-761-3361 or 800-426-6530).

Tiki Condominiums. 6608 Padre Boulevard, South Padre Island (800-551-8454 or 956-761-2694; www.thetiki.com).

On the Laguna Madre side, check out:

Las Brisas. 227 West Morningside Boulevard, South Padre Island (800-241-5111 or 866-861-5111).

Sunset on the Bay. 5101 Padre Boulevard, South Padre Island (956-761-1399).

For More Information

South Padre Island Convention and Visitors Bureau. 7355 Padre Boulevard, South Padre Island 78597; (800) SO-PADRE; www.sopadre.com.

Corpus Christi and North Padre Island

At the intersections of US 77 and I–37.

Almost in the center of the Texas Gulf Coast, Corpus Christi is a major deepwater port and one of the state's most popular coastal playgrounds. The bracing salt air blankets the city, begging for travelers to slow down and relax and enjoy themselves. Texans usually refer to the town by its first name, and Corpus has a lot to offer visitors, from first-rate museums to some great recreational areas. Each September, a huge family event called **Bayfest** takes over the city. The festival includes an expansive arts-and-crafts show, fireworks, parades on city streets and on the water, a sailboat regatta, and other boat races. Call (361) 887-0868 or visit www.bayfesttexas.com/ for more information.

Bayfront Arts and Science Park (ages 4 and up)

1900 Shoreline Drive, Corpus Christi.

The heart of the city of Corpus Christi can be found in and around the Bayfront Arts and Science Park complex. The **Water Garden** here is a cooling, soothing circle of more than one hundred fountains that are lighted at night. Included in the Bayfront complex are the following attractions:

- The **Art Museum of South Texas** (361-825-3500; www.artmuseumofsouthtexas.org/) features the work of many area artists and has rotating exhibits. Open Tuesday through Saturday 10 a.m. to 5 p.m., Sunday 1 to 5 p.m. $–$$, children under 12 **free.**
- The **Selena Auditorium** in the American Bank Center (361-826-4100; http://americanbankcenter.com/auditorium/) is home to concerts, musicals, and other shows. Times and prices of shows vary.
- The **Corpus Christi Museum of Science and History** (361-826-4650; www.ccmuseum.com/) houses the natural history of the area, including artifacts from sixteenth-century shipwrecks, a live reptile exhibit, and interactive hurricane displays. Open Tuesday through Saturday 10 a.m. to 5 p.m., Sunday noon to 5 p.m. Closed holidays. $$–$$$, children under 5 **free.**
- **Harbor Playhouse** (361-888-7469) has children's shows, summer melodramas, and other theater works throughout the year. $$–$$$.
- **Heritage Park** (361-826-3410) features eight restored century-old homes and a multicultural center with changing exhibits focusing on the city's heritage. **Free.**

Texas State Aquarium (ages 2 and up)

2710 North Shoreline Boulevard, Corpus Christi (361-881-1200 or 800-477-GULF; http://texasstateaquarium.org/). Open daily 9 a.m. to 6 p.m. March 1 through Labor Day, 9 a.m. to 5 p.m. Labor Day through March 1. $$–$$$, children 2 and under free.

The Texas State Aquarium is one way to explore the depths of the Gulf of Mexico without getting your feet wet. Kids and adults will learn about more than 250 species of marine life and the beauty of a coral reef at this facility. Also featured are a rare river otter family and a shark "touch tank" where children can get a feel for this fascinating creature. The aquarium is located on Corpus Christi Beach, across the channel from the Bayfront Arts and Science Park and next to the USS *Lexington*.

USS *Lexington* Museum (ages 6 and up)

2914 North Shoreline Boulevard, Corpus Christi (800-LADY-LEX; www.usslexington.com). Open daily 9 a.m. to 6 p.m. Memorial Day through Labor Day and 9 a.m. to 5 p.m. Labor Day through Memorial Day. $$–$$$, children 3 and under free.

Texas **Weather**

You'll hear Texans often saying that if you don't like the current weather, wait a few minutes and it'll change. Don't believe them. In general, Texas weather is remarkably consistent, even though it varies considerably from north to south because of the size of the state. Temperatures range from a summer mean of 78 degrees and a winter mean of 40 degrees in the Panhandle to 84 degrees and 61 degrees, respectively, in the Lower Rio Grande Valley. Average annual rainfall varies widely across the state, from 59 inches in East Texas to less than 8 inches in West Texas. Only in deep winter can you expect drastic, sudden changes of weather, when what Texans call a "blue norther" blows in on an Arctic front and can drop temperatures 40 degrees in a few minutes.

Texas weather can be violent. An average of 126 tornadoes strike Texas every year (the most of any state), usually from March to May. Also, hurricanes spawn many tornadoes (like the record number of 115 tornadoes that swirled into life with Hurricane Beulah in 1967). Hurricane season is June to November, when you should pay close attention to weather reports if you're traveling along the coast.

The USS *Lexington* Museum is a fascinating tour for any family. Decommissioned in 1991, this old aircraft carrier is steeped in history; it served longer than any other U.S. Navy carrier. Self-guided tours cover most of the ship, including the bridge, the engine room, and the flight deck full of vintage planes. Several maritime exhibits and multimedia programs are also on display, as well as new virtual battle stations with interactive video.

The Selena Museum (ages 8 and up)

5410 Leopard Street, Corpus Christi (361-289-9013; www.q-productions.com/museum.html). Open Monday through Friday 10 a.m. to 12 p.m. and 1 p.m. to 4 p.m. $.

After famed Tejano music star Selena's death, her fans flocked to her native Corpus Christi. Her father, Arthur Quintanilla, opened a museum in her memory at his Q Productions recording studio. You can see outfits Selena wore at concerts and award shows, her Porsche, and other personal memorabilia.

Dolphin Connection (ages 4 and up)

Ingleside on the Bay (361-776-2887; www.dolphin-connection.org/). $$$.

Take a trip into the bay on the Dolphin Connection to watch dolphins in their natural habitat. The boat ride even allows children to feed the cavorting cetaceans. Call well in advance for required reservations.

Flagship Paddle Wheeler (ages 4 and up)

Peoples Street Pier, Slip 49, Corpus Christi (361-884-8306; www.captclarksflagship.com). $–$$, children 3 and under free.

Another enjoyable boat ride is on the paddle wheeler *Flagship*. The boat takes you on hour-long, narrated cruises of the bay and harbor. Evening trips last an hour and a half. Call for schedule.

Playland at the Beach (ages 6 and up)

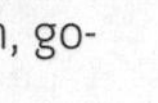

3001 Seagull Boulevard, Corpus Christi (361-884-7251). Open as weather permits, April through October. Prices vary by activity.

Playland at the Beach is an outdoor family park featuring a playground, game room, go-carts, and bumper boats.

Padre Island National Seashore (ages 4 and up)

South of Corpus Christi at the end of Park Road 22 (361-949-8068; www.nps.gov/pais/). Visitor center open 9 a.m. to 5 p.m. $$$.

This 110-mile-long island is one of the last natural seashores in the United States. The tip of the island is developed, but the remainder is a preserve accessible only by four-wheel-drive vehicles or very long hikes. Several beach condos rent four-wheelers. North Padre is a beachcomber's paradise, and the National Park Service will allow your kids to collect seashells, driftwood, and glass floats (from as far away as Portugal or Asia), but not artifacts like flint points or antique coins. The visitor center has information, exhibits, gifts, concessions, a bathhouse, and a picnic area. Although North Padre and South Padre islands are separated by only a narrow channel of water, the two are unconnected by bridge or ferry service, and visitors cannot get to one from the other.

Texas Trivia

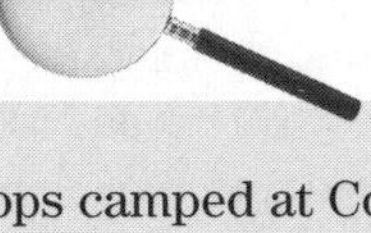

In 1845 General Zachary Taylor and his troops camped at Corpus Christi before marching off to fight in the Mexican War. Among the troops were future Civil War generals Robert E. Lee and Albert Sydney Johnston, future president of the Confederacy Jefferson Davis, and future U.S. President Ulysses S. Grant. The troops put on a performance of *Othello*. Grant, wearing a skirt and carrying a fan, played Desdemona.

Where to Eat

Cracker Barrel. 4229 South Padre Island Drive, Corpus Christi (361-855-1778; www.crackerbarrel.com). A favorite country-style restaurant that offers a varied menu. $–$$

Golden Corral. 1921 South Padre Island Drive, Corpus Christi (361-814-7300). It's difficult to beat all-you-can-eat good food. Special kids' desserts. $–$$

Landry's. 600 North Shoreline Drive, Corpus Christi (361-882-6666; www.landrysrestaurants.com). Well known throughout Texas as the place to go for seafood. Many entrees can be ordered either baked, blackened, fried, or grilled. Children's plates available. $$–$$$

Where to Stay

La Quinta Inn South. 6225 South Padre Island Drive, Corpus Christi (361-991-5730 or 800-527-1133; www.laquinta.com). Pool, **free** high-speed Internet access, **free** breakfast, and children under eighteen stay **free.** $$–$$$

Holiday Inn Emerald Beach. 1102 South Shoreline Boulevard, Corpus Christi (361-883-5731 or 800-HOLIDAY; www.holidayinn.com). On the beach, indoor pool, kids eat **free.** $$$

Best Western Marina Grand. 300 North Shoreline Boulevard, Corpus Christi (361-883-5111; www.marinagrandhotel.net/). Newly renovagted large full-service hotel overlooking Corpus Christi Bay. No smoking, **free** breakfast, high-speed Internet, outdoor pool, fitness center, children 17 and under **free.** $$$

For More Information

Corpus Christi Information Center. 1823 North Chaparral, Corpus Christi 78401; (800) 766-BEACH; www.corpuschristi-tx-cvb.org.

Port Aransas

If your kids can't catch fish in Port Aransas, they just aren't trying. The Aransas Pass area advertises itself as the place "where they bite every day," and that's no exaggeration. You can fish **free** from the beaches, the jetties, and four lighted piers; you can hire a boat for bay fishing; or hop on a group charter boat for deep-sea fishing. Play on the 18 miles of uncrowded beaches, make sand castles, rent a kayak or enjoy other water sports. The town is also full of curio shops, boutiques, and restaurants.

Roberts Point Park (ages 4 and up)

At the ferry landing on Port Street, Port Aransas (361-749-4158; www.cityofportaransas.org/Roberts_Point_Park.cfm).

Big boats and dolphins are usually fascinating to children, so stop by Roberts Point Park located on a peninsula jutting into the ship channel. It's the perfect place to watch cargo ships heading to and from the Port of Corpus Christi and to watch dolphins chase smaller craft across the bay. The park also has picnic areas, a fishing pier, stage, large pavilion, basketball court, sand volleyball, and a children's playground.

Scenic **Drive**

Don't miss the drive along Highway 35 from Port Aransas to Port Lavaca. It's a sunny, refreshing drive with bracing salt breezes and delightful beachfront communities that begins with a ferry ride across Aransas Pass. Depending on the time of year and time of day, you may see dolphins playing in the water or rare whooping cranes overhead. Perhaps most startling are the huge, twisted oaks leaning over almost backward that line the road in the Rockport and Fulton area. In some cases the trees have grown so close together they look like a giant hedge towering above your car.

Mustang Island State Park (ages 4 and up) 

On Park Road 53, 14 miles west of Port Aransas, just north of North Padre Island off Highway 361 (361-749-5246, www.tpwd.state.tx.us/spdest/findadest/parks/mustang_island).

The 3,700-acre Mustang Island State Park is very popular with Texans. In addition to its pristine beaches, it has campsites, shower facilities, and hiking trails.

Where to Eat

Crazy Cajun. 303 Beach Street, Port Aransas (361-749-5069; http://thecrazycajun.com/). Cajun-style seafood served up family style on butcher paper. $$

Seafood and Spaghetti Works. 710 South Alister Street, Port Aransas (361-749-5666). Seafood, steaks, pasta, and pizza; Sunday brunch buffet. $$

Where to Stay

Beachgate Condos and Motel. 2000 On the Beach Drive, Port Aransas (361-749-5900 or 866-749-2565; www.beachgate.com/). Right on the beach, heated pool, Internet access, completely furnished condo suites or motel units. $$$

For More Information

Port Aransas Tourist and Convention Bureau. 403 West Cotter Street, Port Aransas 78373; (800) 45-COAST; www.portaransas.org.

Rockport and Fulton

Rockport, on Highway 35, is more than just a great place to watch birds, go fishing, or swim in the surf. The town is full of crafts shops and art galleries, and each Fourth of July weekend it holds the **Rockport Art Festival,** one of the largest in the state. The festival includes art, food, fireworks, and a special children's art tent. Call the Rockport Center for the Arts at (361) 729-5519 for more information.

Texas Maritime Museum (ages 6 and up)

1202 Navigation Circle at the Rockport Harbor (361-729-1271 or 866-729-AHOY; www.texasmaritimemuseum.org). Open Tuesday through Saturday 10 a.m. to 4 p.m., Sunday 1 to 4 p.m. $–$$, children 5 and under free.

Learn about everything from Spanish explorers to pirates to gulf oil-drilling rigs at the Texas Maritime Museum. The museum also has a number of changing displays and hands-on exhibits for kids. The centerpiece is a new permanent exhibit about the LaSalle Odyssey which tells the story of the French explorer La Salle's expedition to Texas in 1684.

Rockport Beach Park (ages 4 and up)

622 East Market Street, Rockport (361-727-2158).

Your family can relax on the white-sand beach, have a picnic in the shade, fish from the pier, swim in the saltwater pool, or have fun at the playground.

Goose Island State Park (ages 4 and up)

On Park Road 13, 10 miles north of Rockport off Highway 35 (361-729-2858, www.tpwd.state.tx.us/spdest/findadest/parks/goose_island).

Goose Island State Park is another great place for outdoor fun. Located at the conjunction of Aransas, Copano, and St. Charles Bays, the park is noted for its lovely campsites, good fishing, and opportunities to see whooping cranes and other waterfowl. Nearby, you'll also find the Big Tree, the state-champion coastal live oak, a gnarled 1,000-year-old wonder of nature.

Bird **Festivals**

Several local communities sponsor festivals celebrating their most popular local birds.

- **Eagle Fest,** Emory, February (903-473-3913)
- **CraneFest,** Big Spring, February (915-263-7641)
- **Attwater's Prairie Chicken Festival,** Eagle Lake, April (979-234-3021)
- **Migration Celebration,** Clute, April (866-403-5829)
- **Bluebird Festival,** Willis Point, April (903-873-3111)
- **Hummerbird Celebration,** Rockport, September (800-242-0071)
- **Rio Grande Valley Birding Festival,** Harlingen, November (800-531-7346)

Texas Trivia

The top ten state parks for day visits are the San Jacinto Battleground, Cedar Hill, Garner, Caddo Lake, Lyndon B. Johnson, Lake Texana, Bastrop, Mustang Island, Lake Corpus Christi, and Eisenhower.

Fulton Mansion State Historical Park (ages 6 and up)

317 Fulton Beach Road, Fulton (361-729-0386; www.thc.state.tx.us/hsites/hs_fulton.aspx?Site=Fulton). Open Tuesday through Saturday 10 a.m. to 3 p.m., Sunday 1 p.m. to 3 p.m. $–$$, children under 6 free.

Fulton Mansion is special for families at certain times of the year when staff members go all out. They conduct regular historical tours Tuesday through Sunday, but around Halloween they host a two-day event highlighting the mansion's history of hauntings, and every December they celebrate with a traditional Victorian Christmas. The house, built in the 1870s, was an architectural wonder at the time and a tribute to gracious living during the area's cattle-boom days.

Aransas National Wildlife Refuge (ages 4 and up)

Off Highway 35, Austwell (361-286-3559; www.fws.gov/southwest/refuges/texas/aransas). Interpretive center open daily 8:30 a.m. to 4:30 p.m. $.

Aransas National Wildlife Refuge is famous as the winter home for the nearly extinct whooping cranes that fly 2,500 miles from their summer refuge in northern Alberta's Wood Buffalo National Park. More than 300 other species of birds also make Aransas their usual vacation spot, along with native deer, javelinas, and raccoons. The best time to see the rare whooping cranes is between November and March. The **Wildlife Interpretive Center** has mounted specimens and a slide show on the whoopers. Finding the refuge can be difficult if you miss one of the signs, so check out the Web site or call ahead for directions.

The best way for your family to see whooping cranes is from the sea, since you can't walk very far out into the marshlands that make up much of the wildlife refuge. Several boat operators conduct tours with various itineraries. Call the Rockport Chamber of Commerce at (361) 729-6445 or (800) 242-0071 (in Texas) or (800) 826-6441 (outside Texas) to get recommendations.

Where to Eat

Mac's Barbecue. 815 E. Market Street, Rockport (361-729-9388). Great barbecue with choice of several sides; peach cobbler. $–$$

MoonDog Seaside Eatery. 100 Casterline Drive, Fulton (361-729-6868). Burgers, salads, seafood, barbecue. Awesome "loaded fries." $–$$

Hu Dat Restaurant. 61 Broadway, Fulton (361-790-7621; www.hu-dat.com/fulton/). Interesting blend of Cajun and Vietnamese foods. $

Where to Stay

Laguna Reef Hotel. 1021 Water Street, Rockport (361-729-1742 or 800-248-1057; www.lagunareef.com/). Has its own fishing pier and a swimming pool; just 2 blocks from the shops and galleries in downtown Rockport. $$–$$$

Pelican Bay Resort. 4206 Hwy. 35 North, Fulton (361-729-7177 or 866-729-7177; www.pelicanbayresort.com/). Individual cottages, poolside mini-suites, clubhouse with game room and exercise room, pool, lighted fishing pier. $$–$$$

For More Information

Rockport-Fulton Chamber of Commerce. 404 Broadway, Rockport 78382; (800) 826-6441 or (361) 729-6445; www.rockport-fulton.org.

Port Lavaca and Bay City

Port Lavaca Fishing Pier (ages 4 and up)

At the Highway 35 Causeway, Port Lavaca (361-552-5311).

Teach your kids to become expert fisherfolk at the Port Lavaca Fishing Pier at Lighthouse Beach. The pier is actually the old highway causeway and is now one of the most popular and successful fishing spots along the Texas coast, its lighted span jutting 3,202 feet into Lavaca Bay. The family can also cool off with a swim here or take a boat out. The pier has a bait shop, a snack bar, and restrooms, and the city park at the base of the pier has a boat ramp and picnic area.

Matagorda Island Wildlife Management Area (ages 4 and up)

Administrative Office: 1700 Seventh Street, Bay City (979-244-7697; www.tpwd.state.tx.us/huntwild/hunt/wma/find_a_wma/list/?id=48).

Located on a 38-mile-long barrier island, Matagorda Island WMA is one place you're certain to find uncrowded beaches. The fragile island, as narrow as .75 mile wide in some places, remains relatively secluded because the only access is by boat, either your own or

Texas Trivia

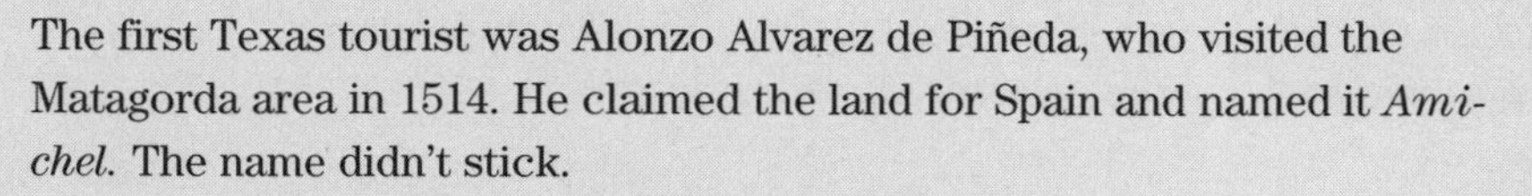

The first Texas tourist was Alonzo Alvarez de Piñeda, who visited the Matagorda area in 1514. He claimed the land for Spain and named it *Amichel.* The name didn't stick.

Texas Trivia

Matagorda Island State Park has recorded 317 species of birds, one of the largest numbers in the nation. Bird-watchers have spotted 110 different species in a single day there.

a rental; ferry service has been discontinued. Once on the island you can fish, hunt, hike, bicycle, comb the beach, swim, get some sun, or camp out.

Matagorda County Museum (ages 4 and up)

2100 Avenue F, Bay City (979-245-7502; www.matagordacountymuseum.org). Open Wednesday through Sunday 1 p.m. to 5 p.m. $.

All the history of this area is here, along with a special Children's Museum section featuring "please touch" exhibits and programs.

Victoria

Texas Zoo (ages 4 and up)

110 Memorial Drive, Victoria (361-573-7681; www.texaszoo.org). Open daily from Memorial Day to Labor Day 9 a.m. to 6 p.m.; Labor Day to Memorial Day 9 a.m. to 5 p.m. $, children 2 and under free.

Your family can get a close-up look at most of the animals of the Lone Star State at the Texas Zoo. Texas has wildly diverse natural habitats from one end of the state to the other, being home to more than 700 species of animals. The Texas Zoo exhibits a wide variety of these native animals: the armadillo, bald eagle, black bear, coati, jaguarundi, margay, ocelot, otter, pelican, porcupine, prairie dog, rattlesnake, tortoise, and red wolf are just a few. Nestled in a curve of the Guadalupe River, the zoo also features a petting zoo, native plants, a wildflower garden, an observation beehive, and special family programs and events.

Victoria Riverside Park and Rose Garden (ages 4 and up)

502 McCright Drive, Victoria (361-485-3200).

If your family likes outdoor fun, they'll find a lot in and around Victoria. Riverside Park and Rose Garden is 562 acres of woodlands bordered by 4.5 miles of the Guadalupe River. The park has an exercise trail, a duck pond, baseball and softball diamonds, a playground, and 200 picnic spots. The garden features 1,500 rose bushes representing 105 varieties, an ornamental water fountain, a gazebo, and walkways.

Saxet Lakes Park (ages 4 and up)

On Timberline Drive, 2 miles south of Victoria off US 59. Open daily from 7 a.m. to 8 p.m. in winter, to 9 p.m. in summer.

More outdoor opportunities exist at Saxet Lakes Park, including fishing, swimming, picnic areas, and boat ramps.

Coleto Creek Reservoir and Park (ages 4 and up)

365 Coleto Park Road (361-575-6366; www.coletocreekpark.com).

Between Victoria and Goliad, Coleto Creek features a 3,100-acre lake, and your family can fish, boat, swim, picnic, camp out, hike along nature trails, or have fun at the volleyball court or playground.

Lake Texana State Park (ages 4 and up)

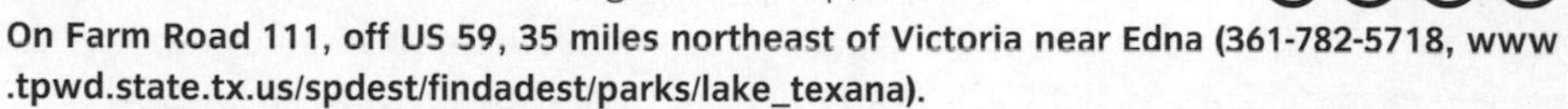

On Farm Road 111, off US 59, 35 miles northeast of Victoria near Edna (361-782-5718, www.tpwd.state.tx.us/spdest/findadest/parks/lake_texana).

Lake Texana State Park has 125 miles of shoreline around the reservoir. Fishing is excellent, as are opportunities to see some of the more than 225 bird species that have been spotted here, along with animals such as deer, rabbits, and raccoons. The park has three fishing piers (two of them lighted), one fishing jetty, a fish-cleaning station, nature trails, campsites, and shaded picnic areas.

Where to Eat

Double J Eatery. 8607 North Navarro Street, Victoria (361-570-7744). The best chicken-fried steak and fresh hamburgers around. $–$$

Golden Corral. 5102 North Navarro Street, Victoria (361-578-9435; www.goldencorral.com). All-you-can-eat buffet and special children's desserts. $–$$

Where to Stay

Comfort Inn. 1906 Houston Highway, Victoria (361-574-9393). Pool, **free** continental breakfast. $$

La Quinta. 7603 North Navarro Street, Victoria (361-572-3585; www.laquinta.com). Pool, **free** breakfast, **free** high-speed Internet. $$

For More Information

Victoria Convention and Visitors Bureau. 3404 North Ben Wilson, Victoria 77901; (800) 926-5774 or (361) 582-4285; www.victoriatexasinfo.com

Goliad

Goliad means a lot to Texans. Not only was it a prime Spanish colonial city, but Colonel James Fannin and 342 men were massacred here after surrendering to Mexican forces just after the fall of the Alamo. Also, General Ignacio Zaragoza was born here. He led the Mexicans in their defeat of the French at the city of Puebla on May 5, 1862. That victory continues to be celebrated in Mexico and Texas as Cinco de Mayo, perhaps the premier holiday for Hispanic Texans.

Goliad State Park (ages 4 and up)

On U.S. Highway 183, 1 mile south of Goliad (361-645-3405, www.tpwd.state.tx.us/spdest/findadest/parks/goliad_and_mission_espiritu_santo).

Goliad State Park is a 2,208-acre park preserving the Mission Nuestra Señora del Espíritu Santo de Zuniga, established in 1749. In addition to interpretive displays, the park has camping and picnic areas. If the kids need a dunking, a city-operated swimming pool across the street is open from noon to 8 p.m. during the summer.

Presidio La Bahia (ages 6 and up)

On US 183, 2 miles south of Goliad (361-645-3752; www.presidiolabahia.org). Open daily 9 a.m. to 4:45 p.m. except Easter, Thanksgiving, Christmas, and New Year's Day. $, children 5 and under free.

Presidio La Bahia, south of town just past the San Antonio River, is the Spanish fort built to protect the mission and the colonists. The fortress has been excavated and restored, and the museum houses many items uncovered during that excavation. Included are artifacts depicting nine levels of civilization at the site. The mass grave of Colonel Fannin and his men is a couple hundred yards south of the Presidio. Also at the Presidio is a reconstructed birthplace of Ignacio Zaragoza who led the Mexican army to defeat the French for Mexico's independence.

For More Information

Goliad Chamber of Commerce. 231 South Market Street, P.O. Box 606, Goliad 77963; (361) 645-3563 or 800-848-8674; www.goliadcc.org.

Gonzales, Luling, and Seguin

You'll discover more Texas history in Gonzales, home to the **Come and Take It! Celebration** in early October. The festival celebrates the first battle flag of Texas, created when Texans stitched the words Come and Take It along with a small cannon on a banner as they protected the village cannon against advancing Mexican troops. The Mexicans retreated after a brief skirmish. The celebration includes a parade, battle reenactment, arts-and-crafts fair, and canoe races. For information on the festival, call (830) 672-6532.

The city of Luling is known for two things. First are the numerous oil-rig pump jacks around town that are painted with a variety of designs or as cartoon characters. Some, like the woodpecker, are fascinating to little kids. Second is the annual **Luling Watermelon Thump** in late June. The Thump, like many such Texas festivals, has a parade, many arts-and-crafts booths, a carnival, musical entertainment, food, dances, and a rodeo, but it also features such contests as watermelon eating and the World Championship Watermelon Seed Spitting Contest. Call (830) 875-3214.

Gonzales Memorial Museum (ages 6 and up)

414 Smith Street, Gonzales (830-672-6350). Open Tuesday through Saturday 10 a.m. to noon and 1 to 5 p.m., Sunday 1 to 5 p.m. Free.

The Gonzales battle is commemorated at the Gonzales Memorial Museum. The star of the museum is the cannon that fired the first shot of the Texas Revolution.

Gonzales Pioneer Village (ages 6 and up)

2122 St. Joseph Street, Gonzales (830-672-2157; www.gonzalespioneervillage.com/). Open Tuesday through Saturday 10 a.m. to 2 p.m. $.

The Gonzales Pioneer Village will help your kids understand the hardships of pioneers on the Texas frontier in the 1800s. The site has several restored buildings, including a log cabin, blacksmith shop, and church. Costumed volunteers demonstrating pioneer skills make the history come to life.

Palmetto State Park (ages 4 and up)

On Park Road 11, off US 183 between Gonzales and Luling (830-672-3266, www.tpwd.state.tx.us/spdest/findadest/parks/palmetto).

Palmetto State Park has a wide diversity of plant life in an area known as Ottine Swamp, where many eastern and western plant species merge. Also, more than 240 species of birds have been identified within the park's 178 acres. The park has picnic areas, campsites, hiking trails, swimming, and fishing. Facilities here were among those built at several Texas state parks by the Civilian Conservation Corps during the Depression.

Max Starcke Park (ages 4 and up)

Highway 123, at the Guadalupe River, Seguin (830-401-2480; www.ci.seguin.tx.us/parks/parks.htm).

Max Starcke Park is a beautiful place to cool off or have a picnic during the summer. Nestled beneath towering oak and pecan trees, the park has a swimming pool and eighteen-hole golf course.

Lake McQueeney (ages 4 and up)

On Farm Road 725, about 4 miles northwest of Seguin (830-557-9900).

Lake McQueeney is a popular spot for swimming, fishing, and especially waterskiing.

For More Information

Gonzales Chamber of Commerce. 414 Saint Lawrence Street in the old jail, Gonzales 78629; (830) 672-6532 or 888-672-1095; www.gonzalestexas.com.

Luling Chamber of Commerce. 421 East Davis Street, Luling 78648; (830) 875-3214; www.lulingcc.org.

Seguin Chamber of Commerce. 116 North Camp Street, Seguin 78156; (830) 379-6382; www.visitseguin.com.

Flatonia and Schulenburg

This area is well known for its Czech heritage, and you can find spicy sausage and kolaches (fruit-filled pastries) just about everywhere. Flatonia celebrates every October with **Czhilispiel,** an elaborate chili cook-off festival with a parade, arts-and-crafts booths, a carnival, and entertainment. Call the Flatonia Chamber of Commerce (361) 865-3920; www.flatoniachamber.com/ or visit www.czhilispielfestival.com.

Where to Eat

Frank's. I–10 at the Schulenburg exit (979-743-3555). Eating here on Sunday after church is a long-standing tradition for most locals. Generous portions; many German and Czech specialties, great pies, reasonable prices. Lobby is filled with country gift items for sale. $–$$

The Brazosport Area

Brazosport is the area around where the Brazos River empties into the Gulf of Mexico and includes the cities of Freeport, Quintana Beach, Surfside Beach, Lake Jackson, Clute, Jones Creek, Richwood, and Oyster Creek. The towns are closely united, and all feature an almost endless variety of outdoor activities perfectly suited to families. Many companies in this area offer charters for freshwater or deep-sea fishing or diving, and others rent boats of nearly all types and sizes.

If you can't beat 'em, celebrate 'em. That's the philosophy behind the **Great Texas Mosquito Festival** in Clute every July. The family event features arts-and-crafts and food booths, live entertainment, a carnival, fun runs, bike tours, kids' contests, and a 25-foot mosquito (he's the bug wearing a cowboy hat and boots). Call (979) 265-8392 or (800) 371-2971 or visit www.mosquitofestival.com.

Texians, Texans, **and Texicans**

It seems that from the beginning of Anglo settlement in Texas there has always been some confusion about what to call its residents. Those of Sam Houston's time, during the Republic of Texas, commonly referred to themselves as "Texians," and you will usually see that term in historic documents of the period. However, after Texas became a state, the term "Texan" was used more often, usually by outsiders. Slowly, "Texan" overtook "Texian," and after the Civil War the older term was seldom heard. John Wayne confused the issue by referring to Lone Star State inhabitants as "Texicans" in several of his movies. A group of Old West shooters in the Hill Country, for example, are the "Texican Rangers," and several Texans who feel strong connections with Texans of old refer to themselves as "Texicans."

San Bernard National Wildlife Refuge (ages 4 and up)

6801 County Road 306, just southwest of Freeport (979-964-3639; www.fws.gov/southwest/refuges/texas/texasmidcoast/sanbernard.htm). Open during daylight hours.

The San Bernard National Wildlife Refuge is a 24,000-acre refuge between Cedar Lake Creek and the San Bernard River along the coast. You'll find more than 400 species of wildlife to watch, including at least 250 types of birds. Mammals include armadillos, bobcats, coyotes, raccoons, and river otters.

Sea Center Texas (ages 4 and up)

On Highway 332 at Plantation Drive, Lake Jackson (979-292-0100; www.tpwd.state.tx.us/spdest/visitorcenters/seacenter). Open Tuesday through Saturday 9 a.m. to 4 p.m., Sunday 1 to 4 p.m. Hatchery tours are available by reservation. Free, donations appreciated.

Sea Center Texas, an aquarium and educational center in Lake Jackson, showcases a 22,000-square-foot fish hatchery for redfish and speckled trout. "Touch tanks" are included especially for children, along with three aquariums that feature freshwater fish, bay fish, and gulf fish in their natural habitats. The hatchery is surrounded by a five-acre wetland site with a nature walk for viewing birds and other wildlife.

Brazoria County Historical Museum (ages 6 and up)

100 East Cedar Street, Angleton (979-864-1208; www.bchm.org). Open Monday through Friday 9 a.m. to 5 p.m., to 3 p.m. on Saturday. Free.

The first Anglo settlers in Texas started out here, and this museum, located in the renovated 1897 courthouse, has comprehensive exhibits on that period of history.

Scenic **Drive**

The 40-mile drive on County Road 257, which changes to Farm Road 3005 from Surfside Beach along barrier islands will certainly give you a close look at the Gulf of Mexico. If you're traveling north, Christmas, West, and Galveston Bays will be on your left, the surf of the gulf on your right. For most of the road, it's all sand dunes and seagulls. It's a peaceful, quiet, sometimes almost secluded drive until you hit the four-lane on Galveston Island, then development picks up with beach homes, condominiums, and, finally, large hotels.

You'll find several spots to access the beach along the road, including the totally undeveloped Christmas Bay State Park at the southern end and Galveston Island State Park near the northern end.

Brazoria National Wildlife Refuge (ages 4 and up)

Office: 1212 North Velasco Street, Angleton; take Highway 332 south from Lake Jackson to Farm Road 523, go north on 523 about 5 miles to County Road 227 and east on 227 for 1.7 miles to the gate (979-849-7771; www.fws.gov/southwest/refuges/texas/texasmidcoast/brazoria.htm).

Brazoria National Wildlife Refuge is another area full of wildlife waiting to be spotted. Brazoria is open to the public only on the first full weekend of each month or by special arrangement. Officials ask that before visiting the refuge you stop by the headquarters on Velasco Street in Angleton.

Center for the Arts and Sciences (ages 4 and up)

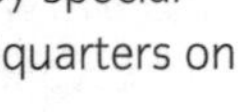

400 College Boulevard, Clute (979-265-7661; www.bcfas.org). Open Tuesday through Saturday 10 a.m. to 4 p.m., Sunday 2 p.m. to 5 p.m. Museum free, planetarium shows $.

Kids will love the South's largest shell collection at the Center for the Arts and Sciences. But that's not all. The museum has fascinating and fun natural-science displays, including dinosaur skeletons, planetarium shows (979-265-3376), a nature trail, live theater productions (many specifically for children), and art exhibits and classes.

Where to Eat

Cactus Grill Steakhouse. 107 West Way, Lake Jackson (979-285-9300). Texas-size steaks done up right. $$$

Taqueria Guadalajara. 921 South Highway 288, Clute (979-265-6676). A large variety of the very best Tex-Mex fare. $–$$

Where to Stay

Best Western. 915 Highway 332 West, Clute (979-388-0055; www.bestwestern.com). Pool, **free** continental breakfast, **free** high-speed Internet access. $$

La Quinta Inn. 1126 Highway 332 West, Clute (979-265-7461; www.laquinta.com).

Rooms are large and quiet, **free** wireless high-speed Internet, **free** continental breakfast, children under 18 stay **free.** $$

Surfside Motel. 330 Coral Court, Surfside Beach (979-233-4585). Kitchenettes, just a few steps from the beach. $$

For More Information

Brazosport Convention and Visitors Council. 300 Abner Jackson Parkway, Lake Jackson 77566; (979)285-2501 or 888-477-2505, www.visitbrazosport.com).

Houston

Houston is the fourth largest city in the United States, and you won't doubt it for a minute when you drive its highways, a spaghetti-like mixture of over- and underpasses where major thoroughfares like US 59 and I–10 and Loop 610 and I–45 converge, and all the drivers seem to be in a hurry. Better know where you're headed beforehand. The city sprawls out from the gulf area nearly to the Piney Woods.

Houston, founded in 1836 by a couple of real estate developers of questionable ethics, was built up on the swampy banks of Buffalo Bayou. Over time it has taken control of its own destiny in a big way by dredging up the remarkable Houston Ship Channel to make the city one of the top ports in the country. Vice President Lyndon B. Johnson ensured that Houston would be the first word spoken from the Moon when he wrangled for NASA's manned spacecraft headquarters to be in the city (NASA returned the favor by naming the space center after him). Oil and gas production made the city boom, and its economy is still strongly based on these two Texas staples.

Visitors will discover more than enough to fill their days with family amusement parks, first-rate museums, professional sports, top-notch performing arts, fun festivals, and lots of recreational possibilities.

Brazos Bend State Park (ages 4 and up)

21901 Farm Road 762, 25 miles south of Houston, Needville (979-553-5101, www.tpwd.state.tx.us/spdest/findadest/parks/brazos_bend).

Brazos Bend State Park is 4,897 acres of coastal plain. This Brazos River bottomland has beautiful oaks draped in grapevines and Spanish moss, small lakes and a marsh, and abundant wildlife that includes migratory and shore birds and more than a few alligators.

Texas Trivia

The county with the largest population in Texas is Harris County (the Houston metropolitan area), with 3,400,578 people, according to the 2000 U.S. Bureau of Census.

Texas Trivia

Approximately 24 million people live in Texas, the second most populated of any state after California. Of those people, 80 percent now live in urban areas. Texas has twenty-one cities with more than 100,000 inhabitants. The top ten (based on the U.S. Census Bureau (web) 2007updates to the 2002 census) are as follows:

- Houston has 2,208,180 people.
- San Antonio has 1,328,984 people.
- Dallas has 1,240,499 people.
- Austin has 743,074 people.
- Fort Worth has 681,818 people.
- El Paso has 606,913 people.
- Arlington has 371,038 people.
- Corpus Christi has 285,507 people.
- Plano has 260,796 people.
- Garland has 218,792 people.

The park has campsites and screened shelters, picnic areas, a nature study and photography tower, fishing, 9 miles of hiking and bike trails, a gift shop and visitor center (open on weekends), and the George Observatory. The observatory features a 36-inch telescope that is open on Saturdays from 3 p.m. to 10 p.m. For information on telescope viewing, call (281) 242-3055.

Stephen F. Austin State Park (ages 4 and up)

Park Road 38, off I–10 at San Felipe, 25 miles west of Houston (979-885-3613, www.tpwd.state.tx.us/spdest/findadest/parks/stephen_f_austin_and_san_felipe).

A portion of the park celebrates the history of Texas, since the town of San Felipe was the center of American colonization in the Mexican state of Texas from 1824 to 1836. A number of old buildings are preserved here, along with historical exhibits. In the wooded, recreational portion of the park, your family can picnic, camp out, or enjoy themselves at the swimming pool or playground. Park facilities include some screened shelters with electricity.

Reliant Stadium (ages 6 and up)

2 Reliant Park, Houston (832-667-2000; www.houstontexans.com). Tours are offered Monday through Thursday on nonevent days. Tours must be scheduled in advance by calling (832) 667-1842. $–$$, children 2 and under free.

Reliant Stadium near the Astrodome dwarfs that famous stadium, which was the first of the giant indoor sports facilities. Reliant seats 7,000 more fans than the old 'Dome, and some of those seats are very close to the action. Artificial turf, now common from high school playing fields to professional ballparks, was invented for the Astrodome, but Reliant has a retractable roof, which allows for a playing surface of natural grass. The **Houston Texans** of the National Football League began their inaugural season in 2002 at Reliant Stadium. Call Ticketmaster at (713) 629-3700 or visit www.ticketmaster.com for tickets.

Reliant Stadium is also the site of the **Houston Livestock Show and Rodeo,** held every February. The rodeo is one of the largest in the United States, featuring top competitors and top music entertainers every night. While the cowboys and singers are going at it in the stadium, livestock competition is taking place in adjacent buildings, where there are also art exhibits and sales booths. The grounds are surrounded by a huge carnival. Call (832) 667-1000 or visit www.hlsr.com.

Houston Astros Baseball (ages 4 and up)

501 Crawford Street, Houston (713-259-8000 for information, 877-927-8767 for tickets; www.astros.com). $–$$$$.

The Astros moved into their new home, now called Minute Maid Park, in 2000. The downtown ballpark is more traditional looking than the Astrodome, their old home, and features natural grass, a retractable roof, and a rushing locomotive that crosses the stands whenever an Astro hits a home run.

The Health Museum (ages 5 and up)

1515 Hermann Drive, Houston (713-521-1515; www.thehealthmuseum.org). Open Tuesday through Saturday 9 a.m. to 5 p.m. and Sunday noon to 5 p.m. $–$$, children 2 and under free, also free on Thursday 2 to 5 p.m.

Through entertaining and interactive exhibits and hands-on activities, the Health Museum offers children of all ages unique health-education experiences.

Houston Rockets Basketball (ages 6 and up)

1510 Polk Street, Houston (713-627-DUNK; www.nba.com/rockets). $$–$$$$.

The Houston Rockets play basketball in the new Toyota Center downtown. The Rockets, twice NBA champions, play from October to April.

Houston Aeros Hockey (ages 6 and up)

1510 Polk Street, Houston (713-974-7825; www.aeros.com). $$–$$$$.

Also quite popular locally, the Houston Aeros, a minor-league hockey team, play in the Toyota Center from October to April.

Texas **Birds**

The bird you're most likely to see while you're traveling Texas roads is the common turkey buzzard. These are the big black birds circling in the sky waiting for you to provide them with lunch. Along back roads, the buzzards become a nuisance. They will wait until the very last second while dining on roadkill before flying off as your vehicle approaches.

Bird-watching is good in Texas almost anywhere, anytime. No other state offers the variety of birds Texas does, with three-fourths of all known American birds represented—about 600 recorded species—many of them very rare like the Colima warblers and whooping cranes.

The state's resident population—varying from gulls to pelicans along the coast, roadrunners to eagles in the west, and flycatchers to woodpeckers in the east—is augmented by hosts of migratory birds in cooler months.

The **Great Texas Coastal Birding Trail** was completed in July 2000. It is a 700-mile marked trail from Port Arthur to Brownsville, including 300 public sites with maps and information on birds.

You can get a checklist of Texas birds, other birding information, and details on the Coastal Birding Trail at most state parks or from the Texas Parks and Wildlife Department, 4200 Smith School Road, Austin 78744; (800) 792-1112.

Zuma Fun Centers (ages 4 and up)

180 Rankin Road at I-45 (281-872-7778) or 6767 Southwest Freeway (US 59) at Hillcroft, Houston (713-981-7888; www.zumafuncneters.com/houston). Hours vary seasonally. Admission varies with each ride or attraction.

Kids want more? Take them to one of the two Celebration Station locations, where they can play miniature golf, zip around on go-karts, try their skill at the batting cages, or play games in the video arcade.

FunPlex (ages 4 and up)

13700 Beechnut Street, Houston (281-530-7777; www.funplex.org). Hours vary seasonally and prices vary with activities.

FunPlex is an indoor family entertainment complex that features a roller rink, bowling, miniature golf, video arcades, three movie screens, and snack bars.

Houston Arboretum and Nature Center (ages 4 and up)

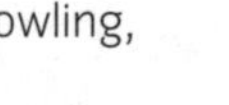

4501 Woodway Drive, Houston (713-681-8433; www.houstonarboretum.org). Trails open 8:30 a.m. to 6 p.m. daily. Visitor center open daily 9 a.m. to 5 p.m. Free.

The Houston Arboretum is an environmental education center with classes and programs for children and adults and a preserve area for plants. Five miles of relaxing nature trails wind through 155 acres of woodlands, ponds, and prairie. Located near Memorial Park and the Galleria area.

Children's Museum of Houston (ages 4 and up)

1500 Binz Street, Houston (713-522-1138; www.cmhouston.org). Open Tuesday through Saturday 10 a.m. to 6 p.m., Sunday noon to 6 p.m. $$.

The Children's Museum of Houston is a fun place. The funky yellow, blue, and pink building, one of the five largest children's museums in the country, is in the heart of the city's museum district. Permanent and traveling exhibits focus on science and technology, environment and history, agriculture and archaeology, culture and art. Many of the displays are interactive and hands-on.

Houston Museum of Natural Science (ages 4 and up)

In Hermann Park at Fannin Street, Houston (713-639-4629; www.hmns.org). Hours and prices vary with attractions within the complex.

The Houston Museum of Natural Science is a first-rate collection of science museums tucked into a bucolic park setting in the middle of the city. Included are the following:

- The **Burke Baker Planetarium** is a sophisticated and entertaining place where your family can travel through a black hole or zip around constellations.
- A six-story glass house is home to the **Cockrell Butterfly Center** where more than 2,000 butterflies live in a tropical rain forest complete with a 40-foot waterfall.
- The **Cullen Hall of Gems and Minerals** displays a collection of more than 750 rare minerals and hundreds of gemstones.
- The **Wortham IMAX Theatre** shows exciting films projected onto a six-story-tall screen with incredible surround sound.
- The **John P. McGovern Hall of the Americas** is a 12,000-square-foot series of galleries with exhibits designed to explain the ways humans inhabited the Western Hemisphere for thousands of years before Europeans dropped in. The hall has one of the best collections of pre-Columbian art and artifacts in the country. Many, such as the full-size Aztec gateway, are breathtaking.
- Also in the park are the **Japanese Gardens,** a golf course, the **Houston Garden Center,** miniature golf, a 4-mile hiking trail, paddleboats, a miniature train that runs around the park, and playground facilities.

Houston Zoological Gardens (ages 2 and up)

In Hermann Park, Houston (713-533-6500; www.houstonzoo.org). Open daily 9 a.m. to 5 p.m. $–$$, free some holidays.

The Houston Zoo will thrill anyone in your family. Not a typical zoo, this one features a Tropical Bird House resembling an Asian jungle, where birds fly freely all around you; a hippo-dome; one of the best gorilla habitats in the United States; a large-cat facility with rare white tigers; and an extensive collection of reptiles and vampire bats. The Wortham World of Primates is a 2.2-acre rain forest habitat for the zoo's primates.

Houston Fire Museum (ages 6 and up)

2403 Milam Street, Houston (713-524-2526; www.houstonfiremuseum.org). Open Tuesday through Saturday 10 a.m. to 4 p.m. $.

Your family can see the history of firefighting, from bucket brigades to horse-drawn pumpers to modern fire trucks, at the Houston Fire Museum, which is housed in a former fire station.

The Orange Show (ages 4 and up)

2402 Munger Street, Houston (713-926-6368; www.orangeshow.org). Hours vary greatly by season. $, children under 12 free.

Any attempt to adequately describe the Orange Show would be impossible. The unique, Rube Goldberg-esque house and grounds were begun in the 1950s by owner Jeff McKissack, who had an obsession with everything orange—the fruit and the color. His stated goal was to encourage families to be healthier by drinking more juice and to be highly amused. Well, you'll definitely be amused here. This amazing place was opened to the public in 1979 and is now a park and performance center.

SplashTown (ages 6 and up)

21300 I–45, Spring (281-355-3300; www.splashtownpark.com). Summer hours 10 a.m. to 7 p.m. $$$–$$$$.

More water-based fun can be found at SplashTown, north of Houston in Spring. This is a large water park, one of the largest in Texas, with more than thirty-five different water slides and pools. It also has snack bars, picnic areas, and a bathhouse.

Where to Eat

Good Eats Grill. 15222 John F. Kennedy Boulevard (inside Holiday Inn), Houston (281-442-2815; www.goodeatsgrill.com). Home-style cooking with huge portions. $$–$$$

Goode Company Barbecue. 5109 Kirby Drive, Houston (713-522-2530) and 8911 Katy Freeway, Houston (713-464-1901; www.goodecompany.com). One of the best barbecue joints in Texas. Exceptional food, Texas-roadhouse atmosphere. $–$$

Wunsche Bros. Cafe. 103 Midway Drive, Spring (281-350-1902; www.wunschebroscafe.com). Local favorite since 1949. Next door is Old Town Spring, a century-old railroad town that features a collection of more than 150 shops, boutiques, museums, and restaurants. $–$$

Where to Stay

La Quinta Inn–Astrodome. 9911 Buffalo Speedway, Houston (800-753-3757; www.laquinta.com). Convenient location. La Quinta has sixteen other hotels in town (call the same number). $$–$$$

Best Western Inn & Suites Downtown. 915 West Dallas, Houston (713-571-7733; www.bwdowntown.com/). Downtown location, covered pool, exercise room, **free** high-speed Internet, **free** hot breakfast, **free** downtown shuttle. $$$

For More Information

Greater Houston Convention and Visitors Bureau. 901 Bagby Avenue, Houston 77002; (800) 4-HOUSTON or (713) 437-5200; www.visithoustontexas.com.

Pasadena, Deer Park, and La Porte

Take Highway 225 east from Houston.

The main highway from Houston through Pasadena, Deer Park, and La Porte isn't what most people would consider a scenic drive, but it is an interesting one. Highway 225 cuts through the heart of the area's oil industry, the largest in the nation and the reason the Houston metropolitan region is as gigantic as it is. You'll see oil tanks and refineries of all sorts. It all takes on an eerie glow after sundown.

If you're in Pasadena in September, don't miss the **Pasadena Livestock Show and Rodeo.** It may not be as big as its cousin in Houston, but the cowboying is just as real, and you get a lot closer to all the competition at the Pasadena Fairgrounds (on Red Bluff Road at Fairmont) than in Reliant Stadium. Call (281) 487-0240; www.pasadenarodeo.com.

Dow Park and Botanical Gardens (ages 4 and up)

610 East San Augustine Street, Deer Park.

The forty-acre Dow Park and Botanical Gardens gives you a chance to cool off in a swimming pool or have a picnic, then stroll through a garden featuring more than 180 flower species, brick walkways, and wooden arches.

San Jacinto Battleground State Historic Site (ages 4 and up)

3523 Highway 134 (Battleground Road), La Porte (281-479-2431; www.tpwd.state.tx.us/spdest/findadest/parks/san_jacinto_battleground). Park open daily 9 a.m. to 6 p.m. Museum open daily 9 a.m. to 6 p.m. $, children 12 and under free.

Texas Trivia

The USS *Texas* had ten 14-inch deck guns that could fire shells weighing as much as a compact car a distance of more than 12 miles.

If your family is interested in Texas history, don't miss San Jacinto Battleground. It was here on April 21, 1836, that Texas won its independence from Mexico. Historical markers provide details of the battle on the actual sites, while the museum, at the base of the monument, preserves hundreds of historic artifacts and documents. New to the museum is the Jesse H. Jones Theater for Texas Studies, where you can see the multi-image presentation *Texas Forever!! The Battle of San Jacinto.* You can also take an elevator ride to an observation room at the top of the monument for a breathtaking panorama of the area. To get to the park, take Highway 225 east, then turn north on Battleground Road (Highway 134). You can't miss the park: You'll see the San Jacinto Monument, towering higher than the Washington Monument, over the prairie. (By the way, although the correct Spanish pronunciation of this place is *San Ha-ceen-to,* Texans have always pronounced it *San Juh-cen-to.*)

The Battle of **San Jacinto**

It was all or nothing that April 26, 1836. Only a ragtag and undisciplined army of Texans, led by a cantankerous general called "Big Drunk" by the Native Americans, would face the man who called himself the "Napoleon of the West" and a regular army that would outnumber the insurrectionists two to one.

After suffering crushing blows delivered by the Mexicans at the Alamo and Goliad, General Sam Houston took what was left of the army and ran. Many of his own men were on the verge of mutiny.

But Houston knew his small band of about 600 men was all that was left to fight for Texas's independence, and he would wait to fight until he was certain of victory.

General Antonio López de Santa Anna's force of 1,300 camped on the banks of the San Jacinto River, leisurely awaiting reinforcements. Houston's force crossed Buffalo Bayou on rafts, and at 3:30 p.m. they caught the Mexicans literally napping. The Mexicans were so surprised that many of their weapons remained neatly stacked in front of their tents after the battle.

The Texas Army killed more than 600 and captured all the survivors, losing just nine men themselves. Now a captive, Santa Anna signed a treaty granting Texas its independence.

The battle lasted just eighteen minutes. Considering the amount of territory eventually decided by the victory—all of Texas and parts of New Mexico, Oklahoma, Kansas, Colorado, and Wyoming—it has been called by historians one of the most decisive battles ever fought.

Texas Trivia

The state highway system has only one tunnel—the 4,110-foot tunnel under the Houston Ship Channel that connects Baytown and La Porte.

Battleship *Texas* (ages 6 and up)

At San Jacinto Battleground, 3523 Highway 134 (Battleground Road), La Porte (281-479-2431; www.tpwd.state.tx.us/spdest/findadest/parks/battleship_texas). Open daily 10 a.m. to 5 p.m., with specially guided tours on weekends. $–$$, children under 12 free.

The battleship *Texas* is the only surviving Navy warship that served in both world wars, and it was a pioneer in naval aviation. The ship has been moored at the San Jacinto Battleground since 1948 but only recently underwent significant restoration. You can now tour the dark-gray behemoth, seeing much of the ship and many excellent historical displays.

Armand Bayou Nature Center (ages 4 and up)

8500 Bay Area Boulevard, Pasadena (281-474-2551; www.abnc.org). Open Tuesday through Saturday 9 a.m. to 5 p.m., Sunday noon to 5 p.m. $.

The Armand Bayou Nature Center is a rare place, a true wilderness in the middle of one of the largest urban areas in the United States. The 1,900-acre park showcases native plant and animal life in three different ecosystems that coexist within the park: hardwood forest, tallgrass prairie, and estuarine bayou. The twisting arms of the bayou give your family the chance to get out in the middle of all the wildness in a canoe. Sightings of blue herons, ospreys, gars, and even alligators are common. Other attractions include a working century-old farm, hiking, picnic areas, and a visitor center with a number of nature exhibits. Located between Pasadena and Clear Lake City, **Windsurfing Sports,** 2300 NASA Parkway, rents kayaks by the hour ($$). Call (281) 291-9199.

Adjacent **Bay Area Park** is a favorite place for local families to get together. It has athletic fields, tennis courts, picnic areas with barbecue pits, and a nature walk. Open daylight hours. Call (281) 326-6539.

For More Information

Pasadena Chamber of Commerce. 4334 Fairmont Parkway, Pasadena 77504-3306; (281) 487-7871; www.pasadenachamber.org.

Clear Lake Area

Several cities all blend together in this area south of Houston, and you won't be able to tell whether you're in Clear Lake City, Webster, Nassau Bay, El Lago, League City, Clear Lake

Shores, Taylor Lake Village, Seabrook, or Kemah if you miss one of the small street signs. The area is surrounded by bays and is full of good restaurants, nice shops and boutiques, and marinas galore. For information call the Bay Area Houston Convention and Visitors Bureau at 800-844-LAKE; www.visitbayareahouston.com/.

Space Center Houston (ages 4 and up)

1601 NASA Parkway, Houston (281-244-2100; www.spacecenter.org). Open Monday through Friday 10 a.m. to 5 p.m., weekends 10 a.m. to 7 p.m. Closed Christmas. $$$.

Space Center Houston is in Clear Lake City at the entrance to the **Johnson Space Center.** Your entire family will be fascinated by the exhibits and displays here, which track the past, present, and future of the U.S. manned-spacecraft program. Interactive exhibits, multimedia programs, shows, an IMAX film, and participation on several devices make space flight come alive. Visitors may also take tours of the Manned Spacecraft Center and visit Rocket Park, where some of the first rockets used in the space program are on display.

Putt-Putt FunHouse (ages 6 and up)

806 East NASA Parkway, next to the Quality Inn, Houston (281-333-0579; www.puttputtfunhouse.com). Open Sunday to Thursday 10 a.m. to 10 p.m. and Friday and Saturday 10 a.m. to midnight. Prices vary by activity.

Putt-Putt FunHouse offers your family miniature golf, bumper boats, go-karts, batting cages, and a game room.

Where to Eat

Frenchie's. 1041 NASA Parkway, Houston (281-486-7144). Where many astronauts and other Space Center folks like to eat Italian food. $–$$

Landry's. #1 Kemah Boardwalk, Kemah (281-334-2513). One of the most popular seafood restaurants in Texas. Located on the renovated Kemah waterfront with shops and other attractions. $$–$$$

Outback Steakhouse. 481 West Bay Area Boulevard, Webster (281-338-6283). Phenomenal steaks. $$

Where to Stay

Holiday Inn–NASA. 1300 NASA Parkway, Houston (281-333-2500 or 800-682-3193; www.holidayinn.com). On the bay next to the Space Center, close to shopping and area parks. Features a pool and exercise room and **free** continental breakfast; children under 18 stay **free.** $$–$$$

Quality Inn–NASA. 904 NASA Parkway, Houston (888-254-0637). Next to Putt Putt FunHouse; children under 18 stay **free.** $$–$$$

For More Information

Bay Area Houston Convention and Visitors Bureau. 20710 Gulf Freeway (I–45), Webster 77598; (800) 844-LAKE; www.visitbayareahouston.com

Galveston

Note:

Galveston received a devastating hit by Hurricane Ike in September, 2008. Some parts of the historic downtown area had up to ten feet of flooding. At press time, most places listed have recovered in part or whole . . . but call before visiting a specific site of interest.

Galveston's sand, surf, sunshine, and seafood are what draw visitors to the city. This island city has miles of beaches, some public lands, some state park lands, some city parks, and some private parks. Some beaches are sandy and broad, others short and rocky. The most popular family-oriented beach is Stewart Beach, at Seawall Boulevard and Broadway on the north end of the island, which is alcohol-free. This area also has a water slide, a bathhouse, concession stands, go-karts, miniature golf, and bumper-boat rides. Galveston is also well known for its well-preserved Victorian architecture, with more than 2,000 buildings listed in the National Register of Historic Places. On the first weekend in December the Strand Historic District turns itself into pre-Christmas Victorian England during **Dickens on the Strand.** Filled with shows, costumed characters, and hundreds of craft booths, it's a true step back in time. You'll find enough food booths that you'll gain weight just walking around smelling all the good stuff.

Bayou Wildlife Park (ages 4 and up)

5050 Farm Road 517, Alvin, about midway between Houston and Galveston (281-337-6376; www.bayouwildlifepark.com). Open March through August 10 a.m. to 4 p.m., September through February 10 a.m. to 3 p.m. Closed Mondays August through February 1. $$–$$$.

Your kids can see and feed animals and birds from all over the world at Bayou Wildlife Park, which not only features exotic animals but has begun to collect endangered ones as well, like the very rare white rhinoceros, ring-tailed lemurs, Bactrian camel, addax, and scimitar-horned oryx. The animals roam free while you ride through the park on a tram with a guide. Frequent stops allow visitors to feed and pet some of the animals. At the Children's Barnyard kids can ride a horse and pet livestock.

Texas Trivia

The Great Storm of 1900 that struck Galveston on September 8 and 9 was the worst natural disaster in U.S. history, responsible for more than 6,000 deaths and hundreds of millions of dollars in damage. Once the second largest port in the nation and Texas's financial capital, Galveston would never completely recover from that hurricane.

Galveston Island State Park (ages 4 and up)

At west end of Seawall Boulevard, 14901 Farm Road 3005, Galveston (409-737-1222, www.tpwd.state.tx.us/spdest/findadest/parks/galveston).

Galveston Island State Park is a 2,000-acre park of sandy beaches and gulf breezes that spans the width of Galveston Island. Activities include swimming, fishing, picnicking, camping, beachcombing, bird-watching, and nature study along 4 miles of walking trails. Facilities include campsites, screened shelters, sixty sheltered picnic tables, a paved boat ramp, and an amphitheater where outdoor musicals are presented.

The Strand National Landmark Historic District (ages 6 and up)

Along Strand Street, Galveston (409-763-4311 or 888-425-4753).

Known as the "Wall Street of the Southwest" before the Great Storm of 1900 devastated most of Galveston, the Strand National Landmark Historic District is a portside area of Victorian buildings now filled with restaurants, shops, factory-outlet stores, jazz and reggae music clubs, art galleries, and more. Although lively anytime, the Strand puts on a great show twice a year, for Mardi Gras and for Christmas.

The Great Storm at Pier 21 Theater (ages 6 and up)

Harborside Drive at Twenty-first Street, Galveston (409-763-8808; www.galveston.com/pier21theatre/ and www.1900storm.com). Open Sunday through Thursday 11 a.m. to 6 p.m., Friday and Saturday 11 a.m. to 8 p.m. $, children 6 and under free.

Feel the fury of the deadliest natural disaster in U.S. history at the Pier 21 Theater in a panoramic, multi-image documentary. Shows begin on the hour. A second film, *The Pirate Island of Jean Lafitte,* is shown on the half hour. $

Texas Seaport Museum/*Elissa* (ages 6 and up)

Located at Pier 21, Galveston (409-763-1877; www.tsm-elissa.org). Open daily 10 a.m. to 5 p.m. $–$$, children 5 and under free.

The Texas Seaport Museum is home to the 1877 Tall Ship *Elissa,* a three-masted sailing ship that serves as a symbol of Galveston and its port. The museum has a number of displays, exhibits, and a multiprojector slide show on what it's like to sail onboard the *Elissa.*

Texas Trivia

Karankawa Indians were the first inhabitants of Galveston. The earliest European settlement of the island was in 1817 by the pirate Jean Laffite; he called the place Campeachy. The U.S. Navy kicked him out in 1821.

Sam Houston's **Big Idea**

The idea for the Gulf Intracoastal Waterway was thought up by none other than Sam Houston in 1846, when he was serving in the U.S. Senate. Houston proposed construction of a navigable channel between the Sabine River and the Rio Grande to stimulate development of Texas's Gulf Coast. But grand ideas moved slowly in those days. Surveying didn't take place until 1873, ten years after Houston died. In 1913 the U.S. Army Corps of Engineers completed the first stretch, a 200-mile segment south from Galveston. The entire 426-mile length from Orange to Brownsville was finished in 1949.

Schlitterbahn Waterpark Galveston (ages 4 and up)

2026 Lockheed Drive, Galveston (409-770-WAVE; www.schlitterbahn.com/gal/). Open during the summer 10 a.m. until 6, 7, or 8 p.m. Heated indoor season during the winter. $$$$.

This family-friendly waterpark features lots of slides, coasters, hot tubs, playgrounds, rivers, and waves. You can take your own picnic (no glass or alcohol) and spend the day.

Ocean Star Offshore Drilling Rig and Museum (ages 6 and up)

Harborside Drive at Twentieth Street on Pier 20, Galveston (409-766-7827; www.oceanstaroec.com). Open daily 10 a.m. to 5 p.m., until 6 p.m. in summer. $–$$, children 6 and under free.

The museum is located on an actual oil-drilling rig and showcases models, information, and interactive exhibits as well as a fifteen-minute orientation film. One of the city's newer attractions, it's also one of the most impressive.

Moody Gardens (ages 2 and up)

One Hope Boulevard, Galveston (800-582-4673; www.moodygardens.com). Open daily 10 a.m. to 6 p.m. $$$$.

Your family can easily spend a day, even a few days, at the phenomenal Moody Gardens. You can't miss its central feature: a ten-story, 40,000-square-foot glass pyramid. The pyramid houses a tropical rain forest with waterfalls, cliffs, caverns, wetlands, and forests and is home to more than 2,000 species of exotic butterflies, birds, plants, fish, and bats. Other attractions include **Palm Beach,** a white-sand beach and blue lagoon swim center for families; landscaped gardens and nature trails; an IMAX 3-D theater, where fish seem to leap out of the six-story screen, and all kinds of tropical fish exhibits, penguins, and sharks at the Aquarium Pyramid.

The Colonel Paddlewheel Boat (ages 4 and up)

At Moody Gardens, Galveston (409-740-7797 or 888-740-7797; www.moodygardens.com/attractions/colonel_paddlewheel_boat/). $$.

For a water-based tour of Galveston, step onto *The Colonel*, a triple-decked paddle wheeler that takes one-hour sightseeing cruises during the day and offers dinner and dancing cruises Friday and Saturday evenings ($$$–$$$$). Departs from Moody Gardens.

Galveston Island Duck Tours (ages 4 and up)

2500 Seawall Boulevard, Galveston (409-621-4771; www.galvestonducks.com/). Tour times vary seasonally. $$–$$$

What a fun way to see the city! This entertaining, narrated land and water tour will introduce you to some of the main attractions in Galveston.

Seawolf Park (ages 6 and up)

On Pelican Island, across the channel from the Port of Galveston (409-797-5114; www.galveston.com/seawolfpark/). Open year round dawn to dusk. $ (parking $).

Your kids can climb aboard an old World War II submarine or destroyer escort, a U.S. Navy jet, and other military vehicles at Seawolf Park. The park has a snack bar, picnic areas, and a playground. It also affords close looks at oceangoing cargo ships passing by. The fishing is good from the nearby pier.

Bolivar Peninsula

For less-crowded beaches, take the twenty-minute ferry ride from Galveston to the Bolivar Peninsula. These ferries are actually a part of the Texas highway system, so there's no charge. Follow Highway 87 north to the dock. The same highway picks up on the other side at Port Bolivar. Kids will love the sand castle-building contests that are the star attraction of the **Texas Crab Festival,** held every May in Crystal Beach. In addition, the festival has a crab cook-off, crab races, arts-and-crafts and food booths, a carnival, and a variety of beach games. Call (409) 684-5940 or visit www.bolivarchamber.org/ for more information on the area.

Where to Eat

Fisherman's Wharf. Pier 22 and Harborside Drive, Galveston (409-765-5708). Waterfront dining, tasty seafood, and steaks. $$–$$$

Gaido's. 3802 Seawall Boulevard, Galveston (409-762-9625; www.gaidosofgalveston.com/). The most popular place in the area for seafood. $$

Mario's Ristorante. 2202 Sixty-first Street, Galveston (409-744-2975). Gourmet pizza, pasta, seafood, and chicken. $$–$$$

Where to Stay

Best Western Beachfront Inn. 5914 Seawall Boulevard, Galveston (888-939-8680; www.bestwestern.com). Walk across the street and jump in the gulf. $$–$$$

Casa del Mar Beachfront Suites. 6102 Seawall Boulevard, Galveston (409-740-2431 or 800-392-1205; www.casadelmartx.com/). Recently renovated condos, great location, two swimming pools. Good value for families. $$–$$$

Hawthorn Suites at the Victorian Resort. 6300 Seawall Boulevard, Galveston (409-740-3555 or 800-231-6363; www.galveston.com/victorian/). Convenient, quiet, great views of the gulf from private balconies, **free** high-speed Internet. You'll also find a pool, barbecue area, playground, and tennis courts; kitchens, bunk beds, and multibed-room suites. $$$

For More Information

Galveston Convention and Visitors Bureau. 2328 Broadway, Galveston 77550; (888) 425-4753; www.galveston.com.

Anahuac, Sabine Pass, and Port Arthur

Anahuac National Wildlife Refuge (ages 4 and up)

On Farm Road 1985, south of Anahuac (409-267-3337; www.fws.gov/southwest/refuges/texas/anahuac).

Anahuac (anna-wack) National Wildlife Refuge is one of the best places in the United States to see all nine species of rails and other marsh birds. Alligators are also common, and you also might see bobcats, river otters, muskrats, and nutria along the 12 miles of road through the refuge.

McFaddin and Texas Point Wildlife Refuges (ages 4 and up)

On Highway 87, between High Island and Sabine Pass (409-736-2371; www.fws.gov/southwest/refuges/texas/mcfaddin).

The McFaddin and Texas Point wildlife refuges are where thousands of migratory geese and ducks use the marshlands. If you're hoping to see or photograph wildlife, you can certainly do it at one of these refuges. McFaddin also has one of the densest populations of alligators in Texas.

Sea Rim State Park (ages 4 and up)

Off Highway 87, 10 miles west of Sabine Pass (409-971-2559, www.tpwd.state.tx.us/spdest/findadest/parks/sea_rim).

Sea Rim State Park offers even more wildlife-viewing opportunities, in addition to beach-combing along the 5.2-mile shoreline. It also has a boardwalk and nature trail through the marshes, canoe trails, fishing, camping, and observation blinds in the 15,109-acre park. A great place for a family to wander about in nature.

Sabine Pass Battleground State Historic Site

(ages 4 and up)

On Farm Road 3322, off Highway 87, Sabine Pass (409-332-8820; www.thc.state.tx.us/hsites/hs_sabine.aspx?Site=Sabine). Open daily. $.

Union forces attempted to invade Texas at Sabine Pass in 1863 but were driven off by a much smaller force of Confederates. The site is now the Sabine Pass Battleground State Historic Site. Dominating the park is a large statue of Lieutenant Dick Dowling, the Texan leader. The 53-acre park also has a boat ramp, picnic facilities, a fish-cleaning shelter, and great views of ships on their way to and from Port Arthur and Beaumont.

Museum of the Gulf Coast (ages 6 and up)

700 Proctor Street, Port Arthur (409-982-7000; www.museumofthegulfcoast.org). Open Monday through Saturday 9 a.m. to 5 p.m., Sunday 1 to 5 p.m. $.

The Museum of the Gulf Coast is filled with relics from this coastal area's past, surrounded by stunning murals. The musical heritage room honors native daughter Janis Joplin, whose psychedelic-painted Porsche sits atop a spinning gold record, and other Port Arthur musical legends like J. P. "Big Bopper" Richardson, Richie Valens, and Tex Ritter. Interpretive displays include a number of children's interactive exhibits.

For More Information

Port Arthur Convention and Visitors Bureau. 3401 Cultural Center Drive, Port Arthur 77642; (800) 235-7822; www.portarthurtexas.com/.

East Texas: The Piney Woods

It's a good thing the signs for Texas's farm and ranch roads have a silhouette of the state on them, otherwise visitors to East Texas might not believe they're in the Lone Star State.

East Texas, often called the Piney Woods, is about as far from the stereotypical Texas landscape as you can get. When you see the red dirt and thick forests of tall pines, you might think you're in Georgia. When you visit the Alabama-Coushatta Indian Reservation, you might think you're in Oklahoma. When you see the multitude of large lakes and rivers, you might think you're in Minnesota. When you see thick moss hanging from trees around Caddo Lake or hear the Cajun lilt of people near Beaumont, you might think you're deep in Louisiana bayou country.

TopAnnualEvents in East Texas

- **Dogwood Festival,** Woodville, March (409-283-2632)
- **Sam Houston Folk Festival,** Huntsville, April (936-294-1832)
- **Stagecoach Days,** Marshall, May (903-935-7868)
- **Tops in Texas Rodeo,** Jacksonville, July (903-586-2217 or 800-376-2217)
- **Black-Eyed Pea Jamboree,** Athens, July (800-755-7878 or 903-675-5181)
- **Texas Renaissance Festival,** Plantersville, October (800-458-3435)
- **Fire Ant Festival,** Marshall, October (903-935-7868)
- **Texas Rose Festival,** Tyler, October (903-597-3130)
- **Wonderland of Lights Christmas Festival,** Marshall, December (903-935-7868)

EAST TEXAS: THE PINEY WOODS

But it's all Texas, a region where timber and oil are king and queen. You won't find any metropolises here. What you will find are many small villages and cities filled with southern hospitality and a region where nature is a prized possession: More than 750,000 acres are set aside in four national forests and the **Big Thicket National Preserve.** If your family likes the outdoors, you're in for a real treat in East Texas.

Orange

You'll find a lot of history in Orange, the first Texas city on I–10 coming from Louisiana. As one example of just how big Texas is, consider that if you started here and drove west along I–10, by the time you reached the western state line just past El Paso you'd have driven 880 miles.

If your family likes Cajun food, don't miss the annual **International Gumbo Cook-Off** held in early May. Sample gumbo, enjoy the carnival rides, watch live entertainment, or wander around the arts-and-crafts booths. Call (409) 883-1011 or (800) 528-4906 for information, or visit the Web site at www.orangetexas.org.

Stark Museum of Art (ages 6 and up)

712 Green Avenue, Orange (409-883-2787; www.starkmuseum.org). Open Tuesday through Saturday 10 a.m. to 5 p.m. Closed major holidays. Free.

Some of the best western art in the country is in the collection at the Stark Museum. You'll find original Audubon bird sketches, sculptures by Remington and Russell, paintings by the Taos masters, Native American pottery and artifacts, and much more.

Heritage House Museum (ages 6 and up)

905 West Division Avenue, Orange (409-886-5385). Open Tuesday through Friday 10 a.m. to 4 p.m., weekends by appointment. $.

The Heritage House isn't some large mansion as are many registered historic landmarks. Instead, this simple home is a century-old middle-class house that features rotating exhibits of early Texas history and family life from a hundred years ago. The museum holds many historical and seasonal events throughout the year where you or the kids can take turns making crafts or participating in pioneer activities.

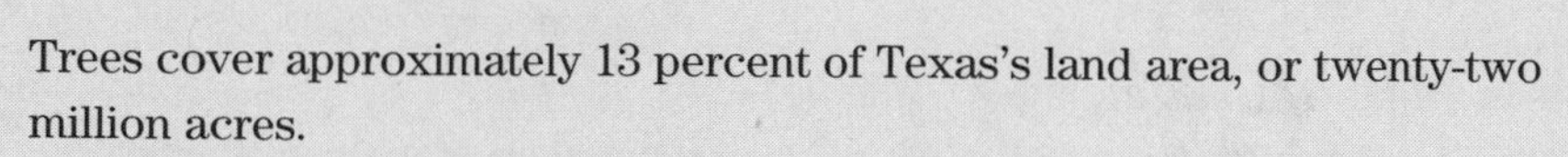

Trees cover approximately 13 percent of Texas's land area, or twenty-two million acres.

Claiborne West Park (ages 4 and up)

On Cow Bayou, west of Orange off I–10 (409-745-2255).

Get personal with nature at Claiborne West Park. This heavily wooded preserve has some of the best bird-watching around, along with nature and hiking trails, picnic areas, campsites, and a playground. You can fish for rainbow trout during the winter.

Beaumont

Beaumont is a city rich in Spanish and French tradition, a city where the Texas oil industry was born, and it's nestled close to both the Gulf of Mexico and the Big Thicket. You'll find a lot to do here, both in museums and outdoors.

Art Museum of Southeast Texas (ages 6 and up)

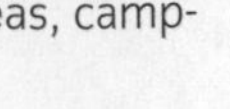

500 Main Street, Beaumont (409-832-3432; www.amset.org). Open Monday through Friday 9 a.m. to 5 p.m., Saturday 10 a.m. to 5 p.m., Sunday noon to 5 p.m. Free.

The Art Museum of Southeast Texas has a permanent collection of art and hosts several traveling exhibits throughout the year.

John Jay French Trading Post (ages 6 and up)

3025 French Road, Beaumont (409-898-0348). Open Tuesday through Saturday 10 a.m. to 4 p.m. $.

The Trading Post is a collection of pioneer artifacts along with a blacksmith shop, tannery, corncrib, and smokehouse.

Spindletop/Gladys City Boomtown Museum (ages 6 and up)

On U.S. Highway 69 at University Drive, Beaumont (409-835-0823; www.spindletop.org;). Open Tuesday through Saturday 10 a.m. to 5 p.m., Sunday 1 to 5 p.m. $.

Your family can see where the oil business in Texas really got started at Spindletop. This wasn't the first well in the state, but the gusher Spindletop produced in 1901 made the industry a reality. You'll see the world's first boomtown re-created here, complete with wooden derricks.

Texas Energy Museum (ages 6 and up)

600 Main Street, Beaumont (409-833-5100; www.texasenergymuseum.org). Open Tuesday through Saturday 9 a.m. to 5 p.m., Sunday 1 to 5 p.m. $.

The Texas Energy Museum will show you just how the petroleum industry evolved, making Texas an oil giant. Displays include many hands-on and multimedia exhibits.

Edison Plaza Museum (ages 6 and up)

350 Pine Street, Beaumont (409-981-3089; www.edisonmuseum.org). Open Monday through Friday 9 a.m. to 5 p.m. Free.

Texas Trivia

In 1899 the U.S. Geological Survey declared that there was "little or no chance for oil in Kansas or Texas."

For the scientists in your family, visit the Edison Museum. This is the largest collection of Thomas A. Edison artifacts west of the Mississippi, including cylinder phonographs and a look at what some of Edison's inventions have led to today and may lead to in the future.

Fire Museum of Texas (ages 4 and up)

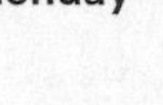

400 Walnut Street, Beaumont (409-880-3927; www.firemuseumoftexas.org). Open Monday through Friday 8 a.m. to 4:30 p.m. Free.

The Fire Museum displays antique bells, buckets, hoses, badges, photographs, and vintage fire trucks in a 1927 fire station. Home of the world's largest fire hydrant.

Babe Didrikson Zaharias Museum (ages 6 and up)

1750 I–10 East, exit 854, Beaumont (409-833-4622; www.babedidrikson zaharias.org). Open daily 9 a.m. to 5 p.m. Closed Christmas. Free.

Mildred "Babe" Didrikson Zaharias was the greatest American female athlete of the twentieth century and the best athlete to come out of Texas. She could do it all: win Olympic medals, play championship basketball, and play championship golf. The Babe Didrikson Zaharias Museum honors this pioneer, exhibiting many of her trophies and personal memorabilia.

Julie Rogers Theatre (ages 8 and up)

765 Pearl Street, Beaumont (800-782-3081; www.beaumont-tx-complex.com/julierogers theatre.html). Prices vary by event.

Beaumont may be a small city, but it is justly proud of its performing-arts organizations. The Julie Rogers Theatre, across from the Civic Center, is home to the Beaumont opera, symphony, and ballet.

Gator Country (ages 6 and up)

21159 Farm Road 365, Beaumont (409-794-9453). Open daily 10 a.m. to 6 p.m.$–$$.

Over 130 American alligators, 6 species of crocodiles/caiman, 4 species of turtles, Sulkata tortoise, snakes, and Savanah Monitor. Home of "Big Al," the biggest alligator in captivity in Texas.

Where to Eat

Carlito's. 2570 Calder Street, Beaumont (409-839-8011). Extremely popular for steaks and Mexican food such as shrimp enchiladas. $$

Don's Seafood and Steakhouse. 2290 I–10 South, Beaumont (409-842-0686). Texans know Don's is the place for great, authentic seafood and steaks done up with a flavorful Cajun twist, heavy on the crawfish. $$

Willy Ray's Bar-B-Q. 145 I–10 North, Beaumont (409-832-7770. Not your typical barbecue joint, this one features great pork loin, pepper turkey, and key lime cheesecake. $–$$

Where to Stay

Best Western. 1610 I–10 South, Beaumont (409-842-0037; www.bestwestern.com). Pool, **free** continental breakfast. $$

La Quinta. 220 I–10 North, Beaumont (409-838-9991; www.laquinta.com). Pool, **free** continental breakfast. $$

For More Information

Beaumont Convention and Visitors Bureau. 505 Willow, P.O. Box 3827, Beaumont 77704; (800) 392-4401 or (409) 880-3749; www.beaumontcvb.com.

Kountze and Lumberton

Big Thicket National Preserve (ages 4 and up)

6044 Farm Road 420, 7 miles north of Kountze (409-951-6725; www.nps.gov/bith/). Open daily 9 a.m. to 5 p.m.

Big Thicket National Preserve is a bewildering, wooded 96,000 acres where eight ecosystems converge to make up what biologists call the "biological crossroads of North America," with thousands of animal and plant life forms. The Big Thicket was designated a "Man and the Biosphere Reserve" by the United Nations in 1981, giving you an idea of just how unique this place is. The park features nine hiking trails ranging from .75 mile to 18 miles. You can also enjoy canoeing, swimming, and fishing. Guided hikes, children's programs, lectures, and boat tours are **free,** but reservations are required.

Village Creek State Park (ages 4 and up)

10 miles north of Beaumont on Highway 96 (Alma Drive), Lumberton (409-755-7322, www.tpwd.state.tx.us/spdest/findadest/parks/village_creek).

Village Creek is a very popular flat-water stream among Texas canoeists. The 63-mile-long creek flows through the heart of the Big Thicket to the Neches River. You'll find a wildness here that is difficult to match. The woods are thick, dotted with baygalls (a kind of miniature swamp) and larger cypress and tupelo swamps. Wildlife including deer, raccoons, armadillos, alligators, rabbits, and possums are common. Birds are plentiful, too. Facilities include tent campsites, a canoe launch ramp, picnic areas, a playground, and plenty of hiking trails.

For More Information

Lumberton Chamber of Commerce. 826 North Main Street, P.O. Box 8574, Lumberton 77657; (409) 755-0554; www.lumbertoncoc.com.

Plantersville and Huntsville

If you're lucky enough to be in Huntsville the first weekend in May, don't miss the Sam Houston Folk Festival, a rousing family event that features costumed characters, demonstrations of pioneer skills and crafts, an arts-and-crafts fair, and entertainment. For information call (936) 294-1832 or visit the Web site at http://samhouston.memorial.museum/FolkFestN/.

Texas Renaissance Festival (ages 4 and up)

21778 Farm Road 1774, 6 miles south of Plantersville (800-458-3435; www.texrenfest.com). $$–$$$$.

On seven weekends in October and November, 237 wooded acres of the Piney Woods are transformed into something out of the Middle Ages. The Renaissance Festival is a wonderful family event, full of parading entertainers, jousting, dancing, entertainment stages, plenty of food booths, and an arts-and-crafts fair.

Sam Houston Memorial Museum and Park (ages 6 and up)

Corner of Nineteenth Street and Avenue N , Huntsville (936-294-1832; www.samhouston.memorial.museum). Open Tuesday through Saturday 9 a.m. to 4:30 p.m., Sunday noon to 4:30 p.m. Free.

Huntsville is one of the state's oldest cities and was home to the biggest Texas hero of them all, Sam Houston. After Houston won independence for Texas and served as president of the republic and governor of the state, he settled here. You can visit his home at the Sam Houston Memorial Museum and Park, near Sam Houston State University. It's also hard to miss that huge statue of Houston, a good place for photos. The statue is the tallest in the world depicting an American hero.

Texas Prison Museum (ages 6 and up)

491 Highway 75 North , Huntsville (936-295-2155; www.txprisonmuseum.org). Open Monday through Saturday 10 a.m. to 5 p.m., Sunday noon to 5 p.m. $, children 6 and under free.

Huntsville is also home to the state's most famous prison. It's here where most of the hard cases go, and its dirty red walls are terrifying. The Texas Prison Museum displays many artifacts pertaining to outlaws and historic methods of punishment. The shop features crafts made by prisoners with a lot of time on their hands.

Texas Trivia

Sam Houston may have had the most unusual career of any politician. As a Tennessee resident, he was elected to the U.S. Congress and served as that state's governor. After moving to Texas, he was elected president of the republic, then to the U.S. Senate, then governor of his adopted state.

Samuel Walker Houston Cultural Center (ages 6 and up)

1604 Tenth Street, Huntsville (936-295-2119). Donations requested.

The Samuel Walker Houston Cultural Center honors a prominent black educator and son of Joshua Houston, a former slave of Sam Houston's. The center depicts life for blacks in the city after the Civil War. Next door is a children's playground.

Huntsville State Park (ages 4 and up)

Park Road 40, Exit 109 off I–45, 6 miles south of Huntsville (mailing address: P.O. Box 508, Huntsville 77342; 936-295-5644, www.tpwd.state.tx.us/spdest/findadest/parks/huntsville).

Huntsville State Park is a beautiful area in the midst of loblolly and shortleaf pines with a lake right in the middle of it all. The park has 11 miles of hiking and biking trails where wildlife and birds can easily be seen. Facilities include campsites, screened shelters, picnic areas, and an amphitheater where rangers give nature talks. You might even see an alligator around the lake. Even if you don't, make sure to get a picture of the DO NOT FEED OR HARASS ALLIGATORS sign.

Sam Houston National Forest (ages 4 and up)

Between Huntsville and Livingston (936-344-6205).

Sam Houston National Forest has a number of hiking and mountain-biking trails and recreation areas. It's an exceptionally beautiful area of Texas, seldom visited except by locals and others in the know.

The Lone Star Hiking Trail is one way to get the family out enjoying nature without crowds or traffic. This is actually several trails that wind for a total of 140 miles through Sam Houston National Forest. You can do short stretches or overnight hikes. Either way, you'll be deep in the Piney Woods, listening to hawks and woodpeckers, feeling cool breezes, and smelling the pungent odor of pine.

For general information on all four of the national forests in East Texas, call the U.S. Forest Service office in Lufkin at (936) 639-8501.

Scenic **Drive**

Several roads through the forest provide you with great woodland beauty. Drive along Farm Road 1374 and Farm Road 1375 and you'll see a Texas you may not have known existed, one of the prettiest drives in the state. The route goes through the heart of Huntsville State Park and Sam Houston National Forest, with so much cooling shade in the summer that you might not want to leave.

The pines are abundant, but they're interspersed with willow, oak, elm, black gum, green ash, dogwood, maple, and sassafras. This thick forest is also thick with wildlife, so drive carefully to let the kids get a glimpse of the white-tailed deer, raccoons, possums, and armadillos that always seem to be alongside the roads.

Where to Eat

Catfish Place. 267 Highway 19, Huntsville (936-295-8685). The best place to taste this Piney Woods staple. $–$$

Chili's. 1406 I–45, Huntsville (936-295-9375; www.chilis.com). This chain serves up scrumptious food with a southwestern flavor. Special kids' meals. $$

Where to Stay

La Quinta Inn Huntsville. 124 I–45 North, Huntsville (936-295-6454). Pool, **free** continental breakfast. $$

Holiday Inn Express. 148 I-45 South, Huntsville (936-295-4300; www.holidayinn.com). Pool, complimentary breakfast. $$

Texas Trivia

Huntsville is the seat of Walker County, originally named for U.S. Treasury Secretary Robert J. Walker, an early Texas patriot. But the state legislature withdrew the honor in 1863 because Walker was a Union sympathizer. Then the legislature renamed the county for Samuel H. Walker, an early Texas Ranger, scout, and codeveloper of the Walker Colt revolving pistol.

Crockett

Davy Crockett National Forest (ages 4 and up)

Between Crockett and Groveton on U.S. Highway 287 (936-639-8501).

Davy Crockett National Forest is the largest of Texas's four national forests, its primary boundary formed by the scenic Neches River. The forest has only a few developed areas but many backpacking trails and primitive campsites. Canoeists in the family will like the Big Slough Canoe Trail.

For More Information

Walker County Chamber of Commerce. The Visitor Center is at the base of the giant statue of Sam Houston at exit 109 from I–45, P.O. Box 538, Huntsville 77342; (800) 289-0389 or (936) 295-8113; www.chamber.huntsville.tx.us.

Palestine

So many dogwoods bloom in this part of Texas that Palestine celebrates with a three-weekend event in late March through early April. The Texas Dogwood Trails Festival includes parades, an arts-and-crafts fair, tours of historic homes, domino tournaments, model-train shows, and hikes and drives through the heart of dogwood country.

Engeling Wildlife Refuge (ages 4 and up)

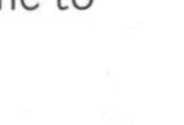

20 miles northwest of Palestine on US 287 (903-928-2251).

Engeling Wildlife Refuge has more than 10,000 heavily wooded acres that are home to several species of birds and many deer, fox, rabbits, squirrels, and wolves.

Museum for East Texas Culture (ages 6 and up)

400 Micheaux Avenue, Palestine (903-723-1914; www.museumpalestine.org). Open Monday through Saturday 10 a.m. to 5 p.m., Sunday 1 to 4 p.m. $.

The Museum for East Texas Culture is a regional museum housed in a circa-1915 high school. Featured are displays on the railroads, local architecture, schools, and pioneers, as well as traveling exhibits.

Davey Dogwood Park (ages 4 and up)

On North Link Street, just north of Palestine (800-659-3484).

Near the Museum for East Texas Culture is Davey Dogwood Park, a 200-acre natural area with 5 miles of scenic roads and hiking trails through a forest of dogwood and other trees. There are several picnic areas.

Fairfield Lake State Park (ages 4 and up)

123 State Park Road 64, south of US 287, about 20 miles west of Palestine or off Farm Road 2570 east of Palestine (903-389-4514, www.tpwd.state.tx.us/spdest/findadest/parks/fairfield_lake).

Get the family wet at Fairfield Lake State Park. You'll find rolling hills of hardwood forest surrounding the lake. Facilities include boat ramps, campsites, picnic areas, a sandy swimming area, and 6 miles of hiking trails. You can see beaver here and, in the winter, bald eagles.

Where to Eat

Herschel's Family Restaurant. 1925 South Loop 256, Palestine (903-729-7811). Lots of choices in a homey atmosphere. $–$$

Where to Stay

Bailey Bunkhouse. 4701 Anderson County Road 441, 8 miles north of Palestine (559-362-5837; www.baileybunkhouse.com/). The spacious log cabin has two bedrooms downstairs, extra beds upstairs, and a kitchen. Rustic location offers excellent fishing on the grounds. $$

For More Information

Palestine Convention and Visitors Bureau. 825 Spring Street, Palestine 75801; (903) 723-3014 or (800) 659-3484; www.visitpalestine.com.

Rusk

About 30 miles east of Palestine on U.S. Highway 84.

Texas State Railroad (ages 4 and up)

Departures from either the Rusk or Palestine depot (888-987-2461; www.texasstaterr.com). $$–$$$$.

This century-old steam train runs for a 50-mile round-trip through scenic forests and pastures and across the Neches River between Rusk and Palestine, over twenty-four bridges. The depots at each end of the trip re-create early twentieth-century stations, and the Rusk depot has a theater that shows a film detailing the railroad's history. This rail line was begun in 1896 using convict labor, and prisoners renovated it when it became a state park in 1972. Engines date from 1901 to 1927.

Texas State Railroad Park and Campground (ages 4 and up)

On US 84, 3 miles west of Rusk and 4 miles east of Palestine (888-978-2461; www.texasstaterr.com/parks.php). $.

Adjacent to the depots, you'll discover the park and campground, which has playgrounds and picnic areas. The Rusk unit also offers overnight camping, fishing, and hiking. The Palestine unit has limited camping and excellent hiking.

Texas Trivia

Texas uses 1.6 million gallons of white and yellow paint each year to paint stripes along its highways.

Jim Hogg Historical Park (ages 4 and up)

Fire Tower Road off US 84, 2 miles northeast of Rusk (903-683-4850; www.rusktexascoc .org/jim_hogg_city_park.htm).

This park is named after James Hogg, the state's first native-born governor. There's a scale replica of Hogg's birthplace here, as well as the family cemetery, picnic areas, nature trails, and a children's playground.

Mission Tejas State Park (ages 4 and up)

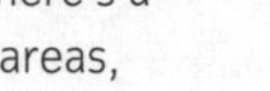

120 State Park Road 44, off US 69 on Highway 21, Grapeland, about 20 miles southwest of Rusk (936-687-2394, www.tpwd.state.tx.us/spdest/findadest/parks/mission_tejas).

Mission Tejas was one of the first Spanish settlements in the area. Historic structures here will transport your family to days of rustic tranquillity. The Civilian Conservation Corps built one log building to commemorate that early mission. The other log building is the Rice family home, which was moved here and restored. Facilities include camping, hiking, and picnicking, with fishing in a pond near the picnic area.

Caddoan Mounds State Historic Site (ages 4 and up)

1649 State Highway 21, Alto, about 20 miles southwest of Rusk (936-858-3218; www.thc .state.tx.us/hsites/hs_caddo.aspx?Site=Caddo). Open Tuesday through Sunday 8:30 a.m. to 4:30 p.m. $.

Caddoan Mounds is a fascinating place, encompassing a Native American village site and the earthen burial grounds of Caddo Indians. The park has two temple mounds in addition to the burial mounds. The park is currently day-use only, and picnicking and camping are not allowed.

For More Information

Rusk Chamber of Commerce. 415 North Main Street, P.O. Box 67, Rusk 75785; (903) 683-4242 or (800) 933-2381; www.rusktexas coc.org.

Jacksonville, Athens, and Canton

Rodeo is always family fun, and the **Tops in Texas Rodeo** in Jacksonville in mid-July will provide you with some of the best. Even though the city is small, the rodeo attracts top Professional Rodeo Cowboy Association riders. The event also boasts a parade, an arts-and-crafts festival, and special children's activities. For information call (903) 586-3285; www.topsintexasrodeo.com.

Lake Palestine (ages 4 and up)

13 miles northwest of Jacksonville on U.S. Highway 175 (903-876-2237).

Go from the woods to the water at Lake Palestine. Here are boating, fishing, hunting, picnicking, skiing, and swimming on a 22,500-acre lake well stocked with fish.

Lake Jacksonville (ages 4 and up)

Off US 69, 3 miles southwest of Jacksonville (903-586-3510).

Water-ski, fish, picnic, camp out, swim, or just relax on the shore of this 1,350-acre lake, which is rated as one of the best bass lakes in all of Texas. Open all year. **Free.**

Cherokee Trace Drive-Thru Safari (ages 2 and up)

1200 County Road 4405, Jacksonville (903) 683-3322; www.cherokeetrace.org). Open March through August Monday through Saturday 10 a.m. to 6 p.m. and Sunday 1 to 6 p.m.and September through February Monday through Saturday 10 a.m. to 5 p.m. and Sunday 1 p.m. to 5 p.m. $$.

This drive-through safari is home to a large variety of exotic and endangered animals living in 300 acres of open habitat in the piney woods of East Texas. The self-guided tour is both fun and educational—take your camera!

Texas Trivia

Next time your family has a round of hamburgers, thank the town of Athens. More specifically, thank Fletcher Davis, who in the 1880s served up a ground-meat patty topped with mustard, onions, and pickles between two slices of bread at Stirman's Drug Store. It was a local favorite for lunch, and in 1904 Davis introduced the hamburger to the world at his booth at the St. Louis World's Fair.

First Monday Trade Days (ages 6 and up)

Off U.S. Highway 64, near the courthouse, Canton (903-567-6556; www.firstmondaycanton .com).

Your family has probably never seen anything like First Monday Trade Days in Canton. Like many small towns in Texas, Canton holds a monthly market day where vendors sell everything from antiques to art, crafts to junk. But Canton's is by far the largest in the state: More than 5,000 dealers gather on a hundred acres to sell their wares the first weekend and Monday of every month. And they've been doing it since 1850. There's something for everyone here. The grounds are full of food and drink booths—and ATM kiosks—to keep you going.

Purtis Creek State Park (ages 4 and up)

14225 Farm Road 316, Eustace, about 15 miles southwest of Canton (903-425-2332, www .tpwd.state.tx.us/spdest/findadest/parks/purtis_creek).

When the family's shopped out, head to Purtis Creek State Park to relax. Good fishing and shady campsites and picnic areas are the attraction here. Facilities include boat ramps, fishing piers and cleaning stations, a playground, and a trout pond.

For More Information

Athens Chamber of Commerce. 1206 South Palestine Street, Athens 75751; (903) 675-5181 or (800) 775-7878; www.athenscc .org.

Canton Chamber of Commerce. 119 North Buffalo Street, Canton 75103; (903) 567-2991; www.chambercantontx.com.

Jacksonville Chamber of Commerce. 526 East Commerce Street, Jacksonville 75766; (800) 376-2217 or (903) 586-2217; www.jacksonvilletexas.com.

Tyler

Municipal Rose Garden and Rose Center (ages 4 and up)

420 South Rose Park Drive, Tyler (903-597-3130; www.cityoftyler.org; www.texasrosefestival .com/museum). Garden open daily dawn to dark; visitor center open daily 9 a.m. to 4:30 p.m.; museum open Tuesday through Friday 9 a.m. to 4:30p.m., Saturday 10 a.m. to 4:30 p.m.; Sunday 1:30 to 4:30 p.m. Free.

Tyler is famous throughout Texas for its roses. One-fifth of all commercial rose bushes in the United States come from this area. The Texas Rose Festival in October celebrates the flower with a parade and show. All you can imagine about roses is at the Municipal Rose Garden and Rose Center. The garden has 38,000 rose bushes of 500 varieties. The museum features educational exhibits about the rose-growing industry.

Brookshire's World of Wildlife Museum and Country Store (ages 6 and up)

1600 Loop 323, at Old Jacksonville Highway, Tyler (903-534-2169). Open from March through September Tuesday through Saturday 9 a.m. to 5 p.m., From October through February Tuesday through Saturday 10 a.m. to 4 p.m. Free.

The museum preserves 250 specimens of animals, reptiles, and fish from Africa and North America, while the store depicts what grocery stores were like in the 1920s, including a 1926 delivery truck. There's also an antique fire truck on display.

Tyler Museum of Art (ages 6 and up)

1300 South Mahon Street, Tyler (903-595-1001; www.tylermuseum.org). Open Tuesday through Saturday 10 a.m. to 5 p.m., Sunday 1 to 5 p.m. $.

The Tyler Museum, near Tyler Junior College, is always changing its exhibits, focusing on a special artist or collection, so you'll never see the same thing twice.

The Discovery Science Place (ages 5 and up)

308 N. Broadway, Tyler (903-533-8011; www.discoveryscienceplace.org/). Open Monday through Saturday 9 a.m. to 5 p.m., Sunday 1 p.m. to 5 p.m. $$.

A hands-on children's learning center with three exhibit halls for kids to explore.

Tyler Skateplex (ages 6 and up)

7922 S. Broadway, Tyler (903-939-3330; www.tylerskateplex.com/) Opening varies. $$.

The largest skating floor in the country! Over 28,000 square feet. This enormous facility also contains a huge Arcade, party room, and skateboard area.

Fire Mountain Amusement Park (ages 6 and up)

14662 Hwy. 155 South, Tyler (903-561-2670; www.firemountainamusements.com/). $$.

A tremendous variety of activities for the entire family—Go-Karts, Bumper Boats, Video Arcade and Miniature Golf.

Caldwell Zoo (ages 2 and up)

2203 Martin Luther King Boulevard, Tyler (903-593-0121; www.caldwellzoo.org). Open March through Labor Day daily 9 a.m. to 5 p.m., Labor Day through February daily 9 a.m. to 4 p.m. $, children under 2 free.

The Caldwell Zoo started as a backyard menagerie, but it's now a thirty-five-acre zoo with elephant and giraffe houses, a monkey island, birds, bears, and alligators. That the zoo was designed especially for children is evident in the milk-cow exhibit.

Tyler State Park (ages 4 and up)

789 Park Road 16, 10 miles north of Tyler (903-597-5338, www.tpwd.state.tx.us/spdest/findadest/parks/tyler).

Like other East Texas towns, Tyler has its own family outdoor getaway, Tyler State Park, where you'll find a spring-fed lake surrounded by a pine and hardwood forest. You can camp, fish, have a picnic, swim, watch wildlife, or wander along the 2.5 miles of hiking trails and the self-guided nature trail.

Where to Eat

Casa Olé. 5105 South Broadway, Tyler (903-534-1991). Top Tex-Mex food. $–$$

Bodacious Bar B Q. 1879 Troup Highway, Tyler (903-592-4148; www.thebodaciousbbq.com/). Best barbecue in East Texas.

Luby's Cafeteria. 1815 Roseland, Tyler (903-597-2901; www.lubys.com). Everyone can find something tasty at Luby's. $–$$

Where to Stay

Hampton Inn. 3130 Troup Highway, Tyler (903-596-7752). Pool, **free** breakfast. $$

La Quinta. 1601 West Southwest Loop 323, Tyler (903-561-2223; www.laquinta.com). Pool, **free** breakfast, children under 18 **free.** $$

For More Information

Tyler Convention and Visitors Bureau. 315 North Broadway Street, Tyler 75702; (800) 235-5712 or (903) 592-1661; www.visittyler.com.

Pittsburg and Daingerfield

North of Tyler on Highway 11.

Getting to these small cities, you'll discover you are surrounded by a heavily timbered area that's a center for farming, poultry, and livestock. You'll also find berry farms almost everywhere, and several offer pick-your-own deals in season. Pittsburg is also one of the largest peach-producing areas in Texas.

Northeast Texas Rural Heritage Museum (ages 6 and up)

At the train depot on Marshall Street, Pittsburg (903-856-1200; www.pittsburgtxmuseum.com). Open Thursday through Saturday 10 a.m. to 4 p.m. $.

Housed in the old Cotton Belt Railroad Depot, the museum exhibits historic artifacts from the time of the town's founding in 1854 along with antique farm equipment and other memorabilia. See the full-sized replica of the world-famous Ezekiel airship.

Lake Bob Sandlin State Park (ages 4 and up)

341 Park Road 2117, about 12 miles north of Pittsburg (903-572-5531, www.tpwd.state.tx.us/spdest/findadest/parks/lake_bob_sandlin).

Are you outdoored out yet? Don't be, because you're in the middle of the best outdoor recreation in the state. Another place where you can find camping, fishing, picnicking, and swimming is Lake Bob Sandlin State Park. The park features many campsites, screened shelters, a fishing pier and cleaning station, and 3.5 miles of hiking trails.

Scenic **Drive**

One of the more unusual drives in Texas is the route between Daingerfield State Park and Caddo Lake, mainly because it doesn't look like what most people figure Texas should look like. Along the way you'll see thick forests, trees turning colors in the fall, scenic lakes and bayous, and, finally, the mysterious-looking Caddo Lake, with its cypress-crowded waters.

Take Park Road 17 out of Daingerfield State Park to Highway 49, head east to Farm Road 250, and drive south. Continue south, then east on Farm Road 729 and east on Farm Road 134 out of Jefferson to Uncertain and Caddo Lake, with its moss-draped cypress and numerous side sloughs.

Daingerfield State Park (ages 4 and up)

455 Park Road 17, 10 miles east of Daingerfield (903-645-2921, www.tpwd.state.tx.us/spdest/findadest/parks/daingerfield).

Families will find an abundance of sights and activities in the park's 550 pine-covered acres, and a spring-fed lake offers excellent fishing and swimming. Hiking trails provide 2.5 miles of wildlife-watching opportunities. Springtime brings blossoming flowers throughout the park. Facilities include campsites, cabins with kitchenettes, picnic areas, and a playground.

Sulphur Springs and Paris

Southwest Dairy Museum and Education Center (ages 4 and up)

1210 Houston Street, Sulphur Springs (903-439-6455; www.southwestdairyfarmers.com). Open Monday through Friday 9 a.m. to 4 p.m. Free.

Sulphur Springs is the largest dairy-producing area in Texas, and your family can get a fascinating look into the industry at the Southwest Dairy Museum. Find out how milk gets from cows to your refrigerator and how it was done a century ago, and help yourself to ice cream at the old-fashioned soda fountain. The museum has several interactive exhibits for children.

Leo St. Clair Music Box Museum (ages 4 and up)

611 North Davis Street, Sulphur Springs (903-885-4926). Open Monday through Wednesday and Friday 9 a.m. to 6 p.m., Thursday 11 a.m. to 8 p.m. Free.

More things to fascinate your family can be found at this gallery, installed on the first floor of the Sulphur Springs Library. They claim the largest collection of music boxes in the world.

Hopkins County Museum and Heritage Park (ages 6 and up)

416 North Jackson Street, Sulphur Springs (903-885-2387; www.hopkinscountymuseum .org). Open Tuesday through Saturday 10 a.m. to 2 p.m. $.

Many restored homes and shops from the nineteenth century were relocated to this eleven-acre site. The museum has displays of area pioneer artifacts.

Lake Crook (ages 4 and up)

On U.S. Highway 271 North, Paris (903-784-9299).

At Lake Crook, your family will find 972 acres of outside fun with fishing, picnic tables, and boating.

Paris Family Fun Center (ages 6 and up)

2625 Spur 139, Paris (903-785-0888). Open daily 11 a.m. to 9 p.m. during summer months. $.

A kid's paradise with a skating rink, go-karts, miniature golf, a game arcade, and batting cages.

Texarkana and Atlanta

Texarkana is one of those few cities in the United States that are split between two states. The name comes from three states, however: TEXas, ARKansas, and LouisiANA. The Louisiana state line is south of the city. For an amusing picture of the kids, head to Photographers Island, in front of the Federal Building at 100 North State Line Avenue. Half the building is in Texas and half is in Arkansas. So as not to play favorites, its address is Texarkana, USA 75501. The island in front of the building shows the state line.

Crystal Springs Beach (ages 4 and up)

On U.S. Highway 67, 18 miles west of Texarkana (903-585-5246). Open Tuesday through Saturday 11 a.m. to 6 p.m. and Sunday noon to 6 p.m. Memorial Day through Labor Day. $–$$, children under 3 free.

This family park surrounding a twelve-acre lake features water slides and paddle boats, a video arcade, and picnic areas.

Museum of Regional History (ages 6 and up)

219 State Line Avenue, Texarkana (903-793-4831; www.texarkanamuseums.org/texarkana historicalmuseum.htm). Open Tuesday through Saturday 10 a.m. to 4 p.m. $–$$.

The Museum of Regional History has a little something for all tastes. Featured are not only the history of the area, from Caddo Indians to the railroad, but also memorabilia honoring native son Scott Joplin, the father of ragtime music.

Ace of Clubs House (ages 6 and up)

420 Pine Street, Texarkana (903-793-4831; www.texarkanamuseums.org/aceofclubshouse .htm). Open Tuesday through Saturday 10 a.m. to 4 p.m. $–$$.

The unusual Ace of Clubs House was built in 1885 with winnings from a poker game. The Victorian house has a central octagonal stair hall with three octagonal wings and one rectangular wing, giving it the distinctive shape of an ace of clubs. Each room represents a specific period in the history of the house, providing insight into the families that lived here.

Discovery Place (ages 4 and up)

215 Pine Street, Texarkana (903-793-4831; www.texarkanamuseums.org/discoveryplace .htm). Open Tuesday through Saturday 10 a.m. to 4 p.m. $.

The kids can amuse themselves and learn something at the same time at Discovery Place, which offers hands-on science and history exhibits, lab demonstrations, and audiovisual presentations and lectures.

Atlanta State Park (ages 4 and up)

927 Park Road 32, 14 miles northwest of Atlanta (903-796-6476, www.tpwd.state.tx.us/sp dest/findadest/parks/atlanta).

Atlanta State Park is nestled in the pine forests bordering Lake Wright Patman. Activities on the lake include boating, fishing, waterskiing, and swimming, and the park has a number of hike and bike trails where you can see abundant wildlife. Facilities include campsites, picnic areas, and a playground with basketball and volleyball courts.

Where to Eat

Randy's Smokehouse. 2504 Richmond Road, Texarkana (903-832-3036). Good hickory-smoked barbecue. $$

Old Tyme Burger Shoppe. 1205 Arkansas Boulevard, Texarkana (870-772-5775). The best burger in town. $

Ole Feed House. 1514 Arkansas Boulevard, Texarkana (870-773-0595). Down-home country cooking with seafood, gumbo, and chicken and dumplings. Special kids' prices. $–$$

Where to Stay

Hampton Inn. 5300 North State Line Avenue, Texarkana (903-832-3499). **Free** continental breakfast buffet, WiFi, pool. $$–$$$

La Quinta Inn. 5201 North State Line Avenue, Texarkana (903-794-1900; www.laquinta .com). Pool, **free** continental breakfast. $$

For More Information

Texarkana Chamber of Commerce. 819 State Line Avenue, Texarkana 75504; (903) 792-7191; www.texarkana.org/.

Jefferson

They call Jefferson "the Belle of the Bayous," and you might think you're in Louisiana or Mississippi here rather than in Texas. The town was once a bustling metropolis, one of the gateways to Texas in the nineteenth century, when it shipped plenty of timber and cotton on passing steamboats.

Jefferson Historical Society and Museum (ages 6 and up)

223 West Austin Street, Jefferson (903-665-2775; www.jeffersonhistoricalmuseum.com). Open daily 9:30 a.m. to 4:30 p.m. $.

Your family will discover a lot about East Texas at the Jefferson Museum. The museum is housed in a restored 1888 federal building, where exhibits fill three floors and the basement. Among the interesting displays are Civil War artifacts; family and household items; Native American artifacts; early tools, weapons, and furniture; an art gallery; and a special collection of children's toys and clothing.

Historic Jefferson Railway (ages 4 and up)

400 East Austin Street, Jefferson (866-398-2038; www.jeffersonrailway.com). Schedules vary with seasons. $$.

To reinforce all that history, take a trip on the Historic Jefferson Railway. The steam locomotive pulls the train beside Big Cypress River and by many historic sites.

Jefferson General Store (ages 6 and up)

113 East Austin Street, Jefferson (903-665-8481; www.jeffersongeneralstore.com). Open Sunday through Thursday 9 a.m. to 6 p.m., Friday and Saturday 9 a.m. to 10 p.m.

While you're downtown, don't miss the Jefferson General Store. Its old-fashioned soda fountain is part of an authentic old-time atmosphere that includes a nickel jukebox, a nickel cup of coffee, and games of checkers. You can even buy an old jukebox or soda machine if you'd like one.

Turning Basin Riverboat Tours (ages 4 and up)

200 Wesst Bayou Street, Jefferson (903-665-2222; www.jeffersonbayoutours.com). Tours April through October at 10 a.m., noon, 2 p.m., and 4 p.m. $–$$.

For a close-up look at Big Cypress Bayou, once a major steamboat route that connected Texas to New Orleans, take a ride on a riverboat. The guided tour provides information on the area's history, nature, and wildlife.

Where to Eat

Lamache's Italian Restaurant. 124 West Austin Street, Jefferson (903-665-6177). Real Italian comfort food; children's menu. $$

Jefferson Old Fashioned Hamburger Store. 203 Market Street, Jefferson (903-665-3251). Awesome burgers. $–$$

Where to Stay

Hotel Jefferson. 124 West Austin Street, Jefferson (903-665-2631). One of the most historic inns in Texas. A cotton warehouse from 1861 to 1900, when it was converted to a hotel. Rooms are furnished with century-old antiques. $$

For More Information

Marion County Chamber of Commerce. 101 North Polk Street, Jefferson 75657; (903) 665-2672; www.jefferson-texas.com.

Uncertain

Isn't Uncertain a great name for a town? It developed because boat captains had a difficult time landing their steamships here. A bit of trivia: Lady Bird Johnson was born in the neighboring town of Karnack.

Whatever you do, don't miss a chance to take the family out on **Caddo Lake,** the most beautiful lake in Texas and one of the few natural lakes in the state. Caddo Lake crosses into Louisiana, but the whole lake feels as if it belongs there, with its moss-laden cypress trees, maze of bayous and sloughs, and swamplands. A canoe trip through the early morning mist is an unforgettable, almost mystical experience. For canoe or pontoon boat rentals, call (903) 679-3743.

Texas **Badlands**

You'll find Caddo Lake so quiet and peaceful today that often the loudest sound you'll hear will be the plop of a jumping fish or squawk of a swamp bird. But once this place was full of outlaws, pirates, thieves, and ne'er-do-wells of all sorts.

After the Louisiana Purchase in 1803, Caddo Lake was the central area of a disputed portion of the purchase. The United States and Spain both claimed it and finally agreed to let it remain neutral territory until the matter was formally decided, and they barred any immigration by either side. But immigrants, usually of the nefarious sort, came anyway. When a man went bad in the United States, he was said to have "gone to Texas," and this area was where he usually went first. The swampy Caddo Lake territory became known as the Texas Badlands, and it had so many outlaws living in it that a common form of greeting was, "What was your name before you came to Texas?"

After Texas won its independence, Caddo Lake remained in dispute, this time by the people living there, who divided into two groups: Regulators and Moderators, who had their own civil war in the early 1840s. Sam Houston finally ended the war with a personal appearance in the area, but many families continued feuding for several decades.

Civilization came to the lake then, with steamboats plying the mazelike bayous and sloughs of the 30,000-acre lake that straddles the Texas and Louisiana border.

Caddo Lake Steamboat Company (ages 4 and up)

Shady Glade Marina on Cypress Drive, Uncertain (877-894-4678; www.gracefulghost.com). The tour schedule varies with the seasons and weather, so call ahead. $$–$$$$.

Your family is certain to enjoy a tour of Caddo Lake on the *Graceful Ghost,* a replica of an 1880s era paddlewheel steamboat. The owners are both master licensed U.S. Coast Guard captains and give enjoyable tours on this mystifying, enchanting lake that seems lost in the mists of time.

Caddo Lake State Park (ages 4 and up)

245 Park Road 2, Karnack, 3 miles from Uncertain (903-679-3351, www.tpwd.state.tx.us/spdest/findadest/parks/caddo_lake).

Caddo Lake State Park was built by the Civilian Conservation Corps in the 1930s, and the period architecture all around only adds to the mystery of the lake itself. The park has campsites, screened shelters, fully furnished cabins, picnic areas, nature and hiking trails, and facilities for boating, fishing, or swimming in the lake.

Where to Eat

Bayou Landing. 300 Cypress Drive, Uncertain (903-789-3394). Steaks and seafood. $$

Where to Stay

Pine Needle Lodge. 400 Park Road 7805, Uncertain (903-665-2911). Log buildings nestled among moss-draped cypress trees. $$

For More Information

Caddo Lake Visitors Center. 724 Cypress Drive, Uncertain 75661; (903) 789-3901; www.uncertain-tx.com.

Marshall and Longview

Celebrate Marshall's history with the Miss Loose Caboose contest, Cow Patty Bingo, parades, arts-and-crafts and food booths, and historical reenactments at **Stagecoach Days** in mid-May. This is one of East Texas's most popular festivals. Call (903) 935-7868.

In mid-October, don't miss the tongue-in-cheek **Fire Ant Festival.** Gather the most ants in the Fire Ant Roundup or try your hand at the Rubber Chicken Chunking (throwing) Contest. Arts-and-crafts and food booths, entertainment, and children's games mean lots of fun. Call (903) 935-7868.

Then, all through December, Marshall really lights up to celebrate the holidays. The **Wonderland of Lights Christmas Festival** is famous throughout the state, even prompting other communities to try to imitate it. In addition to lights everywhere, entertainment is featured Tuesday and Thursday through Saturday. Call (903) 935-7868.

The Capital of Missouri **Used to Be in Texas**

Marshall served as the capital of Missouri during the Civil War. Missouri governor Claibourne Jackson, fearing a Union invasion, moved his staff to Marshall in 1861 and conducted affairs of state there. He was followed by large numbers of Southern sympathizers after several battles were fought in Missouri. When Jackson died in 1862, Lieutenant Governor Thomas Reynolds took office and continued running Missouri from Marshall until Lee surrendered in 1864.

Today, a historical marker commemorates the Missouri capital at South Bolivar and Crockett Streets.

Marshall Pottery and Museum (ages 6 and up)

4901 Elysian Fields Road, Marshall (903-927-5400; www.marshallpottery.com). Open Monday through Saturday 9 a.m. to 5 p.m. For factory tours, call (903) 938-9201.

Marshall is home to the largest manufacturer of red clay pots in America. Marshall Pottery is more than a hundred years old now, still making pots and selling them along with glassware, china, collectibles, pillows, gourmet foods, housewares, books, gadgets, candles, wrought iron, baskets, and more at the giant shop.

Martin Creek Lake State Park (ages 4 and up)

9515 County Road 2181D, off Highway 43 about 20 miles south of Marshall in Tatum (903-836-4336, www.tpwd.state.tx.us/spdest/findadest/parks/martin_creek).

Caddo, Choctaw, Cherokee, and Kickapoo Indians dominated this area until the 1850s, and from the lake's fishing pier visitors can still see Trammel's Trace, a Native American trail that became a major immigration route for Anglo settlers traveling from Arkansas into Texas. Facilities include campsites, screened shelters, picnic sites, hiking and mountain-bike trails, boat ramps, and a lighted fishing pier. You can take a guided tour of the lake or rent a boat from the store. Kids will enjoy the "perch-jerk" contest on Labor Day Saturday. Worship services are held in the park every Sunday morning from Memorial Day to Labor Day.

Gregg County Historical Museum (ages 6 and up)

214 North Fredonia Street, Longview (903-753-5840; www.gregghistorical.org). Open Tuesday through Saturday 10 a.m. to 4 p.m. $.

If your family would like to know what life was like in the 1800s, the Gregg County Museum is a good place to find out. The museum re-creates business offices, a dental office, a school, and several homes, along with offering hands-on activities for the kids.

Lost **Pirate Treasure**

Most tales of Texas treasure are myths, but one is very real. In 1816 pirate Jean Laffite took $2 million worth of silver bars from a Spanish ship in Matagorda Bay. He sent the treasure north in a wagon train, hoping it would reach St. Louis, but Mexican troops overtook the wagons at Hendricks Lake near Longview. In an attempt to save the silver, the wagon master drove the six wagons into the water, where they sank.

Most of the silver was never found. However, three bars were hauled up by fishermen in 1928. Portions of the wagons were discovered in 1959 and 1975, but the bulk of the silver had apparently settled deep into the muck. Laffite's loot is still down there, tempting treasure hunters to this day.

Where to Eat

Bodacious Barbecue. 904 North Sixth Street (903-753-2714), 2227 South Mabberly (903-753-8409), 102 Jet Drive (903-643-9191), and 1402 West Marshall Avenue, Longview (903-236-3215); 2018 Victory Drive, Marshall (903-938-4880). The name and popularity say it all. $–$$

Brenda's Good Eats. 1809 Loop 281 West, Longview (903-297-7474). Home-style cooking. $–$$

Golden Corral. 5012 East End Boulevard South, Marshall (903-927-1934). Steaks or a bountiful, all-you-can-eat buffet can't be beat. $–$$

Where to Stay

Best Western. 5201 East End Boulevard, Marshall (903-935-0707; www.bestwestern.com). Pool, **free** continental breakfast. $$

Days Inn. 3103 Estes Parkway, Longview 75602 (903-758-1113). Pool, **free** continental breakfast, and children under eighteen stay **free.** $$

Express Inn. 3120 Estes Parkway, Longview (903-753-4884). Pool, kitchenettes, **free** breakfast, and cable TV. $$

For More Information

Longview Convention and Visitors Bureau. 410 North Center Street, Longview 75601; (903) 753-3281; www.visitlongviewtexas.com.

Marshall Chamber of Commerce. 213 West Austin Street, Marshall 75670; (903) 935-7868; www.marshalltxchamber.com.

Kilgore

In early April Kilgore is ablaze with red, white, and pink azaleas, so don't miss the annual **Azalea Trail,** featuring some of the area's most beautiful homes and gardens. For information call (903) 984-5022.

Rangerette Showcase and Museum (ages 6 and up)

1100 Broadway, Kilgore (903-983-8265; www.rangerette.com/MessageCenterDetail.aspx?ContentID=40). Open Monday through Friday 9 a.m. to 4 p.m., Saturday 10 a.m. to 4 p.m. Free.

Kilgore is famous in Texas as home of the Kilgore College Rangerettes. You've probably seen a photo of them: cowgirls in white hats cocked to one side of their heads, high-stepping like the Rockettes at Radio City Music Hall. The Rangerette Showcase, on the college campus, documents the group's history in film, photos, scrapbooks, and other displays.

East Texas Oil Museum (ages 6 and up)

U.S. Highway 259 at Ross Street, Kilgore (903-983-8295; www.easttexasoilmuseum.com). Open Tuesday through Saturday 9 a.m. to 4 p.m., Sunday 2 to 5 p.m. $–$$.

Your family can see more history at the East Texas Oil Museum, also on the Kilgore College campus. The museum re-creates an entire boomtown from the 1930s, accompanied by dioramas, artifacts, and films. Don't miss the simulated elevator ride to oil formations 3,800 feet underground.

For More Information

Kilgore Chamber of Commerce. 813 North Kilgore Street, P.O. Box 1582, Kilgore 75663-1582; (903) 984-5022 or (866) 984-0400; www.kilgorechamber.com.

Henderson and Carthage

Families will enjoy the Potlatch festival in Carthage every October. It celebrates the area's heritage with Native American dances, an arts-and-crafts fair, hands-on art exhibits, fun runs, and even an old-time dunking booth. Call (903) 693-6634.

Depot Museum and Children's Discovery Center (ages 4 and up)

514 North High Street, Henderson (903-657-4303; www.depotmuseum.com). Open Monday through Friday 9 a.m. to noon, Saturday 9 a.m. to 1 p.m. $.

Hundreds of hands-on and interactive science and history exhibits will keep the kids busy at the Depot Museum and Children's Discovery Center. Housed in a 1901 Missouri-Pacific

Railroad depot, the museum also has a restored caboose, a log cabin, and the fanciest outhouse anyone in your family has ever seen, including Great-Grandma.

Texas Country Music Hall of Fame and Tex Ritter Museum (ages 5 and up)

300 West Panola Street, Carthage (903-694-9561; www.carthagetexas.com/HallofFame). Open Monday through Saturday 10 a.m. to 4 p.m. $.

Jim Reeves, Tex Ritter, Gene Autry, and Willie Nelson are just a few of the stars in the Texas Country Music Hall of Fame. Born in Panola county, cowboy singer Tex Ritter has a special section of the museum featuring an impressive collection of memorabilia. Another Panola county legendary singer, "Gentleman Jim Reeves" has a memorial statue by his gravesite, about 3 miles east of town on U.S. Highway 79.

Lake Murvaul (ages 4 and up)

On Farm Road 1970, 12 miles southwest of Carthage (903-693-6634).

Lake Murvaul offers boating, camping, picnicking, swimming, and waterskiing. The panorama is a wonder: a pristine blue lake meeting deep blue skies surrounded by the Piney Woods. It's easy to relax here.

For More Information

Panola County Chamber of Commerce. 300 West Panola Street, Carthage 75633; (903) 693-6634; www.carthagetexas.com/chamber.

Rusk County Chamber of Commerce. 201 North Main Street, Henderson 75652; (903) 657-5528; www.hendersontx.com.

Center and Hemphill

Center, on U.S. Highway 96, is known for its timber mills and poultry. Hemphill, at the junction of US 259 and 79, is a commercial lumber center and a gateway to the Toledo Bend Reservoir.

Shelby County Museum (ages 6 and up)

230 Pecan Street, Center (936-598-3613; www.shelbycountytexashistory.org). Open Monday through Friday noon to 4 p.m. Free.

Shelby County was one of the original counties in the Republic of Texas, so its history goes back a long way, and it's all preserved here, from bearskins to bottles, spinning wheels to warbonnets. The museum is housed in a 1905 historic home.

Trail Between the Lakes (ages 4 and up)

In Sabine National Forest near Hemphill (409-625-1940; www.fs.fed.us/r8/texas/recreation/sabine/trailbetweenlakes.shtml).

If your family enjoys hiking, take them to Trail Between the Lakes, a 28-mile hiking trail that winds through the Sabine National Forest. It extends from the Lakeview Recreation Area on Toledo Bend Reservoir to US 96 near the Sam Rayburn Reservoir. The scenery is gorgeous, and many sections are near streams frequented by wildlife. Bicycles and horses are not allowed on the trail.

Toledo Bend Reservoir (ages 4 and up)

Between Jasper and Center off Highway 87 (409-384-9572; www.toledo-bend.com).

Toledo Bend Reservoir is a paradise for fisherfolk and families who want to have fun or relax on a big lake. The reservoir impounds the Sabine River and stretches into Louisiana. It's the largest man-made body of water in the United States, covering about 185,000 acres. With 1,200 miles of shoreline, you can do just about anything here: boating, camping, fishing, hiking, hunting, picnicking, and swimming. Public and private facilities cover the shores.

Nacogdoches

Nacogdoches (pronounced *Nack-ah-doe-chis*) is the oldest town in Texas and was occupied for centuries before Europeans ever settled it. French explorer La Salle passed through in 1687, followed by Spanish missionaries in the early 1700s, and the settlement became a city in 1779. The state's first newspaper was published here, the first oil well pumped here, and Sam Houston, Jim Bowie, and Davy Crockett all slept here. The city is also home to Stephen F. Austin University.

Stone Fort Museum (ages 6 and up)

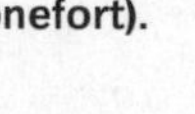

Griffith Boulevard at Clark Street, Nacogdoches (936-468-2408; www.sfasu.edu/stonefort). Open Tuesday through Saturday 9 a.m. to 5 p.m., Sunday 1 to 5 p.m. Free.

The Old Stone Fort on the Stephen F. Austin University campus is where Texas's first two newspapers were set in type. The museum also has many artifacts from a nearby archaeological excavation and other exhibits on pioneer life in the area.

Millard's Crossing Historic Village (ages 6 and up)

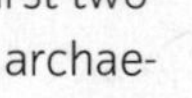

6020 North Street, Nacogdoches (936-564-6631; www.millardscrossing.com). Open Monday through Saturday 9 a.m. to 4 p.m., Sunday 1 to 4 p.m. $.

Millard's Crossing is a collection of nineteenth-century homes, including a Methodist chapel and parsonage. Interiors are furnished with antiques and pioneer artifacts.

For More Information

Nacogdoches Convention and Visitors Bureau. 200 East Main Street, Nacogdoches 75963; (888) 653-3788; www.visitnacogdoches.org.

Lufkin

At the intersection of U.S. Highways 59 and 69.

Lufkin is the heart of the Piney Woods, surrounded by tall timber and between two national forests and the huge Lake Sam Rayburn.

Museum of East Texas (ages 6 and up)

503 North Second Street, Lufkin (936-639-4434; www.metlufkin.org). Open Tuesday through Friday 10 a.m. to 5 p.m., weekends 1 to 5 p.m. Free.

Discover East Texas history at the Museum of East Texas, housed in a 1905 church. In addition to many exhibits on area pioneers, the museum has an extensive collection of works by East Texas artists.

Texas Forestry Museum (ages 6 and up)

1905 Atkinson Drive, Lufkin (936-632-9535; www.treetexas.com). Open Monday through Saturday 10 a.m. to 5 p.m., Sunday 1 to 5 p.m. Free.

If you're in Lufkin, you already know you're in the midst of one of the most heavily wooded areas in the country, certainly the most in Texas. The family can learn all about timber in the Piney Woods at the Forestry Museum. You'll find exhibits of machinery and tools, an antique logging train, lumber oxcarts, a fire lookout tower, and displays on area plant life, wildlife, and the lumberjacks who work the timber.

Ellen Trout Zoo (ages 2 and up)

402 Zoo Circle, Lufkin (936-633-0399; http://cityoflufkin.com/zoo). Open daily 9 a.m. to 5 p.m. and also weekends in summer 9 a.m. to 6 p.m. $.

The Ellen Trout Zoo began with a hippopotamus donated as a gag gift and has now grown to include hundreds of animals from around the world, including ruffed lemurs, Siberian tigers, clouded leopards, bald eagles, Hawaiian geese, Siamese crocodiles, and Jamaican boas.

Texas Trivia

Angelina County is the only Texas county named for a woman. She was a Hasinaii Indian raised at Mission Tejas in the late seventeenth century. She was named "little angel" (*Angelina* in Spanish) by the mission priests. She was later an interpreter for explorers in the area.

Texas Trivia

The first oil well in the state known around the world for its petroleum reserves and refining was drilled in 1866 near Nacogdoches, with production beginning in 1889.

Angelina National Forest (ages 4 and up)

On US 69, 14 miles southeast of Lufkin (936-897-1068; www.fs.fed.us/r8/texas/recreation/angelina/angelina_gen_info.shtml).

Angelina National Forest surrounds Sam Rayburn Reservoir, creating 560 miles of shoreline and offering great places for families to camp, picnic, swim, fish, water-ski, or just relax. Because of the lake, there are a number of developed sites in the forest.

For More Information

Lufkin-Angelina County Chamber of Commerce. 1615 South Chestnut Street, Lufkin 75901; (936) 634-6644; www.lufkintexas.org.

Livingston and Coldspring

Lake Livingston (ages 4 and up)

Between Livingston and Huntsville on U.S. Highway 190 (936-327-4929; www.lakelivingston.com).

Lake Livingston is a mecca for outdoor recreation in the area, drawing families from as far away as Houston. Reaching it is easy from either I–45 or US 59, or from US 190, which connects the two. You can play on the 93,000 acres of lake or relax along the 450 miles of its wooded shoreline, which has many public and private recreational facilities.

Lake Livingston State Park (ages 4 and up)

300 Park Road 65, off Farm Road 3126, 7 miles southwest of Livingston via Farm Road 1988 (936-365-2201, www.tpwd.state.tx.us/spdest/findadest/parks/lake_livingston).

Lake Livingston State Park has a fishing pier, fish cleaning stations, boat ramps, campsites, screened shelters, picnic areas, and about 4 miles of hike and bike trails through the pine and oak forests surrounding the lake. You can get bait, groceries, and gas at the park store.

Double Lake (ages 4 and up)

301 Farm Road 2025, off Highway 150, 4 miles south of Coldspring (936-653-3448; www.recreation.gov/welcome).

For families with small children, Double Lake can't be beat. This is a relatively small area in Sam Houston National Forest that has campsites, picnic areas, a beach house, canoe and paddleboat rentals, a boat ramp, a quiet hiking trail that loops around the lake, and a 5-mile trail that leads to the Big Creek Scenic Area with access to the Lone Star Hiking Trail.

Polk County Memorial Museum (ages 6 and up)

514 West Mill Street, Livingston (936-327-8192; www.livingston.net/museum). Open Monday through Friday 9 a.m. to 5 p.m. Donations accepted.

One of the finest small museums of local history in the state offers exhibits on giant mastodons that roamed the area millennia ago. Other displays cover Native Americans and pioneers, riverboats on the Trinity River, the Civil War, life in the Texas timber country, social development, and a special Main Street collection.

Texas **Forests**

Yes, Texas has forests—lots of them. More than twenty-three million acres in the state are woodlands, and much of it is open for recreation in the form of parklands, preserves, or wilderness areas.

Also, four national forests covering 635,000 acres offer abundant opportunities for outdoor family recreation, whether for day use or over several days. Each forest has its own lakes, streams, and hiking trails.

- **Angelina National Forest**—Home to Boulton Lake, Boykin Springs, Caney Creek, Harvey Creek, Sandy Creek, Lake Sam Rayburn, and the Sawmill Hiking Trail
- **Davy Crockett National Forest**—Home to Ratcliff Lake, Big Slough, Alabama Creek, and the 4C Hiking Trail
- **Sabine National Forest**—Home to Red Hills Lake, Toledo Bend Reservoir, and the Trail Between the Lakes
- **Sam Houston National Forest**—Home to Double Lake, Kelly Pond, Lake Stubblefield, Lake Conroe, and the Lone Star Hiking Trail

For information on the national forests in Texas, contact the Forest Supervisor, Homer Garrison Federal Building, 701 North First Street, Lufkin 75901; (936) 639-8501.

For More Information

Livingston-Polk County Chamber of Commerce. 1001 US 59 Loop North, Livingston 77351; (936) 327-4929; www.lpcchamber.com.

Woodville

Woodville is a quiet little city tucked away in a beautiful forest of pines and dogwoods. The city celebrates its natural heritage with the annual **Dogwood Festival,** which covers a couple of weekends in late March through early April. Each weekend features different activities, like an antique car show, fun run, arts-and-crafts fair, parade, historical play, rodeo and trail ride, western dance, quilt show, and bluegrass music. This is a rousing, old-time celebration. For information call (409) 283-2632.

Heritage Village Museum (ages 6 and up)

On US 190, 1 mile west of Woodville (409-283-2272; www.heritage-village.org). Open daily 9 a.m. to 5 p.m. except major holidays. $.

This is a collection of pioneer buildings and artifacts depicting life in the 1800s, including a giant clock, a blacksmith shop, churches, physician's and apothecary shops, a schoolhouse, a railroad depot, and much more. A gift shop, picnic areas, and a restaurant await upon your exit.

In September the Heritage Village hosts **Ghosts and Legends of Texas Past,** an evening of storytellers presenting legends and folktales of early East Texas that's sure to delight children and fascinate adults. Call the village for dates.

Where to Eat

Elijah's Café. 810 South Magnolia Street, Woodville (409) 331-9090. Good food in large portions. $–$$.

Pickett House. In Heritage Village, Woodville (409) 283-2272). Housed in an old one-room schoolhouse, this restaurant is extremely popular thanks to all-you-can-eat staples like chicken-fried steaks, chicken and dumplings, and its "mess of greens." $$

For More Information

For lodging suggestions, see the listings for Jasper.

Tyler County Chamber of Commerce. 717 West Bluff Street, Woodville 75979; (409) 283-2632; www.tylercountychamber.com.

Jasper

At the junction of US 190 and 96.

Texas Trivia

The largest lake completely in the state is Lake Sam Rayburn, with 114,500 surface acres. Other principal lakes are Amistad, Falcon, Livingston, Texoma, and the Highland Lakes of the Hill Country.

Jasper lies just south of both Angelina National Forest and Sabine National Forest. The city is in the middle of one of the most heavily forested areas of Texas; about 85 percent of the surrounding land grows pines and hardwoods.

Lake Sam Rayburn (ages 4 and up)

On Highway 63, 13 miles northwest of Jasper (409-384-5716; www.swf-wc.usace.army.mil/samray).

Jasper is on the southern end of Lake Sam Rayburn, which is famous in Texas for its great fishing, thanks to the lake's many coves. In addition to fishing, you'll find prime swimming and waterskiing. The shores are covered in dogwood and pine, magnolia, and azalea. The lake lies within Angelina National Forest.

Martin Dies Jr. State Park (ages 4 and up)

On US 190, 12 miles west of Jasper (409-384-5231, www.tpwd.state/tx.us/spdest/findadest/parks/martin_dies_jr).

More lake recreation can be found at Martin Dies Jr. State Park. The park has numerous creeks and the 15,000-acre B. A. Steinhagen Reservoir. The area is filled with beautiful trees like cypress, willow, beech, and magnolia. Facilities include boat ramps, campsites, cabins, canoe rentals, hiking and biking trails through the bottomland forest, and screened shelters. Bald eagles winter here.

Where to Eat

Casa Olé. 2120 North Wheeler Street, Jasper (409-383-8800). Claimed to be the best Mexican food in all of the Piney Woods. $–$$

Where to Stay

Best Western Inn. 205 West Gibson Street, Jasper (409-384-7767; www.bestwestern.com). Pool and spa, **free** breakfast, **free** WiFi, special parking accommodations if you happen to be towing a boat or trailer. You can even check out late on Sunday. $$

For More Information

Jasper-Lake Sam Rayburn Area Chamber of Commerce. 246 East Milam Street, Jasper 75951-4136; (409) 384-2762; www.jaspercoc.org.

Index

A

Abilene, 79
Abilene State Park, 79
Abilene Zoo, 81
Ace of Clubs House, 220
Acton State Historic Site, 51
Adolph Thomas Jr. County Park, 169
Adventure Balloonport, 34
African-American Museum, 39
Agricultural Heritage Center and Cibolo Nature Center, 162
Air Defense and Artillery Museum, 92
Alabama-Coushatta Reservation, 98
Alamo, 120, 128
Alamo Cenotaph, 129
Alamo Village, 114
Alanreed-McLean Area Museum, 70
Albany, 82
Alibates Flint Quarries National Monument, 67
Alice Naylor Art Library, 159
Alpine, 99
Amarillo, 62
Amarillo Dillas, 64
Amarillo Gorillas, 64
Amarillo Museum of Art, 63
Amarillo Zoo, 63
American Airlines C. R. Smith Museum, 28
American Quarter Horse Hall of Fame and Museum, 64
Amistad National Recreation Area, 111
Amon G. Carter Museum, 26
Anahuac National Wildlife Refuge, 201
Angelina National Forest, 231, 232
Angelo State University Planetarium, 77
Animal World and Snake Farm, 138
Anita N. Martinez Ballet Folklorico, 41
Annie Riggs Museum, 106
Anzalduas County Park, 118
Apple Store, The, 160
Aquarena Center, 141
Aransas National Wildlife Refuge, 178
Arctic Wolf Ice Center, 13
Arlington, 30
Armand Bayou Nature Center, 195
Armstrong County Museum, 68
Art Museum of Southeast Texas, 206
Art Museum of South Texas, 172
Athens, 215
Atlanta, 220
Atlanta State Park, 221
Austin, 144
Austin Children's Museum, 145
Austin Zoo, 148
Azalea Trail, 227

B

Babe Didrikson Zaharias Museum, 207
Ballinger, 78
Balmorhea, 89
Balmorhea State Park, 89
Bandera, 161
Bar H Dude Ranch, 70
Barton Warnock Environmental Education Center, 102
Bastrop, 1
Bastrop Museum, 3
Bastrop MusicFest (Concert for CASA), 4
Bastrop Opera House, 3
Bastrop State Park, 4
Bat Emergence, 147
Battleship *Texas,* 195
Bay Area Park, 195
Bay City, 179
Bayfest, 171
Bayfront Arts and Science Park, 172
Baylor University, 17
Bayou Wildlife Park, 197
BC Vintage Flying Museum, 28
Beaumont, 206
Bee Cave, 166
Bell County Museum, 15
Belton, 14
Bend, 151
Bentsen-Rio Grande Valley State Park, 117
Big Bend National Park, 103
Big Bend Ranch State Park, 101
Big Slough Canoe Trail, 212
Big Spring, 82
Big Spring State Park, 83
Big Thicket National Preserve, 205, 208
Blanco, 164
Blanco State Park, 164
Blarney Stone, 71
Blue Bell Creamery, 8
Bluebonnet Festival, 3, 23
Bluebonnet Trails, 8, 23
Bob Bullock Texas State History Museum, 144
Boca Chica State Park, 122
Boerne, 162
Bolivar Peninsula, 200
Border Folk Festival, 91
Border Patrol Museum, 92
Bosque Memorial Museum, 18
Botanical Gardens, 25

Boys Ranch Rodeo, 65
Brackenridge Park, 133
Brackettville, 113
Brady, 152
Brady Lake, 152
Brazoria County Historical Museum, 185
Brazoria National Wildlife Refuge, 186
Brazos Bend State Park, 187
Brazos Drive-In Theater, The, 51
Brazosport Area, the, 184
Brazos Valley Museum of Natural History, The, 12
Brenham, 8
Brenham Heritage Museum, 8
Brookshire's World of Wildlife Museum and Country Store, 217
Brownfield, 54
Brownsville, 122
Bryan, 12
Buckhorn Saloon and Museum, 132
Buddy Holly Statue and Walk of Fame, 54
Buescher State Park, 5
Buffalo Gap, 78
Buffalo Gap Historic Village, 79
Buffalo Springs Lake, 58
Bureau of Engraving and Printing, 29
Burke Baker Planetarium, 191
Burnet, 149

C

Caddoan Mounds State Historic Site, 214
Caddo Lake, 223
Caddo Lake State Park, 224
Caddo Lake Steamboat Company, 224
Cadillac Ranch, 62
Caldwell Zoo, 217
Cameron Park Zoo, 18
Canton, 215
Canyon, 60
Canyon Lake, 140
Capitol Complex Visitors Center, 144
Caprock Canyons State Park, 68
Carthage, 227
Casa Manana, 27
Cascade Caverns, 162
Castaway Cove Waterpark, 47
Castroville, 126
Castroville Regional Park, 126
Cattleman's Steak House, 96
Cattle Raisers Museum, 26
Cavanaugh Flight Museum, 36
Caverns of Sonora, 75
Cave Without a Name, 163
Cedar Hill State Park, 32
Cedar Ridge Preserve, 37
Celebration Station, 35
Center, 228
Center for the Arts and Sciences, 186
Central Texas Museum of Automotive History, 4
Chamizal National Memorial, 91
Championship American Indian Pow-Wow, 32
Chappell Hill, 10
Chappell Hill Historical Museum, 10
Cherokee Trace Drive-Thru Safari, 215
Chihuahuan Desert Research Institute, 98
Children's Art Museum, 77
Children's Museum of Houston, 191
Children's Museum of the Brazos Valley, 12
Choke Canyon State Park, 125
Christmas at Old Fort Concho, 76
Christmas in Chappell Hill, 3
Cinco de Mayo, 128
Claiborne West Park, 206
Clarendon, 69
Claude, 68
Clear Lake Area, 195
Cleburne, 51
Cleburne State Park, 52
Clifton, 17
Cockrell Butterfly Center, 191
Coldspring, 231
Coleman Park, 54
Coleto Creek Reservoir and Park, 181
College Station, 12
Collin Street Bakery, 22
Colonel Paddlewheel Boat, *The,* 200
Colorado Bend State Park, 152
Colorado City, 82
Comanche County Pow-Wow, 3
Comanche Trail Park, 83
Come and Take It! Celebration, 182
Comfort, 162
Commemorative Air Force Headquarters and American Airpower Heritage Museum, 85
Commemorative Air Force Museum, 150
Comstock, 111
Concan, 160
Confederate Reunion Grounds State Historical Park, 21
Copper Breaks State Park, 71
Corpus Christi, 171
Corpus Christi Museum of Science and History, 172
Corral Theater, The, 143
Corsicana, 21
Cowboy Poetry Gathering, 99
Cowtown Coliseum, 27
Cowtown Rodeo, 27
Crockett, 212
Crystal City, 114
Crystal Springs Beach, 220
Cullen Hall of Gems and Minerals, 191
Czhilispiel, 184

D

Daingerfield, 218
Daingerfield State Park, 219

Dalhart, 65
Dallas, 36
Dallas Aquarium, 38
Dallas Arboretum and Botanical Gardens, 40
Dallas Black Dance Theatre, 40
Dallas Cowboys, 33
Dallas Firefighters Museum, 39
Dallas Heritage Village at Old City Park, 37
Dallas Mavericks, 38
Dallas Museum of Art, 40
Dallas Opera, 40
Dallas Stars, 38
Dallas Symphony, 40
Dallas Theatre Center, 40
Dallas World Aquarium, 37
Dallas Zoo, 37
Davey Dogwood Park, 212
Davis Mountains State Park, 97
Davy Crockett National Forest, 212, 232
Deaf Smith County Historical Museum, 59
Deer Park, 193
Del Rio, 112
Denison, 44
Denton, 42
Depot Museum and Children's Discovery Center, 227
Devil's Bowl Speedway, 35
Devil's Rope Museum, 70
Dickens on the Strand, 197
Dinosaur Valley State Park, 52
Discovery Place, 221
Discovery Science Place, The, 217
Dogwood Festival, 233
Dolphin Connection, 173
Don Harrington Discovery Center, 63
Double Lake, 232
Dow Park and Botanical Gardens, 193
Dr Pepper Museum, 18
Duncan-McAshan Visual Arts Center, 159
Duncanville, 32
Dyno-Rock Indoor Climbing Gym, 31

E

East Texas Oil Museum, 227
Edinburg, 120
Edinburg Coyotes, 120
Edinburg Municipal Park, 120
Edinburg Waterparks, 120
Edison Plaza Museum, 206
Eeyore's Birthday, 3, 7
E. H. Danner Museum of Telephony, 76
Eisenhower Birthplace State Historic Site, 44
Eisenhower State Park, 44
Eldorado, 75
Eldorado Woolens, 75
Elgin, 6
Elkins Ranch/Cowboy Mornings and Evenings, The, 62
Ellen Noel Art Museum of the Permian Basin, The, 86
Ellen Trout Zoo, 230
Ellis County Courthouse, 23
El Paso, 90
El Paso Centennial Museum, 93
El Paso Museum of Art, 93
El Paso Museum of History, 94
El Paso–Juarez Trolley, 91
El Paso Patriots Soccer, 94
El Paso Trolleys, 91
El Paso Zoo, 94
Enchanted Rock State Natural Area, 156
Engeling Wildlife Refuge, 212
Ennis, 23

F

Fabens, 96
Fairfield Lake State Park, 213
Fair Park, 38
Falcon State Park, 116
Famous Mineral Water Company, 49
Far Flung Outdoor Center, 103
Festival of Lights, 4
Fiesta de Amistad, 112
Fiesta de las Luminarias, 128
Fire Ant Festival, 224
Fire Mountain Amusement Park, 217
Fire Museum of Texas, 207
First Cavalry Division Museum, 17
First Monday Trade Days, 216
Flagship Paddle Wheeler, 174
Flatonia, 184
Fort Bliss Museums, 91
Fort Concho Frontier Days, 76
Fort Concho National Historic Landmark, 76
Fort Croghan Museum, 150
Fort Davis, 96
Fort Davis National Historical Park, 97
Fort Griffin State Historic Site, 82
Fort Hood, 17
Fort Inge, 114
Fort Lancaster State Historic Site, 107
Fort Leaton State Historic Site, 101
Fort Martin Scott, 155
Fort McKavett, 74
Fort McKavett State Historic Site, 74
Fort Parker State Park, 21
Fort Richardson State Historic Site, 48
Fort Stockton, 106
Fort Worth, 24
Fort Worth Herd, The, 28
Fort Worth Nature Center and Refuge, 25
Fort Worth Zoo, 24
Fossil Rim Wildlife Center, 52
Frank Buck Zoo, 43
Franklin Mountains State Park, 92
Fredda Turner Durham Children's Museum, 84
Fredericksburg, 154
Fritch, 66

Frontiers of Flight Museum, 36
Frontier Times Museum, 161
Fulton, 176
Fulton Mansion State Historical Park, 178
FunPlex, 190

G

Gainesville, 42
Galveston Island Duck Tours, 200
Galveston Island State Park, 198
Garland, 34
Garner State Park, 160
Gator Country, 207
George Bush Presidential Library and Museum, 12
Georgetown, 149
George Washington Carver Museum, 147
George Washington's Birthday celebration, 115
George W. Bush Childhood Home, The, 85
Ghosts and Legends of Texas Past, 233
Gladys Porter Zoo, 123
Glen Rose, 51
Globe Theatre of the Great Southwest, 86
Goliad, 182
Goliad State Park, 182
Gonzales, 182
Gonzales Memorial Museum, 183
Gonzales Pioneer Village, 183
Goose Island State Park, 177
Grace Cultural Center, 81
Granbury, 51
Granbury Live Theater, 51
Grand Prairie, 32
Grapevine, 32
Grapevine Vintage Railroad, 28
Grapevine Vintage Railroad and Heritage Center, 33
Gray Line Lone Star Trolley Tours, 128
Grayson County Frontier Village, 44
Great Storm at Pier 21 Theater, *The,* 198
Great Texas Mosquito Festival, 184
Gregg County Historical Museum, 225
Gruene Market Days, 140
Gruene River Co., 140
Guadalupe Mountains National Park, 90
Guadalupe River State Park and Honey Creek State Natural Area, 163
Guadalupe River, the, 140

H

Hagerman Wildlife Refuge, 45
Hallie's Hall of Fame, 105
Hall of State, The, 39
Hamilton Pool Nature Preserve, 166
Harbor Playhouse, 172
Harlingen, 122
Harry Ransom Center, 146
Health Museum, The, 189
Heard Natural Science Museum and Wildlife Sanctuary, 46
Heart of Texas Country Music Museum, 153
Heart of Texas Historical Museum, 152
Heart of West Texas Museum, 82
Heart o' Texas Fair and Rodeo, 17
Hemphill, 228
Henderson, 227
Henkel Square, 7
Hereford, 59
Heritage House Museum, 205
Heritage Museum, 83
Heritage Park, 172
Heritage Village Museum, 233
Hill Country Arts Foundation, 159
Hill Country Flyer, 145
Hill Country State Natural Area, 161
Hill Country Wildlife Museum, 153
Hip Pocket Theatre, 27
Historic Brownsville Museum, 122
Historic Brownsville Trolley Tour, 122
Historic Fort Stockton, 107
Historic Jefferson Railway, 222
Holiday River Parade, 128
Holland Lake Park, 50
Hondo, 126
Hopkins County Museum and Heritage Park, 220
hot springs, 104
Houston, 187
Houston Aeros Hockey, 189
Houston Arboretum and Nature Center, 190
Houston Astros Baseball, 189
Houston Fire Museum, 192
Houston Livestock Show and Rodeo, 189
Houston Museum of Natural Science, 191
Houston Rockets Basketball, 189
Houston Texans, 189
Houston Zoological Gardens, 191
Hudspeth County Courthouse, 96
Hueco Tanks State Historic Site, 91
Hunt, 158
Huntsville, 209
Huntsville State Park, 210
Hurricane Harbor, 31

I

Imaginarium of South Texas, 115
IMAX Theater, 129
Indian Spring Park, 18
Ingram, 158
Inks Lake State Park, 150
Inner Space Cavern, 149

Insights, El Paso Science Museum, 94
Institute of Texan Cultures, 131
International Butterfly Park, 118
International Gumbo Cook-Off, 205
International Museum of Art and Science, 118
International Museum of Cultures, 40
International Racetrack, 121
Interurban Railway Station Museum, 34
Irving, 32
Island Equestrian Center, 170
Iwo Jima War Memorial, 123

J

Jacksboro, 47
Jacksonville, 215
Jasper, 233
Jefferson, 221
Jefferson General Store, 222
Jefferson Historical Society and Museum, 222
Jim Hogg Historical Park, 214
John E. Conner Museum, 124
John Jay French Trading Post, 206
John P. McGovern Hall of the Americas, 191
Johnson City, 165
Johnson Space Center, 196
Joyland Amusement Park, 57
Juarez Chamizal Park, 91
Judge Roy Bean Visitor Center, 108
Julian Bivins Museum, 65
Julie Rogers Theatre, 207
Junction, 74

K

Kerrville, 158
Kerrville Folk Festival, 158
Kerrville-Schreiner Park, 159
Kickapoo Reserve, 98
Kiddie Acres, 147
Kiddie Park, 131
Kidsville, 32
Kilgore, 227
Killeen, 16
King Ranch, 124
Kingsville, 124
Kountze, 208

L

Lady Bird Johnson Wildflower Center, 148
Laguna Atascosa National Wildlife Refuge, 169
Lajitas, 102
Lake Amistad Resort and Marina, 112
Lake Arrowhead State Park, 48
Lake Belton, 15
Lake Bob Sandlin State Park, 218
Lake Buchanan, 149
Lake Casa Blanca International State Park, 115
Lake Colorado City State Park, 83
Lake Crook, 220
Lake Fort Phantom Hill, 81
Lake Granbury, 51
Lake Jacksonville, 215
Lake Livingston, 231
Lake Livingston State Park, 231
Lake McQueeney, 183
Lake Meredith Aquatic and Wildlife Museum, 67
Lake Meredith National Recreation Area, 67
Lake Mexia, 21
Lake Mineral Wells State Park & Trailway, 49
Lake Murvaul, 228
Lake Palestine, 215
Lake Rita Blanca, 66
Lake Sam Rayburn, 234
Lake Somerville, 9
Lake Texana State Park, 181
Lake Texoma, 45
Lake Weatherford, 50
Lake Whitney State Park, 53
Landa Park, 139
Landmark Inn State Historic Site, 126
Langtry, 108
La Porte, 193
Laredo, 114
Las Posadas, 128
La Villita, 130
Ledbetter, 6
Lefty Frizzell Country Music Museum and Pioneer Village, 22
Legends of the Game Museum, 30
Leo St. Clair Music Box Museum, 219
Lewisville, 42
Lewisville Lake, 42
Lions' Park Kiddieland, 20
Livingston, 231
Llano, 152
Llano County Museum, 153
Llano Estacado Museum, 59
Lone Star Hiking Trail, 210
Lone Star Motorcycle Museum, 160
Longhorn Cavern State Park, 150
Longview, 224
Los Ebanos Ferry, 118
Lost Maples State Natural Area, 160
Lost Mine Peak Trail, 104
Louis Tussaud's Palace of Wax and Ripley's Believe It or Not! Museum, 32
Lubbock, 54
Lubbock Lake Landmark, 57
Luckenbach, 154
Lucy Park, 47
Lufkin, 230
Luling, 182
Luling Watermelon Thump, 183
Lumberton, 208
Lyndon B. Johnson National Historical Park, 165
Lyndon B. Johnson Presidential Library and Museum, 146
Lyndon B. Johnson State and National Historic Park, 165

M

Mackenzie Park and Prairie Dog Town, 57
Magoffin Home State Historic Site, 94
Maize, The, 58
Malibu Grand Prix, 134
Malibu Speedzone, 37
Mansfield, 30
Marathon, 105
Marble Falls, 151
Marfa, 99
Marfa Gliders, 100
Marfa Lights Viewing Area, 100
Market Square, 131
Marshall, 224
Marshall Pottery and Museum, 225
Martin Creek Lake State Park, 225
Martin Dies Jr. State Park, 234
Martin Luther King Jr. Park, 18
Mason, 152
Matagorda County Museum, 180
Matagorda Island Wildlife Management Area, 179
Maxey Park and Zoo, 89
Max Starcke Park, 183
Mayborn Museum Complex, 19
Mayfest, 25
McAllen, 117
McDonald Observatory, 97
McFaddin and Texas Point Wildlife Refuges, 201
McKenna Children's Museum, 139
McKinney, 44
McKinney Falls State Park, 147
McLean, 70
Medina, 160
Medina County Museum, 126
Mercado Juarez, 122
Mercado Zaragosa, 117
Meridian, 51
Meridian State Park, 53
Mesquite, 34
Mesquite Championship Rodeo, 35
Mexia, 21
Mexic-Arte Museum, 145
Midland, 84
Midland Rockhounds Baseball, 84
Millard's Crossing Historic Village, 229
Miller Springs Nature Center, 15
Million Barrel Museum, 88
Mill Pond Park, 152
Mineral Wells, 49
Mission, 117
Mission Concepción, 132
Mission Corpus Christi, 95
Mission Espada, 132
Mission San José, 132
Mission San Juan, 132
Mission Tejas State Park, 214
Monahans, 88
Monahans Sandhills State Park, 88
Monarch Collectibles, 134
Monastery of St. Claire, 9
Moody Gardens, 199
Mother Neff State Park, 14
Mountain Home, 158
Muleshoe, 59
Muleshoe National Wildlife Refuge, 59
Municipal Rose Garden and Rose Center, 216
Museum for East Texas Culture, 212
Museum of Archaeology at Wilderness Park, 92
Museum of East Texas, 230
Museum of Nature and Science, 39
Museum of Regional History, 220
Museum of Science and Natural History, 26
Museum of South Texas History, 121
Museum of Texas Tech University and Moody Planetarium, 56
Museum of the American Railroad, 38
Museum of the Big Bend, 99
Museum of the Gulf Coast, 202
Museum of the Noncommissioned Officer, 92
Museum of the Southwest, 84
Museum of Western Art, 158
Music Hall at Fair Park, 39
Mustang Island State Park, 176
Mustangs of Las Colinas, 33

N

Nacogdoches, 229
National Cowgirl Museum and Hall of Fame, 28
National Mule Memorial, 59
National Museum of the Pacific War (formerly the Admiral Nimitz Museum), 155
National Ranching Heritage Center, 56
National Scouting Museum, 33
Natural Aquarium of Texas, 141
Natural Bridge Caverns, 136
Natural Bridge Wildlife Ranch, 138
New Braunfels, 136
Northeast Texas Rural Heritage Museum, 218
North Padre Island, 171

O

Ocean Star Offshore Drilling Rig and Museum, 199
Odessa, 86
Odessa Meteor Crater, 86
O. Henry Home and Museum, 146
O. H. Ivie Reservoir, 78
Old Fort Parker Historical Park, 21
Old Jail Art Center, 82
Old Suspension Bridge, 17

Old Tascosa and Cal Farley's Boys Ranch, 65
Old Tunnel Wildlife Management Area, 154
Opera House, 108
Orange, 205
Orange Show, the, 192
Overland Trail Museum, 98

P

Pace Park, 16
Padre Island National Seashore, 174
Paint Rock, 78
Paint Rock Excursions, 78
Palestine, 212
Palm Beach, 199
Palmetto State Park, 183
Palo Duro Canyon State Park, 61
Panhandle, 66
Panhandle-Plains Historical Museum, 60
Paris, 219
Paris Family Fun Center, 220
Pasadena, 193
Pasadena Livestock Show and Rodeo, 193
Patriotic Festival, 4
Pawnee Bill's Wild West Show, 27
Pecos, 88
Pedernales Falls State Park, 166
performing arts, the, 40
Permian Basin Petroleum Museum, 84
Pharr, 117
Photographers Island, 220
Pine Springs, 90
Pioneer Farm, 144
Pioneer Museum and Vereins Kirche Museum, 155
Pioneer Park, 113
Pioneer Town, 143
Pioneer West Museum, 71
Pittsburg, 218
Plainview, 59
Plano, 34
Plantersville, 209
Playland at the Beach, 174
Plex Family Entertainment Center, The, 47
Polk County Memorial Museum, 232
Popeye the Sailor, 114
Port Aransas, 175
Port Isabel, 167
Port Isabel Lighthouse State Historic Site, 167
Port Lavaca, 179
Port Lavaca Fishing Pier, 179
Possum Kingdom State Park, 49
Poteet, 125
Poteet Strawberry Festival, 125
Potlatch festival, 227
Presidential Museum, 86
Presidio, 100
Presidio County Courthouse, 100
Presidio La Bahia, 182
Prince Solms Park, 139
Promise, The, 52
Purtis Creek State Park, 216
Putt-Putt Fun Center, 31
Putt-Putt FunHouse, 196
Pythian Home, 49

Q

Quanah, 71
Quitaque, 68

R

Railroad and Cultural Heritage Museum, 23
Railroad and Heritage Museum, 15
Railroad Depot Hudspeth County Museum, 96
Railroad Museum, 47
Rangerette Showcase and Museum, 227
Ray Roberts Lake State Park, 43
Red River Railroad Museum, 44
Red River Rodeo, 3
Red Steagall Cowboy Gathering, 3, 27
Reisen Park, 152
Reliant Stadium, 189
Republic of the Rio Grande Museum, 115
Rio Grande City, 116
Rio Grande Valley Museum, 123
Rio San Antonio Cruises, 128
Ripley's Believe It or Not! and Plaza Wax Museum, 129
Ripley's Haunted Adventure, Guinness World Records Museum, and Davy Crockett's Tall Tales Ride, 130
Rita Blanca National Grassland, 66
River Legacy Living Science Center, 31
Riverside Nature Center, 159
River Walk, 77
Roberts Point Park, 175
Robert Wood Johnson Museum of Frontier Medicine, 76
Rockin' R River Rides, 140
Rockport, 176
Rockport Art Festival, 176
Rockport Beach Park, 177
Roma, 116
Rosanky, 1
Round Rock, 149
Round Rock Express Baseball, 149
Round Top, 6
Rusk, 213

S

Sabal Palm Grove Sanctuary, 122
Sabine National Forest, 232
Sabine Pass Battleground State Historic Site, 202
Saints' Roost Museum, 69
Salado, 16
Salado Art Fair, 16
Sam Houston Folk Festival, 209
Sam Houston Memorial Museum and Park, 209
Sam Houston National Forest, 210, 232

Samuel Walker Houston Cultural Center, 210
San Angelo, 75
San Angelo Museum of Fine Arts, 76
San Angelo Nature Center, 77
San Angelo State Park, 78
San Antonio, 128
San Antonio City Tour, 128
San Antonio Missions Baseball, 134
San Antonio Missions National Historical Park, 132
San Antonio Museum of Art, 132
San Antonio River Walk, 128
San Antonio Spurs Basketball, 135
San Antonio Stock Show and Rodeo, 128
San Antonio Zoo and Aquarium, 133
San Bernard National Wildlife Refuge, 185
San Felipe Springs and Moore Park, 112
San Jacinto Battleground State Historic Site, 193
San Marcos, 141
San Saba, 151
Santa Ana National Wildlife Refuge, 121
Saxet Lakes Park, 181
Scarborough Faire, 3, 23
Schlitterbahn, 139
Schlitterbahn Beach, 171
Schlitterbahn Waterpark Galveston, 199
Schulenburg, 184
Science Spectrum and Omni Theater, 57
Sea Center Texas, 185
Sea Rim State Park, 201
Seawolf Park, 200
Sea World San Antonio, 133
Second Armored Division Museum, 17
SegCity Tours, 128
Seguin, 182
Selena Auditorium, 172
Selena Museum, The, 173
Seminole Canyon State Park and Historic Site, 111
Seminole Negro Indian Scout Cemetery, 113
Shakespeare at Winedale, 7
Shamrock, 71
Sheffield, 106
Shelby County Museum, 228
Sherman, 44
Sierra Blanca, 96
Six Flags Fiesta Texas, 134
Six Flags Over Texas, 30
Sixth Floor Museum at Dealey Plaza, 38
Smith-Ritch Point Theatre, 159
Smithville, 1
Smithville Jamboree, 4
Smithville Railroad Historical Park and Museum, 5
Smitty's Juke Box, 118
Sonora, 75
Southfork Ranch, 34
South Llano River State Park, 74
South Padre Island, 170
South Padre Island Windsurfing Blowout, 170
Southwest Dairy Museum and Education Center, 219
Southwestern Exposition and Livestock Show and Rodeo, 3, 24
Space Center Houston, 196
Spencer's Canoes, 142
Spindletop/Gladys City Boomtown Museum, 206
Splash Amarillo, 64
SplashTown, 192
Splashtown USA, 133
Square House Museum, 67
Stagecoach Days, 224
Stage West, 27
Stark Museum of Art, 205
Star of the Republic Museum, 11
State Fair of Texas, 3, 36, 38
Stephen F. Austin State Park, 188
Stillwell, 105
St. Louis Day Festival, 126
Stockyards Historic Area, 27
Stockyards Historic District, 27
Stone Fort Museum, 229
Stonehenge II, 158
Stonewall, 165
Strand National Landmark Historic District, The, 198
Study Butte, 103
Stuermer Store, 7
Sulphur Springs, 219
Summer Fun Water Park, 15
Sun Metro, 91
Surf and Swim Wave Pool, 34

T

Tascosa, 65
Temple, 14
Temple Lake Park, 15
Terlingua, 103
Terlingua Cemetery, 103
Terlingua Trading Co., 103
Terry County Historical Museum, 56
Texarkana, 220
Texas, 61
Texas A&M University, 12
Texas Country Music Hall of Fame and Tex Ritter Museum, 228
Texas Crab Festival, 200
Texas Discovery Gardens, 39
Texas Dogwood Trails Festival, 212
Texas Energy Museum, 206
Texas First Ladies Historic Costume Collection, 42
Texas Folklife Festival, 131
Texas Forestry Museum, 230
Texas Independence Day, 11
Texas Maritime Museum, 177
Texas Motorplex, 23
Texas Motor Speedway, 29
Texas Natural Science Center, 146
Texas Prison Museum, 209
Texas Ranger Hall of Fame and Museum, 19
Texas Rangers, 30

Texas Renaissance Festival, 209
Texas Rose Festival, 216
Texas Seaport Museum/ *Elissa,* 198
Texas Sports Hall of Fame, 20
Texas State Aquarium, 172
Texas State Arts and Crafts Fair, 158
Texas State Capitol, 144
Texas State Railroad, 213
Texas State Railroad Park and Campground, 213
Texas Trolley Tour, 128
Texas Zoo, 180
Third Armored Cavalry Museum, 92
Three Rivers, 125
Tigua Cultural Center, 94
Toledo Bend Reservoir, 229
Tom Landry Mural, 117
Tops in Texas Rodeo, 215
Trail Between the Lakes, 228
Tube the San Marcos River, 142
Turning Basin Riverboat Tours, 222
Tyler, 216
Tyler Museum of Art, 217
Tyler Skateplex, 217
Tyler State Park, 217

U

Uncertain, 223
University of Texas, 146
USS *Lexington* Museum, 172
Uvalde, 113

V

Vanderpool, 160
Vanishing Texas River Cruise, 151
Victoria, 180
Victoria Riverside Park and Rose Garden, 180
Village Bowl, 47
Village Creek State Park, 208

W

Waco, 17
Waco Water Park, 20
Walter Buck Wildlife Management Area, 74
Washington, 10
Washington-on-the-Brazos State Historical Park, 10
Waxahachie, 23
Weatherford, 49
Weatherford City Library, 50
Weslaco, 120
Weslaco Museum, 121
West Cave Preserve, 166
Western Days and Rodeo, 6
Western Heritage Classic Rodeo, 80
Westfest, 18
West of the Pecos Museum and Park, 89
West of the Pecos Rodeo, 88
West Side Neighborhood Park, 152
Wet 'n' Wild Waterworld, 93
Whitehead Memorial Museum, 112
Whitney, 51
Wichita Falls, 47
Wichita Falls Museum of Art, 48
Wichita Falls Waterfall, 47
Wildlife Interpretive Center, 178
Wildseed Farms, 154
Wimberley, 142
Wimberley Glass Works, 143
Wimberley Market Day, 142
Windsurfing Sports, 195
Winedale Historical Center, 7
Winedale Oktoberfest, 3
Witte Museum, 132
Women's Museum, The, 39
Wonderland Amusement Park, 63
Wonderland of Lights Christmas Festival, 224
Wonder World, 141
Woodville, 233
Woodward Ranch, 99
World Birding Center, 117
World's Largest Jack Rabbit, 86
World's Largest Roadrunner, 107
World's Largest Strawberry, 125
Wortham IMAX Theatre, 191

X

XIT Museum, 66
XIT Rodeo and Reunion, 66

Y

Yellow Rose Express Train Ride, 24
Ye Old Clock Museum, 118
Yesterfest, 4
Y.O. Ranch, 158
Ysleta del Sur Pueblo, 98

Z

Zilker Park, 146
Zuma Fun Centers, 190

About the Author

A freelance travel writer and guidebook author, Sharry Buckner has written extensively about her Texas travels. She lives with her husband, Al, in the Texas Hill Country.